PANAMA

PANAMA

FOUR HUNDRED YEARS OF DREAMS
AND CRUELTY

David Howarth

McGRAW-HILL BOOK COMPANY

New York   Toronto   London

Acknowledgments

Almost the whole of this book is based on firsthand accounts: a list of them is at the end. I found these written sources in the London Library, the library of the Panama Canal Company, the National Library of Scotland and the British Museum. The observations of the isthmus at the present time are my own. In making them, I was helped by the government of the Republic of Panama, the Panama Canal Company, the U.S. Air Force Tropic Survival School, the U.S. Atomic Energy Commission, the Cia. Frutera Internacional de Panama (which helped me to go to Caledonia Bay), and many kind people in the republic, the Canal Zone and the United States. I offer my thanks to them all.

Contents

PANAMA

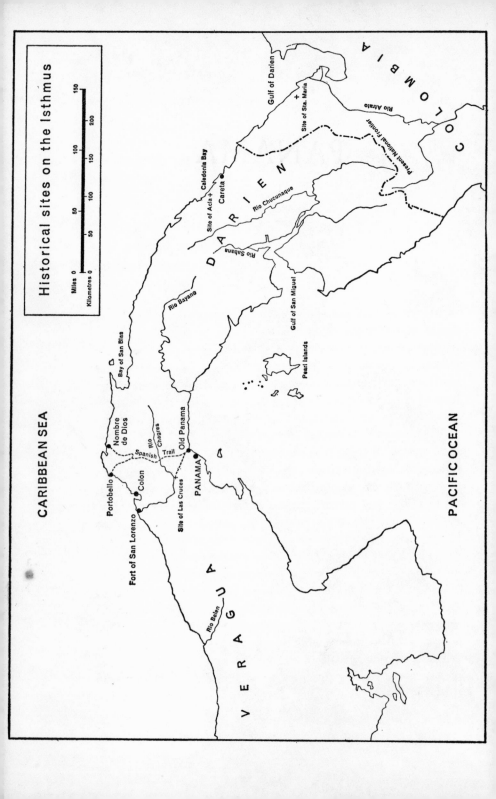

Historical sites on the Isthmus

(*i*)

The Spanish Explorers

> Gold is most excellent; he who possesses
> it may do what he will in the world, and may
> so attain as to bring souls to Paradise.
>
> Christopher Columbus

DOWN IN THE FAR SOUTHWESTERN CORNER of the Caribbean Sea, a wall of green mountains rises abruptly over coral shores. Sailing towards it, one sees that the wall extends both east and west to the far horizon. More often than not, in contrast to the sunlit sea, gray thunderclouds stand heaped above the mountains, lines of rain and sunshine slant across them, and vapor rises from the valley bottoms and clings to the slopes. As one's boat approaches nearer, one can see that every acre of this land is hidden by a canopy of trees. The shoreline, and the little coral islands lying off it, are covered by coconut palms. Mangroves choke the shallow inlets and the low salt-water marshes, standing on stilts in the water. And beyond, dense steaming jungle, intensely alive, writhes up and over the highest of the peaks. It is very quiet and hot. The sweetly rotten smell of jungle drifts across the sea. Pelicans fly silently in flocks, low on the water, seeming to be intent on important errands. Eagles and vultures watch from far above. Now and again, a dugout canoe under sail appears from behind an island, and disappears behind another; and sometimes, on the shallow reefs, a solitary Indian may be seen, dark, stocky and almost naked, standing in his canoe with his fish-spear poised to throw, timeless and motionless, like a primitive statue. He takes no notice of a passing stranger, although few strangers ever pass this way.

3

This is the coast of Darien. And here the Spanish adventurer Balboa, in 1513, was told by the chief of the Indian fishermen about another sea beyond the mountains, and put his men ashore and marched across to find the Pacific Ocean—and started a passionate dream, the dream of cutting a canal to join the seas, which was only fulfilled 401 years later. The coast that one sees today is exactly the same as it was when he saw it: it is only one's knowledge that is different. One knows now that the mountains extend not merely so far as one can see, but all the way from Alaska to Argentina, joining the Rocky Mountains and the Andes. And one knows that away to the west, out of sight, the shipping of the world is converging on the Panama Canal, and that there, on a narrow strip across the isthmus, are cities and civilization. But Darien is primeval, a jungle 350 miles long and forty or fifty across. Nobody lives there excepting two tribes of Indians which were living there before Balboa came: the Cunas on the Caribbean coast and the Chocos on the Pacific side—and excepting also a few intrepid missionaries, a few of the lost descendants of Negro slaves, and among the Chocos a very few dejected planters, trying to keep the jungle back from groves of bananas.

But Darien has not always been deserted. It is only within the last hundred years, since the interests of mankind were concentrated on the route of the present canal, that Darien has been left alone to return to its primitive kind of peace. Before that, centuries of turbulent history flowed across it. Here, on this coast and in this jungle, abominable crimes were committed in the name of Christianity, and dreadful cruelties in the greed for gold—and also, from time to time, the kind of heroic deed which has no easy explanation. On the whole of its Caribbean coast today, there is only a score or so of Indian or Negro villages, and only one that claims to have more than a thousand inhabitants. Yet on this coast was the first Christian settlement on the mainland of America, Santa Maria de la Antigua del Darien. Here was Acla, the city Balboa founded, and Caledonia, the Scottish colony of 1699. Here, at the western end of the coast, were the Spanish fortresses of Nombre de Dios and Portobello, which tempted the Elizabethan seamen and the buccaneers. And here was the secret, guarded Spanish trail which was the only permitted crossing for three hundred years—the trail by which the pearls of the South Sea islands, and the inestimable treasure of the Incas, were carried on muleback to the galleons which waited for them on the Atlantic side.

All this has vanished, or very nearly all. Santa Maria has disappeared, and so has Acla—the later so completely that nobody knows exactly where it was. Of Caledonia, nothing is left but a moat which the Scotsmen dug round a fort they named after St. Andrew. Nombre de Dios, where Columbus took refuge in a storm and Drake suffered his final failure, is a destitute huddle of shacks. In Portobello, once the third strongest and proudest fortress of Spanish America, the mossy bastions and the roofless treasure house still stand, with a poor Negro village scattered over them, and the Spanish guns still lie in rows among the weeds, each opposite its own embrasure, where they fell when their carriages rotted under them 200 years ago. And inland from Nombre de Dios and Portobello, arched over by the jungle, parts of the ancient trail can still be found and followed. But these few stone walls, these rusty guns, this tangled ghostly trail, are the only remains of all the adventure and strife. And over them hangs the hot dank air of swamp and jungle, the miasma the Spanish garrisons thought was the cause of their fatal diseases.

There are not many places anywhere on earth where so much of the history of the civilized world has been enacted and so little trace is left. Sailing in peace along the coast today, one knows that to go ashore and walk across, until one could see the Pacific from a peak, would be just as difficult as it was when Balboa did it, or when the first scientific explorers tried to do it in the early nineteenth century. One would chop a path through the same thick undergrowth in the twilight under the trees, sweat up the same interminable hills, curse the same insects, smell the same smell and meet the same primitive people—a little more sophisticated perhaps, a little less apt to let fly their spears and arrows, but no more inclined than they have ever been to surrender their sovereignty. And so, by penetrating as far into the Darien jungle as courage or prudence dictate, one has a chance, unusual in the world today, of understanding the feelings of adventurers long ago.

Most of the adventurers in Darien went there with one of two intentions: either to make a way across to the ocean Balboa saw—a trail, a road, a railway, or best of all a canal—or to capture a way that somebody else had made. The idea of a way across, especially of a canal, is the theme of this book. It is an idea that began as soon as the sixteenth century navigators knew the Pacific existed and had to admit to themselves, unlikely as it seemed, that America was a barrier of land some 8,000 miles in length but less than forty miles wide in the middle. Since then, the idea has fired extraordinary passions, and drawn a succession of extraordinary people into the jungle: soldiers and sailors, financiers and engineers, politicians, pirates, swindlers, cranks and idealists—and in addition, hosts of humble laborers, of whom at least 25,000 have died there, far from home. And the idea has been pursued by many nations: Spain, England, Scotland, France and the United States of America. All of them had to contend with the jungle, and all were defeated by it except the Americans, who won a narrow victory.

But the jungle of Darien may not be there much longer. The canal the Americans built is over fifty years old now, and too small for modern traffic. It might conceivably be redesigned and enlarged. But it would be cheaper now to blast a new canal straight through the mountains with nuclear explosives. If that devastating experiment is made, as it may be in the next ten years, the likeliest place for it will be the most deserted place: the middle of Darien, where nobody will be put to much inconvenience except the two tribes of Indians. The long history of the idea of a canal has not been finished yet, and it may come back in the end to the place where it all began.

It began with Balboa, but to put the idea in perspective one must look further back than that. Balboa was the first commander who braved the jungle and saw the Pacific Ocean, but he was not the first who saw the hills of Darien. Twelve years before his great discovery, in 1501, two ships commanded by Rodrigo Bastides of Seville approached from the east, along the northern coast of South America, and cruised up the shore of Darien as far as the bay which was later named Nombre de Dios. Balboa was on that expedition, but only as an ordinary seaman. And in December 1502, Christopher Columbus, on the fourth and last of his voyages, approached from the opposite direction and also saw Nombre de Dios, and sheltered there, still seeking, as he sought all his life, for a westward pasage to the kingdoms of the East and round the world. If Columbus had known that Bastides had been there already, he would have known there was no way out of the Caribbean to the westward. But he did not, and as he coasted down Darien he still believed that Cuba, which he had left behind him, was part of China, and that he was somewhere on the east side of the Malayan peninsula. He expected at every moment to sight the cape where Singapore now stands, and sail round it and find himself close to the River Ganges.

Columbus supported this belief with quotations from the Bible and clung to it till he died. In common with most people then, he thought the earth was smaller than it is. There was no room on the globe as he would have drawn it for another ocean, between the land that he discovered by sailing west and the land that Marco Polo discovered by marching east. The Pacific Ocean had not only never been seen: nobody even suspected it could possibly exist. Nevertheless, there was an event on that very early voyage which had a bearing on everything that has happened in Darien since. This was the first encounter of any length between the Indians of the isthmus and the Spaniards, and it was a perfect example in miniature of what always happened when the races met.

Columbus, by that stage of his career, seems a pitiable figure. He was fifty-two, an old man by the standard of his time, often confined to his bunk with gout, or arthritis, and malaria, sunk in self-pity, and subject to hallucinations, perhaps through the

strain on his mind of all the accumulated disappointments of his
life. He was a man at odds with the world, always brooding angrily on the injustice of mankind. And when he saw the bay of
Nombre de Dios, and led his fleet of four small ships to anchor
there, his chronic distress of mind was increased by immediate
worries. Coming down the coast, he had weathered the longest
storm he had ever known. Sails had been torn and rigging damaged, and anchors and boats swept away. The hulls of his ships
had been strained by the heavy seas, and so eaten by teredos that
they were all in danger of sinking. And the crews were terrified
to the point of mutiny, as his crews had often been before. As a
minor source of distress, they were almost out of provisions, and
the ship's biscuits which were left were so full of weevils that even
when they were made into porridge, most of the men could only
bear to eat them in the dark.

It needed a special loyalty to sail under Columbus on his
later journeys, not only because of the fear of unknown seas
and the obvious chance that his expeditions would never reach
home again, but also because other commanders, who merely followed the routes he pioneered, made much bigger profits for themselves and for their crews. He himself had a double motive for
his journeys: the pure inquisitiveness which impels all true explorers, and the ever-pressing need to find gold to placate the king
and queen on whose capricious favor he depended. But gold was
the only aim of most of the Spaniards: a consuming, irrational,
overriding lust. His illiterate seamen had only the vaguest idea
of what else their admiral was looking for. It was always his fate,
or his nature, to press on further; but both he and his men knew
all the time that easy fortunes were being made behind them by
the people who were exploiting the lands he had found. On his
final journey, as he passed through the Caribbean islands he had
discovered years before, he had even been refused permission to
shelter from a hurricane in Hispaniola, the largest and richest
of them all.

It was this knowledge that had driven Columbus almost out
of his mind by the time he reached Darien: a jealous rage that

men who had slandered him to the king were reaping the profits
he believed were rightly his, and a righteous rage at the wholly
unscrupulous way they were doing it. He was a very pious man,
and although piety and charity did not always go together in that
era, he was kinder than most of the Spaniards who followed him.
Towards the Indians of the places he discovered, he could be
ruthless, fighting them by every means he had when they tried
to oppose him, forcing them to labor and shipping them to Spain
as slaves—and always excusing himself with the thought that he
was bringing them to Christianity. But he was not cruel for the
sake of cruelty. He might be said to have given Indians the same
consideration a herdsman gives his cattle; but the men who came
after him gave them less than a hunter gives his prey. In Hispaniola, his successors had already slaughtered most of the native
population and had taken nothing but delight in doing it.

The same knowledge which infuriated him discontented his
crews, and in Nombre de Dios Bay the divergence of aim between
him and his men reached a crisis. The crews for this fourth expedition had been recruited in a hurry, but they had a loyal core.
His brother Bartholomew was with him, and a good many of the
officers and petty officers had sailed with him before. Of the
ninety-eight hands, more than half were boys between twelve and
eighteen years old, which was thought a good age for adventure;
among them was his own illegitimate son Ferdinand, who was
thirteen. But there were some officers he had had to accept for
political reasons, and some of them were untrustworthy—two
brothers, for example, who had only been given their posts because their sister was the mistress of the Treasurer of Castile, who
controlled the source of the expedition's funds. Somewhere among
these people, as they rested after the storm, defiance grew against
the admiral's plans. They had had enough exploration. Farther
back on the coast, in the country called Veragua, just on the other
side of the site of the present canal, they had come across Indians
who wore solid golden breastplates and were happy to exchange
them for a few hawk's bells, which cost a penny each. Columbus
had hardly paused to exploit these bargains, but had eagerly

sailed on; and here in Nombre de Dios and Portobello, the Indians who came inquisitively to the shores offered cotton and food for barter, but did not bring any gold. So Columbus was pressed by his men to go back to Veragua, and abandon the search for the strait and the Indian Ocean.

One can only imagine what he really suffered, there in Darien. His own description of this part of the voyage, in a letter to the king and queen, is hardly coherent, a long repetitive self-contradictory story of the raging seas, the endless rain and the damaged ships. "For nine days I was lost," he wrote, "without hope of life: eyes never saw the sea so high, so rough, so covered with foam. The wind did not allow us to go forward, nor to run under any headland. There was I held, in a sea turned to blood, boiling as a cauldron on a mighty fire. Never did the heavens appear more terrible. For a day and a night they blazed like a furnace, and the lightning darted forth in such flashes that I wondered every moment whether it had destroyed my masts and sails; the flashes came with such terrifying fury that we all believed the ships must be consumed. All this while the water from heaven never ceased; it cannot be said that it rained, but rather that there was a second universal deluge. The crews were already so broken in spirit that they longed for death as a release from such martyrdom. The ships had already twice lost their boats, anchors and rigging, and were stripped bare, without sails."

The agony seems exaggerated, page after page of it. One cannot quite believe in it all. Lifelong sailors do not write like this about the sea, if they are still in their right minds, and none of the other men who wrote journals of the voyage, not even the thirteen-year-old Ferdinand, were so struck by the horrors of the storm. Yet Columbus' story never seems to touch the deeper agony of the choice he had to make: it seems rather to be an unconscious attempt to excuse the choice, either to the king or more likely to himself. For he had to turn back. Darien was the farthest he ever reached, the place where he had to give up his life's ambition and face his own failure. Sometimes he pretended to himself that he would be able to make another voyage, to discover what he had looked for all his life. But in his heart he must have known that Nombre de Dios was his journey's end, and that he was too old and infirm to try again.

He went back to Veragua, because he had to go home with something—if not with dramatic discoveries, then with enough gold to make the king forget the failure. On Christmas Day he sheltered in the bay which is now the mouth of the Panama Canal, and on January 6, 1503, he towed his ships across the bar at the mouth of a river he named Rio Belen, or Bethlehem, because it was the day of Epiphany. This river, and Portobello, are among the few places on the coast today which still have the names he gave them. And Rio Belen is still the same as it was on the day he named it. It is a short, insignificant river: the wall of mountains rises as sharply there as in Darien. Its mouth is no more than a narrow gash in the jungle: nobody since Columbus has made any use of it. And to him, it proved a trap. Whenever the sea was rough, waves broke on the bar and made it impassable; when the rain stopped and the river fell, the bar was too shallow to cross; and when the river rose suddenly, the ships broke their moorings and collided with one another. But there was gold.

As the four ships approached the river mouth, Indians on the banks made a hostile demonstration, but as soon as the Spaniards explained by signs that they were good men who had come in peace, the hostility changed to trustful friendliness. Naked men in canoes brought fish as presents, and gladly took off the golden ornaments which were all that they wore, and exchanged them for glass beads and bells. When the Spaniards asked where they found the gold, they made signs that it came from a neighboring river where the principal chief or *cacique* had his village. And after a few days, Bartholomew Columbus embarked in armed boats to visit the *cacique.**

It was a cordial meeting. The *cacique* came down his river with a fleet of canoes to greet the strangers. His name was

---

* *Cacique* was the word for a chief in the language of the Indians of Hispaniola. The Spaniards adopted it and used it in all their dominions.

Quibian—Columbus calls him el Quibian, as if it were a title:
a tall, powerful painted man, impeccable in naked dignity, who
also stripped off his gold and gave it to Bartholomew, and gravely
accepted the tawdry European trinkets in exchange. On the following day, he returned the visit and was entertained by Columbus himself on his flagship. It was not a long ceremony, because
they could not understand a word of each other's language, but
more presents were exchanged, to the satisfaction of both sides
and the vast profit of the Spaniards.

This appearance of innocent friendliness was always shown
by Indians who had never met Spaniards before, except by the
warlike cannibals of the southeast islands and the southern mainland. It was true that the Indians fought among themselves, and
even collected the heads of rival tribes. But on meeting the
Spaniards—beings as strange to them as visitors from Mars would
be today—they behaved like children who have always been
treated with kindness and do not know that treachery exists. Of
course, nobody now can analyze the thoughts and motives of
savages who lived so long ago, and it would be absurd to search
for qualities in them which happen to be admired as virtues now.
Very few of the Spaniards ever bothered to wonder what the
Indians thought, and those who did were apt to see in them the
worst of their own incentives: fear, greed, revenge and cruelty.
And yet, in every Spanish narrative, the actions of the Indians
suggest that by nature, though sometimes naïvely cunning, they
were innocent, generous and gentle, and less afraid of the Spaniards than the Spaniards were of them.

So it was with Quibian. Columbus, absorbed by his own
misery, left the active command of the expedition to his brother.
So far as one knows he never went ashore. But Bartholomew took
sixty-eight armed men—more than half of the whole complement
—to Quibian's village, where Quibian received them with all his
subjects, unarmed and making signs of peace, and treated them
with all the pomp and hospitality he knew. During the feasting,
Bartholomew asked for guides who could lead him to the gold
mines. He was taken a day and a half's march up the river, to a

place where his sailors were able to pick up grains of gold from the earth below the trees, and from the top of a hill he was shown other places, even farther away, which were said to be full of gold. But this was where the cunning showed. It was a ruse which occurred to every *cacique,* and it nearly always worked. They were content to barter gold they already possessed, but they did not want the Spaniards to mine it on their own account, and make no payment for it. So, when this question was asked, they always pointed out mines in the territory of other rival *caciques,* and kept quiet about their own. It was only common sense, and Quibian had probably done it.

However, the profits Columbus made from Quibian's tribe were so easy that he came to believe King Solomon's mines were somewhere close at hand, and he decided to found a permanent post on the Rio Belen. "I saw greater evidence of gold on the first two days," he wrote, "than in four years in Hispaniola." Bartholomew agreed to stay there with eighty men while Columbus went back to Spain for supplies and reinforcements, and they built a dozen huts on the river bank, a cannon-shot in from the coast, and thatched them with palm leaves.

Columbus must have been very sick to have made such a hopeless plan. Spaniards and Indians had never lived anywhere side by side in peace. A year later, wiser after the event, he wrote: "I knew that harmony would not long continue; they were primitive and our people were very importunate, and I had assumed possession within his (Quibian's) territory." But if he knew this —and he must have known it, from all his experience—it was strangely unwise to think of leaving such a small body of men, who had to live off the country, in a cluster of unfortified huts. Sooner or later, there would be war, and they would not have a chance.

The clue to what happened first is his word "importunate." The same sort of thing always happened. The Spanish desire for gold could never be satisfied, but the Indian desire for beads and hawk's bells could. When everybody had a little bell, and everybody's wife a string of beads, the things lost their value and the

barter rate of gold began to rise. And of course there was another
thing the Spaniards wanted: women. So they began to sneak
ashore at night with pistols and muskets, to get these things
for themselves the easiest way: the gold by robbery and murder,
and the women by rape.

Probably the officers took no part in these unofficial forays,
but they knew what was going on, and it made them uneasy. It
was not a matter of conscience. Few Spaniards saw any moral
problem in robbery or rape—or in torture or massacre—if the
victims were heathen; and if they had any qualms the church
itself had provided arguments they could easily twist to set
their minds at rest. But they expected the Indians to be as re-
vengeful as they would have been themselves. In the European
Christian world they knew, men who were affronted did not turn
the other cheek—they hit back, as hard and quickly as they
could. Meekness was a quality so long fogotten that they did not
know it when they saw it, but called it cowardice.

At the beginning of March, when the fleet had lain six weeks
in the narrow river and the huts on shore were ready, the level
of the water fell, and Columbus could not get his ships across the
bar. After praying all winter for the rain to stop, they began to
pray for it to start again; but until their prayers were answered,
they were prisoners in the river. At about that time, they began
to see parties of Indians, armed as they always were with spears
and bows, crossing the river from east to west, and paddling past
the mouth of it in canoes. They asked them where they were
going, and understood they were joining Quibian for battle
against two other tribes to the westward. But a man called Diego
Mendez, who had shipped as a notary, tried to persuade Columbus that Quibian was assembling an army to attack the ships
and settlement. Columbus was reluctant to believe it, and Mendez
offered to take a boat along the coast to find out what the Indians
were doing.

A few miles up the coast, according to his own account, he
found a band of a thousand men in camp. He landed alone and
tried to talk to them, but he did not understand much of what

they said, except that they were repeating the story of a tribal battle. So he embarked again, and watched them all night from the boat. At daylight, he went back to Columbus and told him an attack had only been prevented because the Indians knew he was watching them.

A few days later, Mendez went on another spying expedition, this time with a single companion, all the way to Quibian's village. If he really believed what he said, this was an act so brave as to be stupid. He found the Indians there in battle array. The village was decorated with 300 heads of slain enemies, and Quibian had been shot in the leg by an arrow and would not come out of his house. "As I crossed the whole open space," he wrote, "there was a great uproar among the women and children who were at the gate, and they went screaming into the palace. Out of it came a son of the *cacique*, very furious, uttering angry words in his own language, and laying hands on me, he sent me with one push far from him." To calm him, Mendez brought out a pair of scissors and a comb and mirror, and told his companion to comb and cut his hair. This amazed everybody. The *cacique's* son consented to have his hair cut, and afterwards Mendez gave him the barber's instruments and asked for something to eat. "They brought it at once, and we ate and drank in love and good-fellowship, and became friends. I took my leave of him and came to the ships, and gave an account of all this to my lord admiral, who was no little pleased."

Nevertheless, Mendez still insisted to Columbus that an attack was imminent. To forestall it and subdue the tribe, he recommended that Quibian and his leading men should be taken as prisoners and slaves. And Columbus agreed. "It was therefore thought fit," his son Ferdinand wrote later "as a punishment to Quibian and a terror and example to others, to make him a prisoner, with all his chief men, and send them into Spain, and that his town should remain at the disposal of the Christians."

It was a barbarous decision even by the standards of sixteenth century Europe. And what the Spaniards did was worse than what Mendez proposed. Bartholomew Columbus went to the

village, with Mendez and seventy-five armed men. He hid the
men in ambush, and pretended he had come as a surgeon to cure
Quibian's wounded leg. The *cacique* sent a messenger asking him
not to come into his house, and saying that he would come out
to talk to him, in spite of his wound—"which they do," Ferdinand
Columbus wrote, "that their women may not be seen, being wonderful jealous of them." The two men sat down and talked about
the wound and the affairs of the country, using as interpreter a
captured Indian of another tribe who had learned a few words
of Spanish. Then bending down to look at the wound, Bartholomew seized Quibian's arm. That was the signal to attack the
house, and they took not only the *cacique* and his leading men
but the whole of his family, his wives and children and grand-
children, nearly thirty people altogether. All were bound and
hustled to the boats, and Quibian was put in charge of a Spanish
pilot who lashed him to a thwart and jocularly told Bartholomew
he could pull off his beard if he let the *cacique* escape.

But in the dark that evening, as the boats dropped down the
river, Quibian persuaded the pilot to loosen the ropes which tied
him to the thwart, and then with his hands and feet still bound,
he jumped overboard and sank. And in the confusion, nobody
could tell if he had reached the bank or drowned.

During this expedition, the Rio Belen had risen and on a
calm day three of the ships were safely towed out to sea, scraping
their keels across the soft sand of the bar. The fourth was left
for the use of the settlers who were to stay behind. Quibian's
family was taken out to the fleet and locked in the forepeak of
one of the ships for Spain, while Columbus, on the flagship,
divided the loot. Bartholomew had plundered Quibian's house
and had taken 300 ducats' worth of golden ornaments. A fifth
share was reserved for the king, which was the general rule. The
rest was parted among the men who assaulted the village, and
Bartholomew was given Quibian's coronet as a "token of victory."

There the story might well have ended: Quibian's family
would have died in slavery, as hundreds of thousands of other
Indians died, and the settlers would never have been heard of

any more—for Quibian had not drowned, and the loss of his whole family, far from subduing him or his tribe, had roused him at last, as anyone more subtle than the Spaniards would have foreseen, to a desperate effort at rescue or revenge. Columbus had to wait offshore for a favorable wind, and he would never have heard what happened in the river but for chance—a chance the Spaniards claimed as God's miraculous intervention to save the settlers' lives. He needed water, and he sent a boat to fetch it.

The boat arrived at the river mouth in the middle of a battle. Ferdinand Columbus wrote: "The Indians having not been discover'd by reason of the thickness of the woods, when they came within ten paces of our men's houses, fell on with great shouts, casting javelins at those they spied, and at the very houses, which being covered with palm-tree leaves, were easily struck through and through, and so sometimes they wounded those within. Having thus surpriz'd our men thinking of no such thing, they wounded four or five before they could put themselves into a posture of defence. But the lieutenant being a man of great resolution, he went out against the enemy with a spear, encouraging his men, and falling furiously on the Indians, with seven or eight that followed him, so that he made them retire to the wood which (as we said) was close to the houses. Thence they returned and skirmish'd, casting their javelins and then retiring, as the Spaniards use to do in the sport they call *Juego de Cannas,* many of them flying from the Christians after they had felt the edge of their swords, and the teeth of a dog, who furiously fell in among them; so that at length they fled, having killed one Christian and wounded seven."

Mendez, who claimed to have been in command in this encounter, although Bartholomew was the captain of the settlement, wrote a different version: "They gave a shriek and then another and again another, and, thanks be to God, they thus gave me time to prepare for the battle.... They began to shoot their arrows and to hurl their darts as if they were attacking a bull, and the arrows and missiles were as thick as hailstones and continuous. Some of them separated from the rest and came to attack us with clubs, but none of them got back, for they were left there, with their arms and legs cut off with swords and dead. This fight lasted three full hours, and Our Lord gave us a miraculous victory."

The man in charge of the boat watched the whole affray with his crew from the safety of the river; and when the battle was won and the winners asked him angrily why he had not come to help them, he replied that he had been sent to fetch water, and that was what he intended to do—not to have the admiral's boat swamped by everybody trying to climb into it. Thereupon, he rowed up the river out of sight, in spite of the warnings of the men on shore, to fill his casks beyond the point where the water was brackish. The next that was seen of him and his men was their bodies drifting by, covered with wounds and followed by vultures. One man, who had had the good fortune to fall overboard, escaped through the jungle and brought the story of the Indian ambush they had met upstream.

Columbus, still lying at sea, waited anxiously for his boat to come back. After being stuck so long inside the river, now he was stuck outside: an onshore wind had sprung up and the sea was breaking on the bar, so that he could not risk his last remaining boat. He watched for day after day, and saw no sign of life in the river mouth. But one night there was a sudden commotion on the ship where Quibian's family was imprisoned, splashes and shouts that the prisoners were escaping. And when it subsided, the report was brought to the admiral. Some of the crew slept on deck, because it was hot below. That night, some had been sleeping on top of the forepeak hatch, and they had forgotten to fasten it. The Indians in the forepeak underneath had heaped up stones from the ballast, and stood on the heap and suddenly heaved the hatch open, scattering the sleeping men on top. But only a few of the men had escaped and jumped overboard: the hatch had been slammed down on the rest, and made secure. All the women and children and some of the men were still safely inside.

And in the morning, when the hatch was opened, all were

dead. Some had succeeded in hanging themselves from the beams, although their legs were trailing on the floor. The rest were strangled: some had strangled themselves by winding a cord round their necks and pulling it tight with their feet.

The Spaniards had often been annoyed, in Hispaniola and the other islands, by the Indians' tendency to hang themselves. They often did it, sometimes alone and sometimes in groups, because the Spaniards often drove them to grief and despair they found unbearable: and it was not at all uncommon for mothers to hang their children rather than let the Spaniards have them. One cannot tell from the Spanish reports of this particular incident whether anyone was upset to imagine the depth of human misery it represented. Ferdinand Columbus called it an added misfortune, but only because the dead people might have been useful: "Tho' this loss was not material to the ships, it was fear'd it might be hurtful to those ashore: because Quibian would willingly have made peace with them to get his children, and now there being no hostage left, there was cause to suspect he would make war with the greater fury." Perhaps Columbus himself was ashamed of it, for in his letter to the king he mentioned the escape of the men but not the deaths of the women or the children. But perhaps it did not seem to him worth mentioning; or possibly he had even forgotten it, because while he waited off shore he was at the height of his delirium. "I was outside on so dangerous a coast," he wrote, "utterly alone, in a high fever and in a state of great exhaustion. Hope of escape was dead. I toiled up to the highest point of the ship, calling in a trembling voice, with fast-falling tears, to the war captains of your highnesses, at every point of the compass, for succor, but never did they answer me. Exhausted, I fell asleep, groaning. I heard a very compassionate voice saying: 'O fool and slow to believe and to serve thy God, the God of all.'" And the voice went on so long that he filled a whole page of his letter with its very words. In the name of God, it promised him the rewards which the world had denied him, and it said nothing at all about the totally innocent people he had just driven to despair and suicide.

But the escape of the prisoners did have one effect on the Spanish crews: it gave them the idea of swimming ashore to find what was happening there. Nobody knew whether the men who jumped overboard had reached the land: the Indians were good swimmers, but it was rough that night, there were sharks, and the ships were a league off shore, which was over three miles. But one of the pilots volunteered, and was taken by boat to the edge of the surf and succeeded in swimming through it. He found that the settlers had already mutinied against Bartholomew and quarrelled among themselves. They were all determined not to stay, and begged Columbus to wait till the sea subsided. This he did. A week later, all the survivors ashore crossed the bar in canoes, abandoning the ship which was still in the river; and from somewhere in the jungle, one must suppose, Quibian watched the fleet set sail and draw away, and knew for certain he would never see his family again.

This then, was the first experience the Indians of the isthmus had of Christians, and it deserves a closer look than historians have given it in the past. The men who wrote firsthand journals of the voyage took it for granted that Quibian was planning to attack them. But it is clear that he had not committed any hostile act before his family was seized. The whole suspicion rests on the stories Mendez told of his two reconnaissances, and biographers of Columbus have accepted a version he wrote thirty-two years later. But his own account shows him to have been a boastful man. It formed part of his will, and he wrote it to prove that his "great and distinguished services" had never been recognized, and should be rewarded by offices of state for his sons. It was a story to suit his purpose: if the Indians were hostile, he was a hero who had saved the expedition; if they were not, he was only a busybody. But the story is impossible to believe. The Indians had said they were assembling to fight another tribe, and he found no proof on either of his journeys that they had ever thought of attacking the Spanish camp. On the contrary, the 300 heads displayed in the village, and Quibian's arrow wound, were proof that they had been busy fighting somebody else. He never explained why hostile Indians should have let him go. And the rest of his observations were irrelevant. There was every reason by then for women and children to run away screaming when they saw a Spaniard, and no reason at all why the wounded *cacique* should have let Mendez come into the privacy of his house.

One can understand the feelings of Columbus' men imprisoned in the river and afraid of the result of their own misdeeds— the jungle well within bow-shot on either side, and the teredos in spite of the brackish water, inexorably eating away the bottoms of the ships. It was a situation to strain a sailor's nerves. But one cannot avoid the conclusion. Mendez said the Indians were hostile in order to inflate his own importance, and everyone believed him—Columbus unwillingly, and the sailors because they knew they deserved revenge. In fact, so far as one can possibly judge, the pagan *cacique* behaved towards the Spaniards exactly as Christians have always been taught to behave. In spite of what Columbus called the Spaniards' importunities, he had never taken revenge and never planned it. And he can never have understood why the Christians suddenly turned on him with such abominable treachery and bereaved him of his wives and sons and daughters.

Even so, he was fortunate. Under many other Spanish commanders, the treachery would not have stopped where it did. The sailors would have been allowed to make a sport of it—to hang the Indians with slow fires under them thirteen at a time, in honor, as they used to say, of Christ and the twelve apostles, and to make the women watch while they fed their living babies to the dogs. And he was fortunate, too, in the danger of the harbors on his coast. For the Spaniards never succeeded in founding a colony there; after one more abortive attempt they gave up trying. Quibian's neighbors a little farther east, at Portobello and beyond, might well have envied him.

(*ii*)

The Way Across

> ...Or like stout Cortez when with eagle eyes
> He star'd at the Pacific—and all his men
> Look'd at each other with a wild surmise—
> Silent, upon a peak in Darien.
>
> Keats: "On First Looking into Chapman's Homer"

AFTER COLUMBUS went away—leaving one derelict worm-eaten ship in the Rio Belen and another in Nombre de Dios—the Indians of Darien had six years without a sight of a Spanish sail; and no doubt they began to hope they would never see one again, for the story of what had happened to Quibian must have spread along the coast. But in December 1509, three ships appeared again. They revisited the places Columbus had sheltered in, Rio Belen, Portobello and Nombre de Dios, and finally they reached the Gulf of Darien, where they met with another fleet which approached from the east. And their crews went ashore there, and captured and occupied an Indian village.

This was the real beginning of the Spaniard's conquest: the country was never free of them again. But the conquest began with a series of disasters, and was only saved from failure by the personality of a stowaway who had joined the expedition for no better reason than to escape his creditors. This was Vasco Nuñez de Balboa.

Balboa led a life of romance and adventure, but it was full of undeserved misfortune, and the misfortune has followed him into posterity. It is bad luck that four of the best-known lines of English poetry should have given added fame to his one superb moment of triumph, and yet given the credit for it to another

man—for Cortes, the conqueror of Mexico, never went to Darien
in his life, and only saw the Pacific years after Balboa. Nobody
seems to know why Keats got it wrong, but it should have been
Balboa's eagle eyes and Balboa's men—and his name would have
scanned, without the ambiguous adjective.

But in any case, his achievement was not strictly speaking
the discovery of the Pacific. That was the reward of the achievement. The achievement itself was first to unite a colony which
was at war with itself, and then, almost alone among Spanish
commanders, to come to friendly terms with Indian *caciques,*
and finally to dare to be the first to enter the jungle of Darien.
And it is to set the proper value on these deeds that one should
take a close look at the jungle nowadays.

Of course, there is an easy way to see the inside of Darien
now. It is not by road: there is still no road in any of this
formidable stretch of country. The Pan-American Highway,
which otherwise runs all the way from Alaska to Argentina,
peters out when it comes to Darien, and is shown by a dotted
line on the maps, about 300 miles in length, which indicates
nothing more than a hopeful intention. But you can fly, low over
the trees, in a light aircraft or a helicopter from the airfields near
the Panama Canal. A flight like this creates impressions of its
own, not all agreeable. You see that the mountains Balboa crossed
are not the simple ridge they seem from the sea: they are a maze
of isolated hills and winding valleys. And you cannot help seeing
the size and solid continuity of the jungle. There are much more
extensive jungles in South America, but Darien's seems big
enough. Below, the surface is uniformly green and billowy. But
this surface is not the ground, it is the treetops: the ground is a
hundred feet or so beneath it, and quite invisible. After an hour
or two above the jungle, you begin to long for a break in its menacing monotony—a clearing, a glade, a lake or an outcrop of rock.
But all you are likely to see is a glitter of water through the
branches which overhang a river, or perhaps a landslide which still
shows a scar of red earth. Even the hardiest flier begins to have

mournful thoughts of engine trouble, the aircraft impaled on the treetops, and the insoluble problem, if he happens to survive the crash, of climbing down to the ground far underneath.

But whatever there is to be said for a bird's eye view, it is always one-sided, and this is especially true of a bird's eye view of jungle, because a traveller in a jungle, on the ground, hardly ever has any view at all. The view of the treetops no more shows what the jungle is really like than a seascape shows the coral and the fishes. It was the bottom of the jungle, not the top, that concerned the adventurers, and the only way to see what they saw is still to walk—to go boldly ashore on one of the long white Caribbean beaches and walk inland. It does not matter where; it is all the same. And luckily, because it is all the same, you do not have to walk very far. After a day's march from the sea-coast, or for that matter a week's march, there is nothing much to be seen that could not be seen in the first few miles, and nothing much to be felt except the degrees of exhaustion and, if you are prone to it, a kind of claustrophobia.

You start up a river. Perhaps in the long wet season it may be possible to use a canoe, and in the dry season, which lasts roughly from January to March, the river bed is the easiest place to walk. But the rivers on the northern coast are short, and on the southern coast so meandering and so often choked with jungle debris that you soon have to leave their course. And then, as all the early explorers discovered, it only takes a few steps for the jungle to wrap you round in its endless twilit sameness.

All the time in the jungle, you are walking on mud or on wet squashy leaf-mold which feels alive, and you are scrambling over or under fallen rotten treetrunks full of ants. You are always sweating prodigiously, not because it is very hot—it may be only 85 degrees—but because the air is saturated and perfectly still. You are always being bitten by mosquitoes and other creatures which you feel but seldom see. And almost all the time, you are using a machete, the heavy two-foot knife which is the only piece of equipment you must take with you, to chop off branches and fronds of palms or gigantic ferns, and creepers as thick as your arm which cross your way. This is not precisely because you could not push them aside or force a way through them: there are not many places, except perhaps mangrove swamps, which really deserve the word impenetrable. It is rather because experience tells you not to touch the jungle plants if you can help it. Some have poisonous juice which raises blisters, some four-inch spines, some blades as long and sharp as swords; and in the dim light among the tangle it is hard to see which is which.

When you pause to look round, you can seldom see more than ten yards, and seldom see more than a glimpse of sky. The palms and the half-grown deciduous trees make a roof, and other enormous trunks rise through it, as bare and straight and untapering as columns in a temple, to branch and bloom far out of sight above. Creepers hang looped like bellropes in a church, and feel for the earth to plant their aerial roots. On every growth there are other growths—mosses, fungi, ferns and orchids. Parasitical trees take root on other trees, and climb up and strangle their hosts. Over it all is the smell of hot, wet, rotten vegetation. And the undergrowth flops back into place across the way you came.

Here, unlike the coast, it is never silent. There is an underlying hum and rustle, and the sound of dripping water. Birds squawk and chatter high above, things crash and crackle just beyond the limit of your vision—living things perhaps, or perhaps dead branches falling. And cicadas trill incessantly. It is said that a single cicada can be heard a quarter of a mile away, and there are billions. It is a daunting, pervasive, irritating noise which comes from everywhere and numbs your sense of direction so that it sometimes seems to be inside your head. It is made by the male insects, and is said not even to attract the females, which appear to be deaf. It may not really be very loud, but it is so shrill that it inhibits your sense of hearing, just as the stink of decay inhibits your sense of smell.

It may be this inhibition of the senses which makes the jungle a rather alarming place, especially if you are alone and night is falling. There is no particular danger, but when you cannot see or hear very well you feel acutely inadequate. Other animals know what to do, they run on all fours underneath the thickets or climb above them; but an animal which has to walk upright and cannot climb or crawl is at an absurd disadvantage— it is simply not designed for this terrain. And there may be another more subtle reason for alarm. The jungle is so virile, its life is so prolific, that death can be seen more plainly than usual here as a part of a cycle. The struggle for life is shown in every twist of the plants which grope and cling and thrust themselves up to the light. Everywhere are those which have failed or are clearly doomed to fail, to die and rot and feed the roots of those which have succeeded. The value you put on your own spark of life seems exaggerated. You know that if you had to lie down and die, the jungle would almost instantly convert you into humus. On the spot that you chose, it would grow just a fraction taller, and you would have fulfilled your natural function.

All adventurers and explorers of Darien started in ignorance of the jungle, and all of them must have had to overcome this feeling of alarm. Some of them frankly describe it in their narratives, and those who do not, one suspects, were only ashamed to admit it: the toughest of parties went warily and stuck together, and were overjoyed when they found the coast again. The more intelligent of them came to terms with the jungle, and learned that almost the only serious danger in it is getting lost. This is easy; a good many people have done it and died of it. Of course, the Indians who live in there have trails, mostly along the ridges, but they are so obscure that nobody untrained could follow them, and the ignorant are likely to be caught in their animal traps. And of course, the rivers are a guide, as they are anywhere else in the world. But in Darien they are not a very good guide. They are surprisingly difficult to find, and some of them are unbelievably tortuous. On a river called Rio Chucunaque, which Balboa himself must have crossed, there is a point which is only twenty miles in a straight line from the sea, but nearly 200 by the course the river takes. It is not even easy to follow a compass course: there is always something in the way, a thicket worse than usual, or a sudden precipitous hill up or down, and you cannot see far enough to know if the hill is a hundred feet high or a thousand, whether to try to climb it or go round. You long for a distant view, something to show you where you are and where you are going. But you never find it. Balboa had to be taken by Indians to the celebrated peak to see the Pacific in the distance, and it was probably a peak they had cleared as a permanent lookout. When Drake did the same thing sixty years later, he had to climb a tree which was shown him by runaway slaves.

As for animals, it is quite possible to march right across the Darien jungle from one ocean to the other without seeing anything much bigger than a six-inch butterfly. The jungle is full of animals, but it is so easy to hide in. The feeling of always being watched may add a little to the traveller's alarm. But most of the animals, far from being dangerous, are among the engaging oddities of evolution: sloths, monkeys, armadillos, anteaters, porcupines, iguanas, agoutis, kinkajous, opossums, turtles and tortoises. The biggest of them is the tapir, a blundering, foolish and rather pathetic creature, and the commonest is probably the peccary, which the Indians hunt for food. The only large predators, apart from crocodiles, are the pumas, jaguars and cougars. Some of the early explorers said the jaguars (they called them tigers) were fierce enough to attack a canoe, but if they ever were, they are certainly not so now. The animals to avoid, so far as possible, are the snakes and insects, and the vampire bats which, true to tradition, drink your blood at night if you sleep soundly enough in the open—a process harmless in itself, but likely to give you rabies. Tarantulas, scorpions and stinging centipedes are extremely unpleasant but not deadly, and many people would say the same of boa constrictors. There are a good many kinds of poisonous snakes: the bushmaster and fer-de-lance are the quickest killers, and snakebite is the commonest fatal accident, next to getting lost. But much the most dangerous animals of all are—or were—the smallest, which killed more Europeans than anything else in Darien in the 400 years before they were suspected: the mosquitoes which carry yellow fever and malaria.

The nightmarish qualities of the jungle are certainly strong, but they are made stronger by too much imagination. Reason, if it is given a chance, will tell you the jungle can provide everything a human being needs to live on. The Indians live in it, with very little husbandry and only the simplest weapons—and even their weapons, except the modern machete, are jungle products: the spears and arrows, and the bows and bowstrings. It is only a matter of knowing how. You can hunt, but even without the patience or stamina for hunting, you can eat. The young shoots of almost all these millions of palms are edible, even raw; so are ferns, and some kinds of cacti. At most seasons, there are fruits and nuts—palm nuts, avocados, pumpkins, wild pineapples, and several things like plums. The coconuts are only on the shores, where the nuts are washed ashore and root themselves. Bananas and plantains are not indigenous, but Indians have been planting them for centuries, and you find them round abandoned village sites. And there are other amenities. A yard chopped off the water vine provides a pure, cool drink. Some palms seem designed by nature for making instant huts or rainproof hats. Some vines no thicker than a piece of string are just as strong and supple; and some trees have fibrous bark, which can easily be stripped off and twisted into rope or plaited into hammocks. It is even possible to light a fire. On the ground, you would never find anything dry enough to kindle, but with any luck, if you pull on the bell-rope creepers, a shower of dry, dead sticks will fall down from above.

Unluckily, no traveller could find out how to live on the jungle for himself. Among the fruits and nuts, there are some that are deadly poison. Some of the adventurers in Darien died by experimenting; more died of starvation, because they did not dare to experiment. But all of them could have learned if they had not been too proud or too belligerent, or perhaps too frightened, to ask the Indians.

This is the clue to survival in the jungle of Darien, as it is in any unfamiliar place: to learn from the people who live there. Two kinds of adventurers succeeded. One kind blundered arrogantly through in armies, taking their own food and weapons and even armor, surviving by sheer weight of numbers and being content to leave their dead behind them. The other kind went humbly, depending on the innate kindness of the jungle Indians.

Balboa, the first of them all, was clever enough to use both these successful techniques, first ruthlessly fighting and beating each *cacique* he met, and then making them all his allies.

The ships which entered the Gulf of Darien in 1509 were the remnants of a dual expedition. The king of Spain had granted two licenses, one to settle the coasts of Darien and Veragua which Bastides and Columbus had discovered, and the other to settle the adjoining coast of what is now Colombia, on the mainland of South America.

The king's licenses were always tremendous gambles for commanders who received them. The possible profits were huge, and so were the dangers. The commanders were empowered to claim their territories in the name of the king, and then given a free hand, as governors, to do practically anything they liked. The only firm condition was that one-fifth of all the treasures they discovered was the king's. But in both these expeditions, the gamble had failed. In less than a year, nine-tenths of the colonists had died.

Their fates were different. Those in Colombia started by attacking the first Indians they saw, in order to capture a cargo of slaves they could sell in Hispaniola. But the Indians there were of cannibal Carib stock, a different proposition from the meek and timid tribes of the northern islands. They used poisoned arrows. Men only slightly wounded by them died in agony, and their raving unnerved the rest. The colony was reduced to fifty demoralized men, starving inside a stockade they had named San Sebastian, in the hope that the martyr who was killed by arrows would protect it.

But the other expedition, in Darien and Veragua, did not

have much contact with the Indians. Quibian's tribe and its neighbors had not discovered the art of poisoning arrows, and on the whole they kept out of the Spaniards' way. These colonists simply died. They did not know what they were dying of. But they were the first to make the harsh and important discovery which decimated Spanish garrisons ever after, and finally was the cause of the desolate emptiness of the coast today—the discovery that no European could safely live for long on the coast of Darien. These men were weakened by hunger and exhausted by incompetent leadership—for the governor lost his way and was shipwrecked, and then set off in the wrong direction along the coast to find the main body of his men. But undoubtedly it was malaria, yellow fever and dysentery that reduced them in a year from 780 robust, ambitious men to sixty emaciated wretches, too weak to finish the work they had begun of building a fort in Nombre de Dios Bay.

It was on the ruin of these expeditions that Balboa rose to power. He first emerged from obscurity among the starving mutinous survivors in the stockade of San Sebastian. There, at the crucial moment when the last shreds of hope were disappearing, he said that on Bastides' voyage he had seen a prosperous Indian village on the other side of the Gulf of Darien, and that the people over there did not use poisoned arrows. All the survivors abandoned San Sebastian, followed him across the gulf and found the village. Its owners fled to the jungle as soon as they were threatened, and the Spaniards occupied it. There was food in the abandoned huts, and standing crops of maize—and, what was more, there were golden ornaments the Indians had left behind. And here, by degrees, the remnants of both the expeditions coalesced, just over a hundred tough, determined men, made tougher by having watched so many companions die. This was the place they dedicated to the Blessed Virgin. Santa Maria de la Antigua was a church at home in Seville. They added del Darien to the name when they found that this was the Indian name of the river the village stood on. And since this was the first settlement, Darien came to be used as the name of the whole country.

The Spaniards, like many other people, were united in danger and quarrelsome in peace. After all they had suffered, Santa Maria seemed a haven, but as soon as they settled there a struggle began for command of the colony. There were two men with the king's authority: the deputy governor of the San Sebastian venture—for the governor had gone back to Hispaniola and died there—and the governor of the other settlement, who had had to be rescued, destitute, from Nombre de Dios Bay. Each of these men in turn tried to govern the unruly band they were left with. But each had already made a failure of his own expedition, and each made himself more unpopular by forbidding the colonists to make any private collections of gold. Balboa had no authority at all, but in this situation he rose to the top like a bubble of oil in water. He was that kind of man. The colony could not appoint its own governor—that was the king's prerogative—but it elected Balboa leader, deposed the king's men and gave both of them ships to go home. One disappeared at sea and was never heard of again. The other, who was a lawyer called Enciso, made all the speed he could for Spain to lay a complaint before the king against the colonists, and especially against Balboa.

The early life of Balboa was so obscure that nobody even remembered afterwards when he arrived in the fated stockade of San Sebastian—whether he came with the original expedition or joined it in a relief ship. But the story told about him was that he had lived in Hispaniola since Bastides' expedition, and had run himself so far into debt that he had to hide in a cask and stay in it until it was loaded on a ship and was safely at sea. The story fits in with everything else he did: he always appears— except in a few moments of bestial cruelty—as a gay, eager, rather feckless, charming adventurer. It is easy to believe he would have cheerfully got into debt, and would have found some picturesque and memorable way of getting out again. "He was thirty-five years of age, tall, well-shap'd and limb'd, strong, of

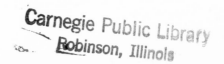

a good Aspect, fair-hair'd, ingenious, and patient under Hardship." This was written by the Spanish historian Herrera in 1601. It is certainly true that he was ingenious, and long-suffering in a physical sense, and one would like to believe he was handsome too: he ought to have been. But it must be admitted that nobody knows exactly what he looked like. Several portraits of him exist, and a large statue of him stands on the sea front of Panama City today, staring out across the ocean he discovered. But he left Spain to seek his fortune in the Indies when he was an unimportant young man of twenty-five, and he never went back. After he won his fame, he never even left Darien, and there was no portrait artist there. So probably the portraits show an idealized conquistador: the gleaming breastplate, the aggressive torpedo beard, the classically shapely nose and, of course, the eagle eyes, focused like all explorers' eyes on the farthest distance. What his contemporaries wrote about him depended on whether they were his friend or his enemies, and he had plenty of each: some saw him as a knightly hero and some as the blackest of villains. And by the time the enmities had died away and he could be seen as an historic figure, the verbal portraits, like Herrera's, had become as stylized as the statues. So one can only give him the benefit of the doubt, and assume he was as dashing and brave in appearance as he was in action.

By accepting the power the colonists offered him and usurping the royal governor's, Balboa was treading dangerously close to treason. He was worried enough about it to send a friend of his back to Spain with Enciso to put his own case at court. But of course, it would be months before the king's opinion, whatever it was, could be sent back to Darien; and in the meantime, under his leadership, the fortune of the colony changed completely. Men caught his own spirit of energy and optimism, and began to talk again of glorious conquests and dream of a golden future.

The direction the conquest took was decided by a chance encounter. Balboa began like any other Spaniard with bloodthirsty raids against the Indians near Santa Maria. But one of his ships, coasting along to look for more survivors of the settlement at Nombre de Dios, picked up two Spaniards, naked and painted like the Indians. They had deserted to escape the punishment of a crime, and they told Balboa they had taken refuge with an Indian chief called Careta and lived with his tribe for a year. He had treated them with every kindness and made one of them a captain in his army: now, with the treachery of Spanish sailors—so barefaced as to seem almost innocent—they proposed that Balboa should attack Careta and take his store of gold. Balboa agreed: he also was a man of his time. But in these two deserters he had an asset few other Spanish captains had enjoyed, and one that was to change his whole behavior; for they had learned the Cuna Indian language, and with them as interpreters Balboa, from that early beginning, was able to understand the people he conquered.

With an escort of ruffians, he sailed along to Careta's territory, which was a hundred miles west of Santa Maria, landed there and was received with hospitality. After the feast, he demanded supplies of provisions, but Careta demurred at that. He said he would always be willing to entertain any Christians who were passing by, but he could not afford to supply the whole colony: he was having a war at the moment with a neighbor, and was short of food himself. Balboa pretended to accept that explanation and went away. That night, when Careta and his people were asleep, he went back, put the village to the sword, seized all the tribe's provisions and all the gold he could find, and took Careta and his family, just as Columbus had taken Quibian, into captivity.

Balboa may not have been consciously copying Columbus: this was a normal practice, and Balboa, new to command, was only following the usual rules of conquest. But what happened next was unique. After taking Careta back to Santa Maria, Balboa began to talk to him. One has to imagine the scene: the bearded Spaniard, relaxed perhaps at the end of an active day, talking at first in idle curiosity; the naked Indian, knowing his life and his family's were at stake; the two traitorous interpreters; the smoky light in an Indian hut Balboa had fitted

roughly as his home and headquarters; outside in the stolen village, the voices of the armored Spanish watchmen and the sounds
of the sea and jungle. Nobody divulged what the two men talked
about. But slowly in those long laborious conversations, through
the inept interpretations of the two deserters, a revelation must
have come to Balboa's agile mind: the revelation that here was
not merely a savage to be enslaved, but a man of intelligence,
perhaps of charm, a man with values and customs and beliefs
which deserved respect. Careta, whatever he said, brought his
antagonist to see that he had done wrong to enslave him. He
offered forgiveness, alliance and friendship in return for his freedom, and as a binding token of them he offered Balboa his
daughter as a wife. This was a girl who all the Spaniards agreed
was beautiful. Unluckily they never described her further: not
even her name is known. But since she was a Cuna Indian and a
maiden, one may be sure she was very young—perhaps fourteen
—small, delicately formed, brown-skinned, black-haired, wide-
eyed.

What was it that changed Balboa? Perhaps, at the lowest
estimate, it was only a degree of shrewdness and an eye for a
good proposition: both he and Careta were rulers, and they may
both have seen that they would be stronger together than apart.
Yet one feels there must have been something more than that,
because other Spaniards were shrewd, but Balboa did something
that none of them had done. Perhaps it was the pretty and doubtless almost naked girl: it was a very long time since Balboa had
seen such a sight. Yet it was not only lust, because the girl was
already a captive, and if that had been all Balboa felt, her
father's offer would have been superfluous. Perhaps Balboa was
put to shame for all the horrors of Spanish conquest, because
Careta's promise certainly revealed a standard of honor which,
without any Christian basis, corresponded strangely to the chivalry the Spaniards had almost forgotten.

Whatever the reason, Balboa set his captives free. And in
those conversations, a totally new relationship was founded between a Spanish commander and the Indians, a relationship with

trust and respect in it. Afterwards, Balboa was perfectly loyal to Careta and every other *cacique* who was willing to make a pact with him. As for the girl, Balboa took her, not just for an hour but as a mistress he cherished and protected all his life. So far as history records such affairs, this also was unique. Careta believed they were married, and so they were by Indian custom. To have married her by Catholic rites would probably have made a scandal, even if Balboa could have found a priest to do it. But there was only one conceivable reason why he should have kept her ever after, in a place and time where innumerable Indian girls were taken by force and discarded. In defiance of all the conventions, he fell in love with her, and she with him.

The alliance soon had successful tests. Careta, safely home, made his surviving people plant crops to feed the Spaniards, and Balboa joined him in his tribal war. The rival chief, whose name was Poncha, retreated into the jungle at this dual threat, and the allies ravaged his country with profit to them both.

Balboa's next encounter was purely peaceful. Another *cacique,* an elderly man called Comagre, heard of the Spaniards' prowess and invited them to visit his capital, which lay on the coast a little beyond Careta's.

This visit showed that Balboa's change of heart had influenced his men. For the first time, in Comagre's village, they behaved like respectable tourists and looked at things with an interest beyond mere rape and plunder; and to their own surprise they found something to admire, in Comagre himself and his community, and especially in his sons, of whom he had seven. His house impressed them. It was 150 paces long and eighty wide, and it had carved ceilings and decorated floors. They wandered peacefully through it, marveling. Among its many rooms they found a buttery stocked with food, and a wine cellar with red and white wines made from roots, maize and palms, which they tried and found excellent. They also peered into a private room and saw dried human bodies hung up by cotton cords, dressed in rich mantles and masks of gold and precious stones. These were Comagre's parents and ancestors, preserved by curing

over slow fires and treated with care and veneration. The Spaniards respectfully left them where they were. The golden masks,
on any previous expedition, would have been torn off them in a
moment.

But it was Comagre's sons who won their highest admiration. They described the eldest, naked though he was, as wise,
genteel, discreet and virtuous. And they even allowed him to
make them ashamed of themselves. He had given them some
gold ornaments, perhaps through generosity or perhaps to ap-
pease them, and they immediately gathered in the vestibule of
the house and set up scales and melting pots and began to try
to divide the gifts by weight and to set apart the fifth for the
king. And of course they began to wrangle and quarrel about it.
The boy watched the quarrel grow, and then he suddenly knocked
over the scales with his fist, scattered the gold and started to
make them a speech which the two interpreters translated—a
speech which none of them ever quite forgot.

How could they be so foolish, he asked them, as to quarrel
over gold? What use was it, when they destroyed the beauty of
the ornaments? If they really had such a craving for it that they
would leave their homes and bring calamity to peaceful people,
he would show them a country where they could satisfy this
thirst that tormented them.

This of course was enough to silence all the Spaniards and
make them listen. It would not be an easy journey, he went on.
They would need a thousand men to conquer powerful rulers.
And there were cannibals, fierce men who had no country of
their own. These were the goldsmiths who made the ornaments
they had seen: they traded them with his own tribe for food,
including prisoners of war, whom they ate. "But if you succeed
in crossing those mountains," he added, pointing towards the
south, "you will find another sea. The people there go naked and
live as we do, but they have ships as big as yours, with oars and
sails, and even their cooking pots are made of gold."

The Spaniards by now were gathered round the boy, excited

and amazed. Suppose they could bring a thousand men, they asked, what then? He reflected for a moment, like an orator preparing for a hard debate, and then he spoke again.

"Christians," he said emphatically, "we people who go naked are not troubled by greed, but we are ambitious. We fight each other. My ancestors have always been warriors. Sometimes we win and sometimes we lose, and wars are the source of all our misfortunes." And he offered a statesmanlike bargain. He would guide the Spaniards, leading his father's men. They could hang him from the nearest tree if he had not told them the truth. Between them, they would shatter his father's enemies. The Spaniards would have all the gold they wanted. His reward would be the end of the fear of attack: his people would be able to live in peace.

"After these wordes," the contemporary chronicler Peter Martyr wrote, "this prudente younge Comagre helde his peace. And oure men, moved with greate hope and hunger of golde, beganne again to swalowe downe theyr spittle." Balboa hastily rewarded Comagre and his family by having them baptized—the old *cacique* was christened Don Carlos after a prince of Spain—and then he hurried back to Santa Maria.

It is hard to say whether Balboa was more excited by the unlimited gold or the undiscovered sea: both prospects enchanted him. They seemed to offer a chance of wealth and fame beyond any the Indies had given Spain before, and far beyond any he had ever imagined for himself. And all that stood in the way was a range of hills, some reputedly hostile Indians—and the jungle. He was desperately eager to start, but he still had only 150 men. A few more had come in since Santa Maria was founded, but they were only a handful compared with the army the boy had said was needed.

By good luck, he reached Santa Maria to find that a ship had come from Hispaniola, bringing a little food. He sent it back with his epoch-making news. With it he sent gold to the value of 15,000 pieces of eight, which was the king's fifth of what

he had won from the Indians, and he sent an urgent request to
the king for a thousand men. Then he settled down to wait with
his Indian beloved.

By this time, life in Santa Maria had one or two comforts.
Some of the settlers had started to build themselves houses, to
supplement the huts of the Indian village, and they had planted
gardens on the river banks. Property was being bought and sold.
A few horses had been imported. One or two of the newcomers
had brought their wives, and the others had a plentiful supply
of Indian women, who were humble and undemanding. Balboa
added to his own harem: why not? he would have said. Most
Indians were monogamous, but the *caciques* were not, and he was
a high *cacique*. He could and sometimes did have other women
without offending Careta's daughter or loving her less. Sometimes the place was still not far from famine, and raiding parties
had to be sent to steal the Indian's food. But Careta's crops were
coming in, and slaves in Santa Maria itself were planting. Balboa
used to go out to inspect their work and encourage them, using
on them the same inborn art of leadership he used on his Spanish
troops. But he always went armed and mounted: Indians were
terrified of horses, and to ride was the surest self-defence.

Nor was life dull. The colonists were still quarrelsome, and
the neighboring Indians hostile. Careta and Comagre could afford
to be friendly, because they were far away, but it was a different
matter for the *caciques* who were close to Santa Maria and had
to comply with the Spaniards' incessant demands. Five of them
made a pact to get rid of the settlement, and they raised 5,000
men. But the plot was discovered. A young Indian warned his
sister, who was in Balboa's household, and the warning reached
Balboa. He led out a bloodthirsty punitive expedition, and put
the insurrection down.

But these daily chores of conquest had lost their savor beside the urge to climb the mountain range and claim the sea
beyond. The South Sea, as he had begun to call it, was always
in his thoughts, and at night he had endless talks about it with
his captains. Comagre's son had shown him how it could be done.

The Indians of Darien were clearly an average among the tribes the Spaniards had discovered. They were much less warlike than the Caribs, but not quite so peaceful and defenceless as the people of Hispaniola had been. Most of their *caciques* ruled very small territories, not more than twenty or twenty-five miles across. But each of them was independent, there was no higher authority, and they were all intermittently at war with each other. So he could always win allies by offering them his support in their wars. With Careta and Comagre behind him, he could defeat Poncha. Then he could demand a pact with Poncha, and go on to fight his enemies. With a little diplomacy, the Indians themselves would help him to fight a way forward and a chain of allies could be left behind. It was a plan which no Spanish conqueror had used, because no other had ever won the trust of Indians, or thought of trusting them. And all he needed was a thousand men.

Then a ship came in with news from the court of Spain—but not with the king's commendation, not with the promise of a governorship or the army he wanted. It brought a hundred new colonists, and it also brought a letter from the friend Balboa had sent home with the governor he had deposed, Enciso. He wrote that the king had listened to Enciso's embittered complaint, and would not hear excuses. He was appointing another governor of Darien. Balboa had already been condemned to pay recompense to Enciso, and was to be summoned back to Spain to answer the charges.

Spanish historians say that Balboa was stunned by the news. Possibly he was: the bravest Spanish commanders, even in the utmost colonies three or four months away from Seville, were extraordinarily subservient to their king. But it seems more likely that in private, among the friends he could trust, he was furious. At all events, he made his decision at once with characteristic bravado: he would go to the South Sea, or die on the way, whatever the king's opinion, with anyone who would follow him. And here again his official motive does not quite ring true. It was said he decided to go in order to win the king's favor with great discoveries and treasures. But it is easier to believe that his thoughts,

if one should put them in a modern phrase, were—To hell with
the king and his governor. The news of the South Sea was his. It
was his work, his subtlety with the Indians, that had revealed it.
It was he who had planned the expedition, and he alone, with his
friends among the Indians, who had a chance of succeeding. He
was damned if he would see another man step in and try to take
the glory. So he went: the greatest of all the Spaniards' ventures,
after Columbus, was started despite the king.

He went with 190 Spanish volunteers and a pack of fierce
hounds, in one small ship and a fleet of twelve dugout canoes.
The men were armored and carried shields, crossbows, swords
and muskets. A much larger number of Indians went with him
from Santa Maria, mostly the slaves he had taken in previous
battles, to carry his supplies and ammunition. He landed in
Careta's territory, and was joined by Comagre's son and his
army. And with this motley force, entirely dependent on the good-
will of his Indian allies, he entered the jungle at the end of August 1513.

It must have been one of the hardest marches in history. It
was certainly one of the slowest. The distance was negligible: in
open terrain, a healthy man could have walked it in a day. But
time and distance have other meanings in the jungle. Balboa's
rate of advance was just over a mile a day. Some days were spent
in fighting or diplomacy, or in waiting for the sick and exhausted
men to catch up, but his best days' marches put only another
three or four miles of jungle behind him.

Inland from Careta's territory was Poncha's, and as the combined armies approached it for the second time Poncha retreated
to a hiding place in the farthest and least accessible corner of his
land. Balboa sent some of Comagre's men to persuade him to
come out again, promising him his friendship if he wanted it and
the quickest, most horrible fate if he did not. So Poncha came,
bearing a small amount of gold as an offering—it was all he had
left since the previous raid. Balboa received him with the cheerful bonhomie which won him genuine friends, and he plied him
with mirrors, bells and beads, and an even more desirable gift he

had thought of for Indians: axes. Axes, to them, were really worth more than their weight in gold, because gold was too soft to make a cutting tool. In return, he asked Poncha for men as guides and porters.

With Poncha won over, Balboa pressed on through the hills to the next of the petty chiefdoms. Its ruler was named Quarequa. Here, among the trees and the undergrowth, Quarequa confronted him with a mass of men and asked him what he wanted, and warned him to come no farther. His men were armed with bows and arrows, swords made of palm-tree wood—the ancestors of machetes—and wooden spears, hardened in fire, which they threw from slings: dreadful weapons, the Spaniards noted, against naked people, because they could be flung right through their bodies. Balboa ordered his men to close their ranks. Quarequa, seeing him adamant, attacked with shouts and fury. The Spaniards let off a volley with crossbows and muskets: some Indians fell and the others fled in terror—and no wonder, for in the heat of the moment they had not noticed the muskets and thought the Spaniards were spitting the fire and smoke and thunder out of their mouths. Balboa ordered the pursuit, the dogs were unleashed, and 600 of Quarequa's men were killed.

It seems an unnecessary, and indeed a hardly credible number. But as to necessity, Balboa may have thought this was the moment to establish his supremacy once and for all. He never needed to be so harsh again, and never was. And as to its possibility, the Spanish soldiers were utterly ruthless when they were given a chance, and a sharp Spanish sword could cut a dozen naked men literally into pieces in as many seconds. But what happened next was not excusable: it was the only act of pure stupidity and cruelty recorded against Balboa. Quarequa was dead. It had been noticed that he and his principal men were wearing cotton dresses. This, in fact, was a common ceremonial custom among the Darien Indians, a mark of rank: it was strange that the Spaniards had never seen it among Careta's and Comagre's leading men. Now, to the Spanish eyes, the garments looked effeminate. They jumped to the senseless conclusion that all these

leaders were homosexual, and for this imagined sin, without any
enquiry, Balboa had them all rounded up and bound and thrown
to his dogs, and watched with self-righteous satisfaction while
they were eaten alive.

In spite of this treatment, those of Quarequa's men who were
left alive made peace with Balboa and served him as faithfully
as Comagre's. This was not surprising. They were accustomed to
sudden incursions by other *caciques,* and when they lost a battle
they expected worse treatment than he gave them. Among savages, Balboa was behaving a little better than a savage, and instead of resentment it earned him gratitude. Here he sent Poncha's guides back home, with trifling presents that delighted them,
and took a fresh set who knew the next stage ahead.

By this time, a great many of the Spaniards were lagging
behind, or had fallen out of the march altogether. This was certainly not through weakness: they were a hardy band. Nor was
it really through excessive labor: the Indians were doing most
of the work, carrying the stores and carving a way through the
jungle. Probably some had bouts of malaria, but most of them
must simply have been worn down by the effort of marching
through the jungle, up the Darien hills, in armor. The Indians
wore nothing: the Spaniards wore helmets and breastplates of
polished steel, thick leather breeches, woollen stockings and
thighboots, and they probably seldom felt safe enough to take
them off. To anyone who has walked the way they went, the
thought of the itching sweat inside all that impedimenta is ap-
palling. Even naked in the jungle, one suffers discomfort because
sweat evaporates so slowly in the still, wet air. The thinnest of
shirts sticks on disgustingly. In what the Spaniards wore, the
toughest of men could expect to collapse with heatstroke, and this
was undoubtedly what they did. Balboa urged them along by
showing he could do whatever he ordered them to do, and more.
But he would not wait: he was far too eager to find the final summit. More than half of the men were left in Quarequa's village,
with orders to follow him as soon as they recovered.

It was the dead Quarequa's guides who led him there. On

the edge of their land, they told him, there was another hill, the last. Beyond it were other enemies, but from its top the distant water could be seen. More days of suffering followed, more men fell out, a few more miles were won. On the final day, when the Indians pointed up through the trees to the final slope, only sixty-six men, one third of the force that had started, were still with him. It was September 26th, 1513 at ten o'clock in the morning. They climbed together, but in the last few yards, when the top of the hill was in sight, he told them to wait, and went on alone. They saw him reach the crest, and stand there staring to the southward, and then kneel down and pray.

No explorers since that day have identified the peak, or found the route he followed. There is still a village called Careta on the Caribbean coast, inhabited by descendants of the chief who befriended him. Probably that was the point he started from, although on later journeys he started a little farther west. And the part of the sea he saw still bears the name he gave it—the Gulf of San Miguel. Both these points, the beginning and end of his journey, are over one hundred miles east of the present canal. But precisely where he went in between will never be known: he did not know himself. The Indians led him on, and without them he could not even have found the same way again. The trails they made or followed disappeared. Even the villages were often abandoned or moved. The watershed between the oceans, in that part of Darien, is only ten miles in from the Caribbean side, and south of it there are no conspicuous peaks. But the peak he climbed must have been nearer the Pacific shore, because it took him nearly a month to get there, but only a few days more to reach the sea itself. It must therefore have been some insignificant rise in the dreary low-lying swampland far to the south of the mountains—a place as little touched by civilization now as it was 450 years ago. There is no less dramatic scenery on earth, but it is here that the drama must be pictured.

Kneeling alone on the hilltop, gazing through the topmost branches of the trees below at a misty blue horizon, Balboa had

a moment of pure humility, and gave thanks to God and all the
saints, he said afterwards, for having granted the glory of this
discovery to himself, an ordinary man without experience or
authority. Then he waved to his men to come up and see what he
had seen; and they shouted for joy at the sight, embraced him
and congratulated each other. All of them knelt on the top, and
he prayed to the Virgin Mother to favor his expedition and let
him explore the sea and land which lay ahead. Among the sixty-
six who had kept up with him were a priest and a notary. The
priest led them in chanting the *Te Deum*. The notary drew up a
statement witnessing the discovery, which was signed first by
Balboa, then by the priest, and then by all the others present,
ending with the notary himself. Balboa made a speech in which he
promised boundless riches to his men and gratefully acknowledged the help of Comagre's son. And finally they built a cairn
and carved the name of the king on the trunks of trees. The Indians stood around, astonished to see such excitement.

It was some days later that he reached the shore: in the
meantime, he waited for the men he had left behind, and defeated
and befriended another *cacique*. At the water's edge, he held a
second ceremony: he waded in waist-deep, bearing his shield and
sword, and claimed the ocean and all its coasts, and all that ap-
pertained to them, in the name of the king. And later he embarked on the Gulf of San Miguel in a fleet of canoes. But this
was against the advice of the friendly *cacique,* who said it was
a dangerous time of year, and the first Spanish voyage in Pacific
waters nearly ended in disaster: a storm blew up, and the Spaniards and Indians together were driven onto an island so small
that the tide, or the waves, came up to their waists in the middle
of the night.

From the moment when he saw the sea, Balboa acted with a
new-found confidence, and without the eager haste that had driven
him across. His journey became a sort of triumphal procession
through the jungle. Whenever he came to the border of a new
cacique, a set process was repeated. The *cacique* opposed him,
fought him, and was instantly put to flight by the dogs and mus-

kets. But Balboa never let his men follow up these victories by another slaughter. He always sent out Indians to find the fleeing chiefs, and tell them what their own experience had been: that he was invincible as an enemy but generous as a friend. For a paltry basketful of golden ornaments, they must have explained, Balboa was likely to give a magnificent hatchet. So the *caciques* came in, contentedly bringing him fortunes in gold and also, near the coast, almost equal fortunes in pearls. And he marched slowly on, stopping here and there to rest his men, and leaving behind him *caciques* who had bound themselves to him by solemn promises of friendship. But the process only worked with two conditions: one, that he never lost his battles, and two, that he never broke a promise he had made.

Towards the end, as the column struggled back across the mountains, it was carrying such a load of gold that it could not carry food enough to feed itself. Everyone came near to starvation, and even Balboa fell sick. "The Fatigues he went through were very great," Herrera wrote of him, "because he was always in every Action, and by his example in Marching, Fighting, Passing of Rivers, enduring Hunger, and Watching, he had all his Men submissive, and ready at his Will; all which threw him into a Fever, and yet he would proceed, being carried in a Hamack, on the Shoulders of Indians." And he was not the only man. One has a final glimpse of his expedition, limping home through the jungle, armor tarnished and clothes reduced to rags, some of the Spaniards carried like Balboa, some on crutches, and some supported by Indians who held their arms to guide them—yet all elated at the boxes of treasure on the Indians' backs. Four months they had been in the jungle, and most of them, at one time or another, had been left behind sick or wounded and cared for by the Indians. Yet all of them returned alive to Santa Maria. It was an amazing achievement. It could never have happened without the willing obedience Balboa won from that unruly band of men, and the trust he gave and received from each *cacique* he conquered. Herrera wrote: "He was brave, subtle, diligent, and of a generous Temper, a Commander fit for mighty Enterprizes." It was true. Perhaps the whole episode was immoral by modern standards—perhaps colonization always was—but Balboa, almost alone among his contemporaries, was a man the sternest of moralists can admire for his achievements and forgive for his faults.

Back in Santa Maria, he was embraced with joy by the colonists who had stayed behind, and also, one hopes, by his little Indian mistress. Then he divided the booty to everybody's satisfaction—no small feat in itself—and at last he sat down with a pen to write a report to the king.

To follow his story further, one must turn for a moment to events in Spain. The fortunes of all the Spanish commanders depended to some extent on the whims of the king, and when quarrels broke out in the Indies the winner was often the man who was first to run home to Spain and tell the king his version of what had happened. The first news the king had heard from Darien was Enciso's complaint against Balboa. The second was Balboa's request for a thousand men to march to the sea he had heard of. Together with this request, and the rumors of gold he had heard, he sent an Indian to Spain who told such marvelous stories of rivers full of gold that the country was given the official name of *Castilla del Oro,* Golden Castile. It was not unnatural that the king decided to appoint a new governor, a man with a reputation, to rule a land of such promise. His choice fell on Pedro Arias d'Avila, a middle-aged courtier who had fought against the Moors and had earned the nickname of El Galan for his prowess in the jousts. Pedrarias, as he was also called, was given a fleet and authorized to raise 1,200 men. About four times that number flocked into Seville, some soldiers and some courtesans, all eager to get rich quick. He selected 2,000 and after an abortive start when he was driven back to harbor by a storm, he sailed for Santa Maria in April 1514. His wife insisted on coming with him, leaving their eight children behind; and her devotion is absolutely the only thing that history records to his credit, for he proved to be vain, avaricious, cruel, vindictive and inefficient.

Then, a few days after Pedrarias had left, Balboa's dispatch on his journey arrived in Spain, together with the heaps of gold

and the fabulous pearls he had remitted to the king. At once
Balboa became a national hero. Peter Martyr wrote sardonically:
"Beynge therefore thus tourned from a rasshe royster to a poly-
tyke and discreate capitayne, he was judged woorthy to be advanced to great honoure. By reason whereof, he was bothe re-
ceaved into the kynges favour, and thereupon created the generall
or Lieuetenaunt of the kynges army in those Regions." If only
he had hurried back and written his dispatch a little sooner! Now
it was too late. The king would not recall Pedrarias. Balboa was
to remain his subordinate.

The history of the next few years in Darien is so terrible
that even now it seems best to pass over it briefly. Pedrarias arrived in some trepidation that Balboa would oppose him; but
Balboa, on the contrary, received him with a guard of honor of
his ragged veterans, and handed over what had been his command. Pedrarias was furious to find that Balboa had already won
the glory he had expected, the glory of discovering the new sea.
The news reduced him to a rabid jealousy. He had brought the
lawyer Enciso with him, and they opened judicial proceedings
against Balboa and kept him for a long time under restraint in
Santa Maria. There was a repetition of what had happened in the
islands: the lure of easy gold had brought out entirely the wrong
kind of people. The newcomers could not provide for themselves.
The little settlement, which had just become viable, could not
suddenly absorb five or six times its numbers, and it was reduced
again to famine. Courtiers still in the finery they had worn in
Spain fell down in the streets of the village and died of starvation.
Within a month, there were 700 deaths.

But that was a small matter. What was much worse was that
Pedrarias sent out expeditions of soldiers in all directions with
orders to collect the Indians' gold, and no restrictions on the
methods they used to do it. Every horror which had wiped out
the people of Hispaniola was now let loose in Darien. All the
caciques Balboa had befriended happily greeted the captains
Pedrarias sent. Every one of them was seized and tortured to

death with all the ingenuity of mediaeval Spain. The more gold
they gave the Spaniards, the more they were thought to be hiding
and the harder the tortures. Hundreds of thousands of their people were put to the sword or thrown to the dogs or worked to
death in Spanish slavery. Among the first who were racked and
burned were Careta and the son of Comagre. Of course, the Indians turned on the Spaniards and sometimes achieved a massacre
in their turn, but when all their *caciques* were dead their social
organization fell to pieces and their survivors scattered to hide in
the depths of the jungle. It was only the jungle that saved them
from extermination: the Spaniards could not find them all.

From his captivity in Santa Maria, sometimes in prison and
sometimes under a kind of house arrest, Balboa had to watch this
happening: his promises broken, his allies betrayed, his work un-
done, his ideals forever wrecked in Darien. Nobody knows how
much it hurt him. Perhaps he told his friends, and certainly he
must have told his mistress when her father was tortured to
death; but it was a thing that could only be talked about in secret. Pedrarias was not only madly jealous, he was frightened of
him too; he knew that if the colonists had their say, Balboa
would be chosen their leader again. Balboa wrote secretly to the
king, but that was all he did. He refused to take part in the new
brutalities, and if he ever thought of insurrection he put the
thought out of his mind. Instead, he began to look farther afield,
to think of leaving Darien behind and sailing the South Sea where
he could be his own man again.

In this, he had some unexpected allies. One was a man who
had been appointed Bishop of Darien. He was not a good bishop
—he had far too much interest in gold—but he saw the good in
Balboa. Another was the wife of Pedrarias: perhaps she was
susceptible to his charm. These two between them devised a notable scheme: to reconcile Pedrarias and Balboa by marrying Balboa to Pedrarias' eldest daughter Maria. And while the bishop
and the mother were hatching this plot, a letter came from the
king appointing Balboa Adelantado of the South Sea—a position
of authority at last, but still subservient to Pedrarias.

Nobody asked the daughter, who was still in Spain. But Pedrarias agreed: he knew he could not keep Balboa down forever, and would have to let him take up the king's appointment, and this seemed a way of keeping hold of him, or at least of keeping his successes in the family. And Balboa also agreed. For him, it was blatantly a means to an end. He still had his darling mistress. He cannot have wanted to marry a girl he had never seen. But it meant he could get away to fresh adventures—and it could not take less than a year to send for the girl and bring her to Santa Maria. A lot might have happened by then.

So at last, with the governor's blessing, Balboa was freed and given the royal permission to explore the South Sea. He collected his friends and a quantity of slaves, and sailed away to what had been Comagre's country. There he founded a new settlement which he called Acla—it was significant that he gave it an Indian, not a Spanish, name. And then he set about an almost incredible project: to fell trees and hew out planks and beams for a fleet of ships, and carry them through the jungle and over the mountains by nothing but manpower, with anchors, ironwork, sails and rigging and stores, and put them together on the Pacific side. It is a mystery why he did not fell the timber on the Pacific shore: there must have been—or seemed to be—some compelling reason at the time to justify the prodigious labor of taking it there. He nearly gave up in despair. The first set of timbers that were carried over turned out to be full of worm, and he had to start again. The second set was washed away by a flood and mostly lost. With the third, he built two brigantines, and began two more. And in these ships he embarked, and explored the Bay of Panama, and set up a new headquarters—not in Darien, but on the archipelago he had called the Islands of Pearls, thirty miles away from the ravaged coast.

The months that Balboa spent out there may have been the happiest of his life. His Indian girl was with him: so were a few well-tried companions. The infinite sea was ahead, and Spain and Santa Maria far behind. But in such a world as his, happiness could only be insecure, and love defenceless.

There was a quarrel over the girl, between Balboa and one of his captains, a man called Francisco Garabito. What Garabito had done is obscure, whether he had insulted her or tried to rape her, or whether some deeper feeling for her made him jealous. Hard words were spoken, but Garabito was forgiven.

Next, a rumor came from Acla that a new governor had been sent from Spain to replace Pedrarias. This was unsettling. Pedrarias, however grudgingly, had given Balboa his license to explore. The ships were not quite ready for extensive exploration—they still needed pitch and ironwork. A new man might easily revoke the license, and give it to a favorite of his own. Discussing the risk one night with two companions—one of them was a priest—Balboa said he thought it was best to send a messenger to Acla to fetch the materials, and to find out if the governor had arrived. If he had not, they could afford the time to put the finishing touches to their ships—but if he had, they had better set out on their voyage at once before he could issue new orders. The man he chose as messenger was Garabito.

Garabito betrayed him. For whatever had happened, Balboa had forgiven him, but he had not forgiven Balboa. He told Pedrarias that Balboa had no intention of marrying his daughter. One suspects this was true, or half true; most likely, Balboa was putting off that unwelcome decision until the time came, and hoping it would never come. But Garabito had another accusation: that Balboa was plotting to sail away to some distant place and set up an independent command beyond the governor's jurisdiction. Of this there was no proof at all, but it was plausible enough to reawaken all the old man's jealous fury. He wrote an outwardly friendly letter, asking Balboa to come to Acla to discuss the projected exploration. Innocently, Balboa started at once on the journey. Everyone in Santa Maria and Acla knew what was pending. One man wrote to Balboa to warn him, but the letter fell into the governor's hands. Others went out to meet him on the trail, but he had a clear conscience and would not believe he was in danger. Outside Acla, he was met by a man who had followed him on his journey and stood with him on the peak: Francisco

Pizarro, the uncouth illiterate soldier who went on, years afterwards, to discover and wreck the empire of the Incas. Pizarro, on
the orders of Pedrarias, arrested him.

He was charged with treasonably plotting to throw off the
king's authority. The trial was a travesty. The judge, appointed
by Pedrarias, did what he dared to give justice. But day after
day, Pedrarias brought new variations of the charge and new
evidence—hearsay, surmise, suspicion, but nothing that deserved
to be accepted. Balboa absolutely denied it all. The strongest
evidence was given by a sentry who had sheltered from the rain
below the eaves of Balboa's house and overheard a part of his
conversation with his friends—the part when Balboa had said
they ought to sail at once: but he had missed the point that they
only meant to sail if Pedrarias had been superseded.

There was no proof: but was there any truth? The verdict
of historians has always been that there was not—that Balboa
was a loyal servant of the king and had never dreamed of escaping his authority. Undoubtedly, Balboa was a man with much
good in him, and Pedrarias, his accuser, was as evil as a man can
be; so one would assume that truth was on Balboa's side. But
this very contrast made it likely that Balboa had his dreams.
Certainly, he never tried to give effect to them, he never made a
plot, he never committed the crime he was accused of. But the
temptation was only too clear, and he must have felt it. Ahead,
there was the virgin ocean: behind, the wickedness and dishonor
of Spanish colonization. Ahead again, the chance to rediscover the
simple honesty he had found in Careta and Comagre: behind, a
world where Indian girls were fit for rape and slavery but not for
love. Who knows? What man of ideals, lying awake at night out
there on the Pearl Islands, would not sometimes have thought of
setting a course to the west, with the girl he had dared to love and
the friends who were loyal, and taking a chance on his landfall?
If this was Balboa's waking dream, it was a crime that history
may forgive him.

But not Pedrarias. He forced through a sentence of death.
The judge recommended mercy, but Pedrarias refused it. The

judge insisted on a right of appeal to Spain, but Pedrarias denied
it. In the center of Acla, the town he had founded, Balboa was
strangled by the official executioner.

Nobody knows what happened to his girl: nobody thought
her fate, any more than her name, was worth recording. Perhaps
another Spaniard took her—perhaps Garabito. Perhaps she was
sold as a slave. But Indians often chose death instead of misery,
and Indian women often killed themselves when their husbands
died.

(*iii*)

The Elizabethans

F<small>ROM TIME TO TIME</small>, all through the history of the isthmus and the jungle, a man appears who suddenly seems to light the scene with his personality so that one sees it afresh, either through his eyes or through his deeds. The first is Columbus with his grim self-pity, the second Balboa with his tragic gaiety. And the third is Francis Drake, who descended unexpected on the isthmus and set the whole place in an uproar with his own kind of boyish bravado. But between these flashes of light, the human history of the place went on evolving, and one has to look at the times of dim evolution to be ready for the lightning when it comes. Between Balboa's death and Drake's irruption there were fifty years, and in those years the Spanish colony had moved and shrunk, the Spanish outlook had changed, and the first plans for a Panama Canal had already been promoted and discarded.

The death of Balboa was a crime which affected millions. If he had lived, Peru would have had a tolerably humane discoverer instead of the savage Pizarro: it is even conceivable that the Inca civilization would still exist today. But instead, the wave of conquest, with its slaughter and destruction, after passing through Darien like a wave of the sea through a narrow sound, began to spread out beyond. Pizarro carried it south, and Pedrarias north to the Pacific coast of Nicaragua. On the isthmus, the ebb of the wave left a kind of peace behind, but it was only the peace of death. The terrible rule of Pedrarias lasted for sixteen years until he died in 1530, and the historian Oviedo y Valdes, who was there until he could stand it no longer, made an estimate that he had caused the death or enslavement—or both—of 2,000,000 human beings. The figure seems impossible. But it is true that the Darien

53

Indians disappeared from all historical record for over a century. For all that anyone cared, they might have ceased to exist, like the Indians of Hispaniola. But enough had survived, hiding in scattered remnants in the jungle, to save their race and slowly rebuild the ruins of their simple society. They rebuilt it exactly as it had been before. Even now, it is not much different. But they never forgave the Spaniards.

The first of the processes of evolution was the movement of the colony. In 1519, two years after Balboa's execution, Pedrarias abandoned Santa Maria and founded the city of Panama, on the Pacific shore. Santa Maria and Acla dwindled and disappeared. The reasons for moving across to the other side were health and climate. Mortality from disease, on the Caribbean coast, was so high that it was impossible to maintain a capital city there. Even the earliest Spaniards saw some connection between their constant fevers and the pervading wetness, and they observed that the south coast had less than half the prodigious rainfall of the north. But Panama was bad enough. In the first fifteen years of the city's existence 45,000 people are said to have died of disease. Most of them must have been slaves, but Spain was pouring men into the colony, and few of them ever came home.

The site which Pedrarias chose for his city moved the center of activity on the isthmus farther west, to the area it has occupied ever since. Balboa's route was never used again, except by marauders. A trail was hacked through the jungle due north from Panama, to join the new city to Nombre de Dios Bay, where another but smaller town was founded to become the only port on the Caribbean side. It was a mean, muddy track that joined the oceans, winding up and down among the hills, about fifty miles in length and nine feet wide at its widest—just enough for laden mules to pass each other, brushing the virgin jungle on either side. But by 1535 or thereabouts it had the imposing name of *el Camino Real,* the Royal Road, and it was the most important thoroughfare in the Spanish empire.

It was a longer route than Balboa's from sea to sea, but it

had one advantage: only eighteen miles from Panama, it crossed the Rio Chagres, which flows into the Caribbean. A small settlement called Venta Cruces grew up at the river crossing. The Chagres, ever since, has been the most important geographical feature of the isthmus. It is much the biggest of the rivers on the Caribbean side, and from the earliest days it gave an alternative route for the northern two-thirds of the journey. In the dry seasons, trains of mules went all the way; but in the rains, the trail became almost impassably boggy, and at the same time the river rose until boats could go up it all the way to Venta Cruces. At these times, therefore, goods from Spain were landed at Nombre de Dios, and then sent by boat, forty-five miles along the open coast to the river mouth, then up the river to Venta Cruces, and only from there to Panama by muleback. Consignments of treasure, however, which came in the opposite direction, were seldom sent by river: the route was too long and exposed. When the trail was too bad, gold and silver and jewels accumulated in the Treasure House at Panama.

No one has ever computed the enormous wealth that came over this muddy track. All the gold that was seized from the Incas crossed it, all the pearls of the Pacific, all the silver of Bolivia. For the silver, an estimate exists: between 1545 and 1600, 20,000,000 kilograms, 200,000 tons. As for the gold and jewels, even if the quantities were known, one could not possibly give them a modern value. To the successive kings of Spain, the riches seemed to promise world-wide power and dominion. But on the contrary, all they did was disrupt the economy of Europe. Throughout the century, prices rose against the flood of Spanish wealth, a consequence which the Spaniards never understood; and in the upheaval, Spain was worst hit of all. Three times in the second half of the sixteenth century, the king was bankrupt. For all the courage and effort of the conquistadores, for all the pillage and slaughter, Spain was no better or richer a kingdom in the end.

The idea of a canal was first discussed within twenty years of Balboa's discovery. In 1520, Magellan passed through the

strait at the southern end of the continent, and after his death
in the Philippines his ship went on round the world and put the
continents more or less in their proper places on the map. By
that year also, Cordova, Cortes and other pioneers had closed
the last gaps in the exploration of the Caribbean coast and proved
that the strait Columbus had searched for did not exist. It was
hard to believe there was no way through for ships, not even by
rivers and lakes; the isthmus was so absurdly narrow. But when
the explorers reluctantly admitted there was none, it was a very
short step to the idea of making one.

The idea was first mentioned in print in 1555, in a book
called *The Discoveries of the World*, by the Portuguese governor
of Ternate in the Moluccas, whose name was Antonio Galvao.
But it was not his own idea. He attributed it to a man called
Alvaro de Saavedra Ceron, who was a cousin of Cortes; and it
is this man, of whom little else is known, that one must call the
originator of the Panama Canal.

Saavedra sailed from the Pacific coast of Mexico across the
Pacific to the Moluccas in 1528, and it was possibly there that
Galvao heard of him—he had some bloodthirsty fights with the
Portuguese in that far-flung outpost. He picked up a cargo of
cloves and other merchandise and set sail in 1529 to return to
Panama, where he meant to tranship his goods for Spain. If he
had succeeded, he would have been the first man to realize the
dream which had driven Columbus—the dream of a trade route
westward to the east. But his ship was beaten back by contrary
winds. And it was in an account of that journey that Galvao
casually mentioned Saavedra's idea:

"They came backe againe to Maluco very sad, because
Saavedra died by the way: who if he had lived, meant to have
opened the land of Castillia de Oro and New Spaine from sea to
sea.* Which might have beene done in fower places: namely from
the Gulfe of S. Michael to Uraba, which is 25 leagues; or from

* This was the translation published by Richard Hakluyt in 1601. The
Portuguese original said that Saavedra "intended to arrange with the king for
the land to be opened."

Panama to Nombre de Dios, being 17 leagues distance: or through Xaquatur, a river of Nicaragua, which springeth out of a lake three or fower leagues from the South sea, and falleth into the North sea; whereupon do saile great barks and crayers. The other place is from Tecoantepec through a river to Verdadera Cruz in the Bay of the Honduras, which also might be opened in a streight. Which if it were done, then they might saile from the Canaries unto the Malucas under the climate of the zodiake, in lesse time and with much lesse danger, than to saile about the Cape de Bona Speranca, or by the streight of Magelan, or by the Northwest."

So the idea existed, in the mind of a man who died in 1529. And perhaps the most curious thing about Galvao's report is that the Spaniards, so long ago, had already hit on four of the feasible routes—routes of which the merits have been passionately argued ever since. The first, from the Gulf of San Miguel to Uraba, which is the head of the Gulf of Darien, is being resurveyed in the 1960s as a possible route for a new canal dug out by atomic explosives. The second, from Panama, is the route of the present canal. The third, through the Lake of Nicaragua, was the principal rival to Panama in the nineteenth century. The fourth, through the isthmus of Tehuantepec in Mexico, has been proposed on and off for centuries.

Galvao, however, did not say how Saavedra proposed to build the canal. Slave labor, of course, was plentiful, and mere digging was not a problem. He must have intended to build it with locks; otherwise, he could not have thought of the Lake of Nicaragua, which is far above sea level. The theory of locks was known. Leonardo da Vinci had designed and built a canal with locks in Milan in the 1490s, and the Dutch had probably done it earlier. But nobody, even in Europe, had yet built a lock which was big enough for the seagoing ships of the time, and to have made such a pioneering effort in the jungle anywhere on the isthmus would have been immensely difficult. Probably, therefore, Saavedra was the first of the long line of optimists who thought the Panama Canal would be very much easier than it was.

But in any case, his grand idea was annulled before it began, and not only by his death. It is said that the king of Spain opposed it on the ground that if God had intended there should be a strait, He would have made one. But if God was invoked, it was only to support the royal policy; and with the discovery of Peru, that policy changed entirely. Saavedra belonged to the Columbian age of pioneering, but that age and its spirit were waning. The explorers had sought for a route to the riches of the east, but they found incomparably greater riches on the way; and like any treasure-seeker or prospector who finds his hoard, Spain lost the will to seek, and became obsessed with the fear of rivals coming to rob her. With Peru in his hands, the king lost interest in the east. The isthmus, which had been looked on at first as a way of reaching the Pacific, was looked on now as a heaven-sent barrier for keeping people out. A better crossing, or a canal, or even a second trail, could not have let more treasure out, but it might have let rivals in—and by 1555 the thought of rivals sailing the Pacific coast had become a waking nightmare for the Spaniards.

Under this policy, the isthmus became a dismal place to live in, the kind of place—as many travellers still regard it—which people only go to on the way to somewhere else. By the 1560s, the Spaniards in Panama and Nombre de Dios were far from thinking of anything so energetic as building a canal. The fight had gone out of them: the old fire of conquest had died in the heat and wet. The garrisons and merchants who succeeded the conquerors were on the defensive, against rains, diseases, homesickness and discontent—and also, at last, against human enemies more formidable than the Indians: the *cimarrones* and the corsairs.

The *cimarrones* were runaway Negro slaves: the Spanish word, which signified wild men, became shortened in English to maroon and is more familiar now as a verb although it started as a noun. Tens of thousands of Negroes, captured in Africa, had been sold in the Spanish islands, largely by English slave traders, and shipped to Nombre de Dios. They fetched a good price because they had more stamina than the Indians, who so readily killed themselves or died under Spanish burdens. But buying slaves was one thing, keeping them was another. Anywhere on the trail, if vigilance was relaxed for a second or two, they could dash off and vanish in the jungle: even in Nombre de Dios, the jungle pressed round the walls. The Spaniards themselves said that out of each 1,000 imported, 300 were likely to escape. By 1570, these maroons had established a kind of civilization of their own, with at least three secret towns securely hidden in the heart of Darien, from which they sometimes sallied forth in merciless revenge. The largest town was called Ronconcholon, and it was said to keep 1,700 men under arms. So the jungle, which had always been intimidating, now held a genuine menace. Any thicket might hide a gang of Negroes, intent on murder. No Spaniard could venture off the trail alone, and only along it well-armed. Castilla del Oro was reduced to a colony nine feet wide. The rest of Darien, excepting a few stockaded mining camps, was a no-man's land of terror.

The maroons kept the Spaniards in a state of nervous tension all the time. The corsairs, on the other hand, who were Frenchmen or Englishmen, half trader and half pirate, were the cause of occasional intense alarms—as, for example, on July 29th, 1572, when the church bell in Nombre de Dios suddenly rang out at three o'clock in the morning, drums and strange trumpet calls were heard, men were seen marching with torches through the market place—and the townspeople ran for the jungle, preferring to risk the maroons and shouting that Drake was there.

It was true. Drake had sailed out of Plymouth Sound in May, taking seventy-three men in two small ships, the *Pascha* or *Pasco* and the *Swan*, with this very intention: to attack the Spanish treasure-route at its heart. He was only thirty years old. Although everyone knew his name in Nombre de Dios, it was almost unknown in England, and this voyage was a private escapade. All his crew were even younger than he was, except one man of fifty; and in the Darien jungle, and on the Spanish trail, this boyish gang was to set a supreme example of Elizabethan audacity and flair.

Drake's motives were ignoble in themselves; they were theft and revenge. He had already sailed four times to the Spanish Main. The first two voyages, when he served as purser, were in the slave trade, the second of them under the redoubtable John Hawkins. Possibly, in defiance of his times, he disliked this trade; at any rate, he never had anything to do with it again. But in both these voyages he had run across the Spanish claim to exclusive possession of Central America—a claim that all English voyagers thought irritating, arrogant and false. Even trade by other nations was forbidden by the Spanish crown. The colonists were often willing to trade, because the English prices were lower than the royal monopoly's. But it was always a contraband trade, subject to sudden skirmishes and swindles. And on the second voyage, Drake was present at the battle of San Juan de Ulua, on the coast of Mexico, when the Spaniards treacherously tried to seize Hawkins' fleet which had put into harbor for repairs.

One modern American writer has called that battle the Pearl Harbor of Tudor England. The English could not forgive the Spaniards for it: it was the beginning of the enmity which culminated in the Spanish Armada. There were still many years before open war began, but after San Juan the Spaniards and their possessions were always considered fair game for any Englishman brave enough to attack them. And Drake, who had seen the treachery in person and lost his own property and his friends', took to this unofficial warfare with a crusader's zeal and a born adventurer's delight.

He planned the attack on Nombre de Dios with extraordinary thoroughness and patience. His third and fourth voyages were private reconnaissances. He explored the whole of the coast of Darien, deserted now by Spaniards and Indians alike, and found in Careta's country a small landlocked bay which he called Port Pheasant (on account of the large numbers of these "goodlie fowles" which his men had been able to hunt there.) This he equipped as a base. Cruising on the coast, he took a good many Spanish ships, in order to help himself to any provisions or valuables they were carrying, and also to glean intelligence from their crews of Spanish dispositions at Nombre de Dios. But after questioning the crews, he always gave them back their ship or put them ashore with plenty of food in places where he knew they could save themselves. And it was on these voyages that he won his reputation among the Spaniards for swift irresistible attacks and totally unexpected chivalry.

The voyage of 1572 began in drama and continued in drama to the end. No other voyage ever made can have been so exciting for a youthful crew. It was a year and three months of pure adventure, up and down that exotic empty coast, through the jungle, in and out of Spanish harbors, under a captain who could always sail a boat a little better than anyone else alive. It had failures and disappointments, enough to give a glow to its moments of triumph. It had extreme hardship also: half the men died on the way. But adventure does not exist without danger; any Englishman sailing to the Spanish Main would have been content with a fifty-fifty chance of coming back alive. And through it all was the vein of good humor and overflowing self-confidence which was the mark of the best of the Elizabethans, and of Drake above them all when he was young. The aim was to steal—but only to steal what the Spaniards had already stolen. The motive was revenge—but Drake's revenge for the slaughter of San Juan was not to slaughter Spaniards, only to annoy them to the point of ridiculous fury. Certainly, the voyage was profitable; but even more important, it was fun.

They sailed straight from Plymouth to Port Pheasant, only stopping once, on a deserted island coast, for water. But entering his secret harbor there, Drake saw a column of smoke among the trees. He landed cautiously, but there was nobody there, only a dying fire. The jungle had overgrown the clearing he had made the year before. But prowling around, his men found a sheet of lead nailed to a very large tree, with a message scratched on it:

"Captain Drake, if you fortune to come to this Port, mak

hast away, for the Spaniards which you had with you here the last yeere have bewrayed this place, and taken away all that you left here. I departed from hence, this present 7. of July, 1572. Your verie loving friend John Garret."

Five days before. Everyone knew John Garret, he was a Plymouth man, but nobody knew—or knows now—what he was doing there, or where he had gone. Drake's earlier crews, of course, knew about Port Pheasant—it was an open secret in Plymouth—and the Spaniards who had betrayed it were captives Drake had taken there and then set free. He was not much disturbed by the warning. What he meant to do in Port Pheasant was to assemble three pinnaces—heavy eight-oared boats with sails—which had been built for him in Plymouth and taken to pieces and stowed in the holds of his ships: and undismayed he landed the pieces and set his carpenters to work, while the rest of the men built a small stockade around them in case of trouble.

The day after they started, another ship came in: an English barque from the Isle of Wight, Captain Ranse, escorting two captured Spanish vessels. This was a nuisance: the secret port was getting a little too popular. But when Ranse was told of Drake's plan, he wanted to join him, and Drake felt obliged to agree.

In a week, the pinnaces were finished, and the whole fleet sailed west along the coast to a place called the Island of Pines. Here they encountered two Spanish frigates, manned by Negroes who were felling timber. Drake questioned these men, and then put them ashore on the mainland, confident they could not reach Nombre de Dios before him by walking along the shore. "For he was loath," the account of the voyage facetiously explained, "to put the town to too much charge in providing before hand for his entertainment."

From the Island of Pines to Nombre de Dios is 130 miles. Seventy-three men—fifty-three of Drake's and twenty of Ranse's —rowed and sailed this distance in the pinnaces and Ranse's boat, leaving the ships behind. Their arms, packed in casks to keep them dry, were "sixe Targets, sixe Firepikes, twelve Pikes, twentie foure Muskets and Callivers, sixteene Bowes, and sixe Partisans, two Drums, and two Trumpets." Evidently, he had given careful thought to this armament, as to all his other preparations. Bows were unorthodox, but more reliable than firearms in a wet climate. He had had the arrows "made of purpose in England, not great sheafe arrows, but fine roving shafts, very carefully reserved for the service." The drums and trumpets were psychological, and the firepikes, which were ordinary pikes with a twist of tarry tow on the end, were used both as torches and weapons.

For five days they followed the coast, sometimes in the open sea, sometimes between the coral islands and the shore, and always below the wall of jungle-covered hills. On the fifth day they landed, and Drake distributed the arms and made a speech of encouragement. From his captives in the past, he had a fairly clear idea of Nombre de Dios. It was quite a considerable town— larger than their own home town of Plymouth—with streets and a market place, main buildings of stone and houses of wood, and a wall or stockade all round it except on the seaward side, with a single gate where the Royal Road came in: not a small undertaking for seventy-three men in open boats, but not a small prize if they won.

That afternoon, they rowed on, close inshore, and at dusk they saw the watchtower on the point of the bay—the first building they had seen in Darien. They cast their grapnels and waited at anchor until it was dark night, and then rowed again, as silently now as they could, until they were in the harbor mouth below the loom of the hills which enclose it.

Drake meant to attack at dawn. But lying there on their oars, the crews began to whisper about the size of the town and its garrison. Most of them had never been in a fight before; the odds against them in fact were heavy enough, and when there was nothing to do but wait they began to look heavier. So he cut the waiting short. The moon was rising. He told them it was the dawn, and gave them the word to go.

Rounding the point, pulling hard, out in the open now, they

saw a ship in the bay which had just come in—its sail was still
unfurled—and the crew of the ship saw the pinnaces coming and
put off a boat for the shore. Drake cut in between the boat and
the town and ran the pinnaces aground on a sandy beach twenty
yards below the houses. At the head of the beach there were six
brass cannon, but only one gunner, who fled. While they toppled
the cannon off their carriages, the alarm was given; the church
bell rang and went on ringing, shouts came from the town, drum-
mers began to run up and down the streets. Drake spent some
minutes—wasted as it turned out—in climbing a hill which he
had been told had artillery on top, but there was none. Then he
divided his force according to his plan: twelve to keep the pinnaces, sixteen under his brother to double round to the other end
of the town, and himself with the forty-odd others to march up
the main street in formal ranks with firepikes lighted and the
martial sound of drum and trumpet. And in the Elizabethan account of what happened, there is the elation of the torchlit,
moonlit skirmish:

"The Souldiers, and such as were joyned with them, presented us with a jolly hot volley of shot, beating full upon the
egresse of that street in which we marched, and levelling verie
low, so as their bullets oft times grazed on the sand. We stood
not to answer them in like tearmes: but having discharged our
first volley of shot, and feathered them with our arrowes, we
came to the push of pike, so that our fire-pikes being well armed
and made of purpose, did us very great service. For our men with
their pikes and short weapons in short time tooke such order
among those Gallants, some using the but-end of their Peeces in
stead of other weapons, that ... they, casting downe their weapons, fled all out of the Towne by the gate aforesaid."

Giving chase, some of the Englishmen injured themselves by
tripping over the weapons the Spaniards had thrown away, and
they gave it up and came back to the market place, out of breath
and triumphant. One of their trumpeters was lying dead: nobody
else seemed badly hurt. The town was emptied, but the church

bell was still ringing. Drake sent some men to stop it, but the
church was locked and he told them not to force it. Two or three
Spaniards had been captured, and he made them take him to the
governor's house, where the treasure that came from Panama was
unloaded and counted. The door was open, a candle was lighted
at the top of a flight of steps, and a horse stood saddled. There
was nobody there. By the light of the candle, they saw a huge
heap of silver, seventy feet in length, they guessed, ten feet thick
and twelve feet high, piled against the wall of a lower room. It
was in bars which weighed thirty-five or forty pounds. Drake
told them to leave it alone. It was too heavy to carry—there
might be more fighting to do; and the gold and jewels, he believed, were in the King's Treasure House, nearer the water's
edge—more of them than the pinnaces could carry.

After a lull, the uproar in the town began again as fresh
troops came in from the outskirts, and rushed through the streets
shouting "*¿Qué gente?*"—who goes there?—and shooting at random. And then the confusion was stilled by a thunderstorm and
a drenching shower of rain. Everyone took shelter, to keep
matches and powder dry, Drake's men below the eaves of the
Treasure House itself. Nervous muttering began again. They
were better at sailing or fighting than waiting. Drake said he had
brought them to the door of the treasure of the world: if they
went without it now, they would have nobody but themselves to
blame. As soon as the storm began to abate—a long half hour—
he ordered his brother's troop to break open the Treasure House,
and the rest to follow him to hold off the enemy.

Stepping forward, he fainted and fell; and then they saw he
had been wounded in the leg, and standing there all that time
had filled the footprints they had made with blood—more blood
than they could believe one man could spare and live. They tied
his scarf round his leg and gave him a drink, and begged him to
give up the treasure and retreat to save his life. He refused, but
grew weaker; and when he could not resist them any longer,
they carried him—"with force mingled with faire intreatie"—

back to the pinnaces, and launched them and rowed away. Going
out of the harbor, they took the ship which had entered in the
night, and sailed it away. It was loaded with wine.

They only retreated three miles, to an island outside the bay
that Columbus had named Bastiamentos—the Island of Provisions. In Columbus' time, it had been notably fertile; now it was
a sort of market garden for the town, and there, still in view of
the Spanish defenses, they settled down to rest for the next few
days.

It was a strange kind of warfare. On the day after the battle,
the Spanish governor sent out a courtly officer—"a proper Gentleman of meane stature, good complexion and fare spoken"—to
ask after the attackers' health. Drake though he was a spy, but
courtesies were exchanged. The Spaniards, the emissary said, had
been delighted to find the attackers were English, not French:
the English might take their treasure, but the French would be
mercilessly cruel. Was it true he had the honor to meet Captain
Drake? Were the English arrows poisoned, and if they were,
what was the cure? What victuals or other necessities did Captain Drake desire? Drake gave him the obvious answers: it was
never his practice to poison his arrows, and their wounded could
be cured by ordinary surgery. As for his needs, he wanted nothing but the special commodity the country yielded, gold, and he
advised the governor to keep his eyes open, because if God lent
him life and leave, he proposed to reap some of that harvest.
After dinner, the gentleman departed, protesting that he had
never been so honored in his life.

It was all very well for Drake to send a defiant threat to
the governor: at that moment, he had no idea how to carry it
out. All his careful planning had been brought to nothing by a
chance shot in the dark from a Spanish soldier. Once the direct
attack had failed, it was hopeless to try it again. Captain Ranse
lost heart and left, to nobody's regret. But the encounter gave
Drake's men a confidence they never lost: it was their first battle,

and they had won, and it was sheer bad luck that they had missed the treasure. And they had found an ally in the town: a Negro slave, a man called Diego, who had hailed the pinnaces in the middle of the fight and asked if Captain Drake was there, and had begged, in spite of being shot at, to be taken on board. He was a renegade who had joined the maroons and then betrayed them to the Spaniards. Now despised by both sides, he offered his life and service to Drake, and told him the maroons would all be willing to serve him against the Spaniards. It was the germ of a new idea. Six weeks later, in the middle of September, Drake sent his brother John under Diego's guidance through the maze of coral islands in the Gulf of San Blas, about fifty miles east of Nombre de Dios, to a point where the fugitive slaves were sometimes seen. And there, lurking among the trees, they found a few of them, and managed to overcome their suspicion.

The maroons were surprised to meet white men who treated them as human, and Drake, when he met them, was surprised to find them intelligent and well organized. They were also surprised and rather dismayed to hear that he wanted gold: like the Indians, they had never quite understood why anyone should value anything so useless. It was only a pity, they said, that he had come at the wrong time of year. They had often taken gold from the Spaniards, not because they wanted it, but simply because they knew the Spaniards did. They had always hidden it in river beds, but now in the rainy season the rivers were too high to dig it up again. However, it was easy to get more, if he could wait till January. And they explained a fact he had not understood before, that the Spaniards only moved their gold in the dry winter seasons.

He agreed to wait. But he was not a man to wait four months in idleness. He took the *Pasco* in by careful sounding to an anchorage inside the islands where she was perfectly safe— because nobody could sail in there by night, and in daylight only as slowly and carefully as he had. He had already sunk the

Swan, in order to have enough men to man the pinnaces. Now he left his brother to build a fort, and in two of the pinnaces he and forty men went roving.

His successes in those open boats are still astonishing. By that time, there were about 200 Spanish frigates, from 10 to 120 tons, in trade between Nombre de Dios and the other harbors of the Spanish Main, especially the new city of Carthagena, on the coast beyond the Gulf of Darien. Drake's crews claimed afterwards—and he did not deny it—that they captured most of these 200 ships, and some of them twice or three times. It could have been true, because Drake and his Devon captains were incomparably better sailors than the Spaniards—and knew they were —and because the boats they chose to use were smaller, handier and faster than the frigates. It was a foretaste of the nautical outlook that beat the Spanish Armada. And it was not only at sea that he took the Spanish ships. Again and again he sailed into the landlocked harbor of Carthagena, the strongest of all the cities on the Main, capturing ships inside it and sailing them out, and always keeping to windward of his frustrated enemies. Once, in a typical gesture, he jumped ashore there alone, in sight of a Spanish army, simply to be able to say he had done it.

It was the kind of success that breeds success. He never sank or burned the Spanish ships he took, unless they were men-of-war, and never injured the Spanish crews, once the first sharp fight was over. As his reputation spread, his victims began to expect to be given back their ships, or at worst to be set ashore. They had more sense than to risk their lives to defend their cargoes, which probably belonged to merchants, not to them; and so they began to surrender with only a token fight when his pinnaces overhauled them. For Drake and his crews, the sea chases and boardings were immensely exciting in themselves, and there was the excitement too of rummaging in the holds of the captured ships to see what the cargo was. Sometimes there was the fiasco of an empty ship, always the slender hope of a glorious chest full of treasure. They were never short of arms and powder and shot. Most of the rest of the booty was food—maize, wine, sugar, bacon, cheese, often live hogs and hens, once a load of honey, and once, less welcome, of soap. Sometimes they were wet and cold and hungry, sometimes they feasted. They took the food they could not eat and stored it in caches on the Darien coast, until they had enough to feed thousands. And between times, when the pursuit of the Spanish men-of-war grew hot, they vanished into hidden bays to rest, and Drake set half the men each day to hunting and fishing and mending the boats and gear, and the other half to more gentle sports than piracy—bowls, quoits, archery and skittles. There was only one disaster, and it happened when Drake was not there. For once, the self-confidence he bred in his men overreached itself. John Drake, the young brother he had left on the Main, sighted a pinnace when he was sailing his boat with a load of timber for the fort he was building. The men he had with him wanted him to take it. The only weapons they had were a broken rapier, a fish-spear and a rusty musket. It was a stupid risk, and he said so, but they urged him on until he said "If you will needes adventure, it shall never be said that I will be hindermost." So they hove the timber overboard and gave chase and boarded—John Drake in the van with the rapier. But the frigate was well armed with muskets, which were discharged in their faces, and John and another young man called Richard Allen were killed.

The repeated attacks of corsairs, and the knowledge that Drake was among them, reduced the colony to fearful consternation. There were quarrels about the defense of Nombre de Dios. A few extra troops were sent there from Panama, but there were hardly enough to go round. The colonists only agreed in blaming General Diego Flores, the commander of the twice-yearly fleet from Spain, for failing to root out the corsairs when he was there. And whenever dispatches could be sent to Spain, the authorities of Panama begged the king to set up a coastal patrol and strengthen the garrison. These requests were formal, each ending with slight variations of the words "Catholic Royal Majesty, Your Majesty's humble servants and vassals kiss your Catholic

Royal Majesty's feet." But as time went by and nothing except
vague promises came from Spain, their impatience began to show.
"This realm at the present moment is so terrified, and the spirits
of all so disturbed, that we know not in what words to emphasise
to your majesty the solicitude we make in this dispatch, for we
certainly believe that if remedial action be delayed, disaster is
imminent." "May your majesty deign to provide suitably in this
matter, for this place is as good as lost." "Humbly we entreat
your majesty to deign to send prompt relief and defence, the
best form for which we believe would be two galleys to patrol
the coast, as we have many times previously asked your Majesty
to provide." But none of it did any good. The king procrastinated.
And the dry season approached—the time for the visit of the
treasure fleet, and the movement of the gold along the trail.

But Drake's run of success, as the time came near, had ended
in serious trouble—not with the Spaniards, with something he
did not understand: the disease of the coast. In the pinnaces, a
man suddenly died, and many of the rest fell ill. They thought
it was due to the cold and exposure of all those weeks at sea in
the open boats. Perhaps it was. They sailed back to the Gulf of
San Blas to rejoin the party they had left there, and they seemed
to recover. But at the end of the year, when the treasure fleet
was expected any day in Nombre de Dios, a dozen more men
were taken sick, and in two or three days, most of the dozen
were dead. The sickness spread: at one time, more than half who
were still alive were in a fever. Another of Drake's younger
brothers died of it, and Drake had the surgeon cut him open to
try to find what had killed him. Of course, he did not succeed;
and four days later the surgeon died, from taking too much of a
purgative he had made himself. Within two or three weeks, the
epidemic was over; but by then, twenty-eight were dead.

There was no time to grieve about it. The maroons, ranging
up and down the country as far as Nombre de Dios, brought
word that the fleet was in; and in the middle of January, Drake
assembled all the men who were fit—only eighteen—for the new
adventure he had been waiting for: an attack on the Spanish trail.

The maroons had promised to take him to the farthest part of the trail, between Panama and Venta Cruces. It is a mystery why he decided to go so far, when the nearer end of the trail at Nombre de Dios was so close. Perhaps he thought, or they thought, that the treasure might be brought down the Rio Chagres from Venta Cruces, or that the far end of the trail would not be so closely guarded. At any rate, the distance he set himself to march was about 130 miles as the crow flies, and probably twice as much by the shortest route through the jungle. Yet he did it with no more trouble than sore feet, because his approach to the jungle was different from any Spaniard's, even Balboa's. He was not too proud to learn. The maroons had lived there for years, and knew the jungle as well as the Indians had. He made up his mind to trust them, took their advice and put himself entirely in their hands—although he was always unmistakably in command. And they responded by looking after the Englishmen like honored guests. He took thirty maroons, who were under a captain of their own called Pedro. Every day, four of them marched a mile ahead and blazed a trail. The rest formed a vanguard and a rearguard, with the English in the middle. They kept them well-fed by hunting with bows and arrows, and told them which of the fruit they could eat and which they must leave alone. And each evening, they built huts for the whole of the party and lit fires in them—for this was winter, and the nights in the hills were cold. On the whole, these Englishmen found the jungle pleasant: it can be, at that time of the year, when the ground is almost dry and the deciduous leaves have fallen and let some sunlight in. It was all rather like a rich man's African safari.

Three days in from the coast, they came to one of the towns the maroons had established in the depths of the jungle. It was not the capital Ronconcholon, but it was quite a considerable place, and it made a deep impression on the Plymouth men. There were fifty-five households in it, surrounded by a ditch and a mud wall ten feet high, and it was "kept so cleane and sweet that not only the houses but the verie streets were verie pleasant to behold. They lived verie civilly and cleanely, for as soone as wee came thither, they washed themselves in the river, and changed their apparrel, which was verie fine and fitly made (as also their women doe weare) somewhat after the Spanish fashion, though nothing so costly." Drake found that they had no priests but held the cross in veneration. He persuaded them out of what seemed to him a popish practice, and taught them the Lord's prayer; and detesting the Spaniards as they did, they gladly declared themselves Protestants. He was only there one night: it must have been one of the quickest mass conversions ever made.

After four more days of marching, a more famous incident occurred. At the top of a hill, Pedro, the chief of the maroons, took Drake by the hand to a "goodly and great high Tree" in which they had cut steps and built a bower big enough for a dozen men to sit in. Other trees had been felled to north and south, and climbing up to the bower Drake saw both seas—the first Englishman to do so—and prayed God to give him life and leave to sail an English ship in the South Sea: a prayer which was answered years later in the voyage of the *Golden Hind*. Then, like Balboa, he called up his men to see the inspiring sight, and one of them in particular, a man called John Oxenham, declared that unless Drake beat him from his company he would be with him in the voyage he had prayed for.

In the last three days of their outward march—it took them a fortnight altogether—they were in the grasslands at the back of Panama, and whenever they came to the top of a hill they could see the city. Here they went very cautiously, away from what tracks there were, hiding in the six-foot grass, because the maroons had warned them that "the Dames of Panama are wont to send forth Hunters and Fowlers for taking of sundry daintie Fowle, which the land yeeldeth." Still in secrecy, three miles from the city boundaries, they found the trail and hid themselves beside it in a grove. One of the maroons who had served in Panama was dressed in slave's clothes and sent into the city to spy. This intrepid man, who would have suffered the most ingenious tortures if he had been recognized, came back the same evening with a report that set them on their toes: the treasurer of the city of Lima in Peru was leaving Panama that night, with his family on the way home to Spain, taking fourteen mules of which eight were laden with gold and one with jewels—the savings of a profitable post. For the mule-trains travelled by night across the grasslands, which were unbearably hot for travel in the day.

With this entrancing news, the Englishmen and maroons marched up the trail to within a few miles of Venta Cruces, in order to shorten their line of retreat. There they put on their shirts outside the rest of their clothes, so that they would know each other in the dark. Drake divided the party into two, one to lie in wait in the grass on each side of the trail, and gave them the strictest orders: to let the traffic from Venta Cruces pass, and seize the mules that came from Panama.

It was a very still night. They lay in ambush just over an hour, and then they heard bells—the deep-throated bells of the mule-trains far away. They were approaching from both directions. And then on the stones of the trail, the hoofbeats of a single horse, coming down at the trot from Venta Cruces. On Drake's side of the track they had a glimpse of a cavalier, well-mounted, and his page running at his stirrup. And instantly, as he disappeared, the hoofbeats changed from a trot to a gallop.

What had happened? they whispered. Had they been seen? Drake thought they had, but he could not imagine how. They listened again: the bells seemed to pause, but then they came on again.

The train of mules came up to them, chiming through the night. The moment came. Drake blew a whistle, they dashed out and seized the leading mules and overpowered the drivers, and the other half of the party came in behind and cut off the retreat. But this was not a treasure-train, it had far more than fourteen mules. They were only carrying food. And in the melée Drake confronted the muleteers and heard the truth: the horseman had seen a man in white rise up from the grass and galloped on to warn the treasurer, who had turned back to Panama and let the food-train go through. And the other half of Drake's party brought him a shamefaced Englishman called Robert Pike, who had drunk too much brandy without any water while he was waiting, and jumped to his feet in drunken bravado when the horseman came, and done the damage before a maroon, with more sense, pulled him down again and sat on him.

That part of the Spanish trail still exists, because native horsemen have used it on and off ever since, and picking one's way along the remains of it now, one does not need much imagination to see that scene of confusion and disappointment, and the hectic scenes that followed it that night. This is just where the trail leaves the grassland and enters the jungle. Now it is overgrown, but there underfoot are the same worn stones that paved it, and there overhead the same dense growth that arched it over like a small dark tunnel. Now treetrunks lie across it, and here and there one has to cut away the creepers and the fronds of palms and ferns. But then it was regularly cleared, and the jungle cut back like a matted hedge. Then, at that moment, with Panama at one end and Venta Cruces at the other, and Englishmen, maroons and Spanish muleteers all milling about in the dark among the restive mules, and at least a hundred miles to go for safety, it was a very unhealthy place indeed.

There is no record of what Drake said to Robert Pike. It should have been memorable, but he had a way of accepting failure without recrimination, as if the whole thing were a game which did not really matter very much. Clearly, God had not meant them to rob the treasurer: the man must have made his fortune honestly. (The Spaniards also put it down to divine intervention.) The only question was how to get out of the mess. There were two ways: to retreat by the way they had come, or advance up the trail itself, straight through the middle of Venta Cruces. They were tired, but the mules were not; it seemed a pity not to use them. Drake consulted Pedro the maroon, who simply said he would die for him, and they mounted the mules and rode up the trail towards the settlement at the river crossing.

The maroons, among their other useful skills, were able to

smell Spanish soldiers at a distance from the slow matches they used for their muskets. Eagerly sniffing, they smelt them coming a mile from Venta Cruces. Everyone dismounted, sent the mules and their drivers back towards Panama and advanced on foot. From the pitch darkness under the trees ahead, a voice shouted "Ho-oh." Drake answered the same.

"*¿Qué gente?*" the voice demanded.

"Englishmen," Drake shouted back.

"Surrender in the name of the king of Spain, my master," the man ahead of them shouted. And he promised fair treatment on the word of a gentleman soldier.

"In the name of the queen of England, my mistress," Drake replied, and fired his pistol.

His tactics were always the same: to provoke the Spaniards to fire off a volley, and then get them hand-to-hand before they could reload. The volley came, a storm of hail-shot down the narrow track. He and several others were slightly wounded, and one man badly. They charged up the trail, the maroons with their arrows ready in their bows, dancing and leaping forward and loudly singing "*Yo peho, yo peho.*" There was a short sharp fight in the thickets—the enemy were a mixture of soldiers and armed Dominican friars—and then they were through in the town and everyone had fled.

They stayed there till dawn—refreshing themselves, they said. The maroons succeeded in looting some clothes, but there was nothing much of value light enough to carry, and Drake had to spend some time reassuring three pregnant women in a kind of maternity home—they had come up from Nombre de Dios, where the climate was supposed to be fatal to newborn babies. A counterattack from the trail was easily put to flight, and in the first light they crossed the Chagres and took to the jungle beyond. A week later, by forced marches, they were back at the coast again, hungry and footsore and no richer than they had started—but not very much dismayed.

On that long walk back, and in his ship when he found it, Drake kept their spirits up, but he must have privately faced the thought of going home to England empty-handed. He had only thirty-one men left alive—hardly enough to protect themselves, and far too few to attempt a serious fight. It was not just a matter of going without the fortune he had hoped for: if he failed, it would be the end of the career he was starting. He would probably be imprisoned, and possibly lose his head—for the Spaniards would certainly make a complaint to the queen, and she would not offend them by supporting him unless he could bring her a victory bizarre enough to make him a national hero. Those were the rules of the game, and everyone understood them.

For want of a better idea, he put to sea again to hunt for frigates bringing gold to Nombre de Dios from the coast on either side. All he managed to capture was yet another cargo of fat hogs and hens, and the well-designed new frigate which was carrying them. But while he was hunting, he fell in with a French corsair called Captain Tetu, who hailed him and asked for food. Drake had plenty, and gave him what he needed. They mistrusted each other, but when Tetu was told of Drake's escapade on the trail, he offered to lend him twenty men for another attempt, in return for a half share of the spoils. It was a final hope, and Drake took it.*

There was no need to go all the way to Venta Cruces: he had learned that lesson. He sent for his maroons, left his ship among the islands, and landed from two pinnaces in a river mouth which was only fifteen miles east of Nombre de Dios. This time, he had twenty Frenchmen—including Captain Tetu— and only fifteen of his own men: perhaps Robert Pike was one of the three left behind. He told the men who were manning the

---

* Captain Tetu, though Drake may not have known it, was a distinguished maker of maps when he was not engaged in piracy, and he had published an atlas of the world. It was a wonderful production. His seas were full of monsters, ships and splendid wooden-wheeled chariots drawn by dolphins, and every inch of his continents was decorated with whimsical creatures of his own invention, pictures of scenery, and men. His animals always had gentle, amiable expressions on their faces, but his men were often shooting each other with arrows or clubbing each other to death. In the map of the northern part of South America, the cannibals had given him some of his most macabre inspiration.

pinnaces to meet him at the same place four days later, without fail.

They marched in the same formation as before. The jungle, and the whole proceeding, astonished Captain Tetu, who said he would never find his way back again if the maroons deserted him. But it was not very far. By a long day's march, they came within a mile of the trail, and then stopped in hiding for the night—so close to Nombre de Dios that they could hear the hammers of the carpenters in the shipyard, who were working at night to avoid the heat of the day. And in the morning, they heard the bells again, more and more of them, far and near, coming down from the hills towards the town. The maroons rejoiced, and promised them more gold and silver than they could carry away. And creeping down to the trail, they saw the mule-trains coming —three of them, nearly 200 animals tied head to tail, and all of them laden. They were escorted by soldiers. At Drake's whistle, the raiders leaped out of cover and seized the foremost and hind-most mules, halted the train and blocked the track. Some arrows and musket shots were fired, one maroon fell dead and Captain Tetu was badly hit in the stomach by hail-shot. And the escort fled.

The maroons were right: there was far more treasure there than they could carry. Most of the mules were loaded with silver —300 pounds each, nearly thirty tons of it—and some were carrying bars and disks of gold. They took the gold, and spent two hectic hours in burying silver bars, some in the burrows of land-crabs, some under fallen trees, some in the sand of a shallow river bed. Only half of that work was done when they heard more soldiers and horsemen approaching from Nombre de Dios, and they loaded themselves with gold and took to the jungle again.

In the town, when the guards of the treasure-train came panting in with their story, the church bell was rung again, the drums were sounded, and the mayor read a proclamation calling the people to arms. In person, he led a detachment up the trail.

Fifty men were sent overland along the coast to the place where
they guessed the corsairs had landed, and General Diego Flores,
the commander of the treasure fleet, sent all his pinnaces out to
patrol the river mouths. The mayor and his men found the mule-
trains scattered, their boxes broken open, a dead maroon and a
Frenchman (so they said) with his head cut off. A score of soldiers were sent to pursue the raiders through the jungle, and
they caught poor Captain Tetu, who had grown too weak to run,
and killed him. Another Frenchman was captured, and under
torture in the town he confessed where the silver was hidden.
But that night, a storm blew up and torrents of rain came down,
and the chase in the jungle was abandoned.

Drake and his gang marched all the next day, learning that
gold is much heavier than it looks. At evening, hungry, tired and
wet to the skin, they came to the coast where the pinnaces should
have been. But they were not there. Instead, out at sea, they saw
seven of the boats of General Flores. Even Drake thought the
worst—that the Spaniards had taken the pinnaces, and even then
must be putting the crews to torture to learn where the ships
were hidden. Some of the company saw their way home cut off,
and their treasure useless. Drake said this was no time to fear,
but a time to hurry to prevent what was feared: even if the
pinnaces were taken, they might still reach the ships before the
Spaniards—not by land, because of the rivers and thickets, but
by sea. "Let us make a raft," he said, "with the trees that are
here in readiness, and put ourselves to sea. I will be one. Who
will be the other?" One Englishman and two Frenchmen volunteered. The raft was made overnight, from the trees that the
storm had brought down the river, a sail of biscuit sacks, and a
young tree as a rudder. And in the morning, Drake embarked on
it, and promised the rest that if it pleased God he should put his
foot in safety aboard his frigate, he would, God willing, by one
means or another get them all aboard in spite of all the Spaniards
in the Indies.

Drake could sail anything. With this crazy equipment in
the open sea, he covered nine miles before the storm in six hours,

sitting up to his waist in the water, and up to his shoulders at every surge of the waves. Under the sun and salt water, his skin was "much fretted away." At length, thanking God, they saw two pinnaces, and he cheerfully told his companions they were his. But the pinnaces did not see the raft: they ran into shelter behind a point of land.

What other sea-captain would have had the surplus energy, at a moment like this, to play a practical joke on his crew? Drake did. He put his raft ashore and ran at top speed round the point, pretending he was being chased by the enemy. Successfully alarmed, the crews of the pinnaces hurried to take him on board, and he answered their questions so coldly that they thought there had been another disaster. And then—his great moment—he undid his shirt and pulled out a bar of gold. That night, he rowed right back to the river, against the wind, and rescued the men and the treasure.

It was Drake's genius always to go one step further in sheer audacity than his friends or his enemies ever thought he would. Now, with his fortune made and everything to lose, and the Spaniards ashore and afloat in a state of excited alarm, he did it again. He decided to go back to look for Captain Tetu and dig up the silver. His own men refused to let him go—they believed by then he was the only man with the luck and skill to take them home again. But they agreed to go for him, and it was he who rowed in a week later and put them ashore again. Tetu, of course, was dead, but they found another Frenchman who had been lost in the jungle and now came down to the river bank and fell on his knees to bless God for the time that Captain Drake was born. The maroons had told him 2,000 Spaniards and Negroes had been digging for the silver. Nevertheless, they went. For a mile around the scene of the ambuscade, they saw that every likely place had been well dug over; but they found thirteen bars of silver and several disks of gold, and came back safe and cheerful.

It was high time to think of home. They were loaded with wealth. The English reports are evasive about the amount they had captured, but the Spanish reports put the loss at 130,000

pesos, which was about £50,000—a huge sum of money then.
Drake divided it fifty-fifty with the Frenchmen, in accordance
with his bargain with Captain Tetu. They parted on very friendly
terms with the maroons who had shared their adventures. The
treasure-fleet had sailed from Nombre de Dios and was riding at
the entry of Carthagena harbor, waiting to leave for Spain.
Drake could not resist a gesture. "Thus we departed, passing
hard by Carthagena, in the sight of all the Fleete, with a flag of
Saint George in the maine top of our Fregat, with silk streamers
and ancients downe to the water, sayling forward with a large
wind." On Sunday, August 9th, 1573, they sailed into Plymouth
at sermon time. The news spread through the church, and very
few or none of the congregation stayed to hear the preacher.

*   *   *

Drake's adventure had two sequels, and both of them were
grim. The first was five years afterwards in the Pearl Islands—
where Balboa had made his Pacific base—when a slave girl in a
Spanish house heard her master's dog barking in the night, and
opened the door and gave a shriek which began a new era of
Spanish trepidation. She ran through the house crying "My lady,
the French!"—but the ruffians she had seen outside in the darkness were not the French, they were the English, and they were
led by John Oxenham, Drake's lieutenant who had climbed the
tree with him. What the Spaniards had feared so long had happened: Englishmen were at large in the South Sea.

After Drake reached home, his thoughts had turned away
from the isthmus to wider fields of adventure, and he had started
to plan his voyage round the world. Oxenham, quite independently, had fitted out an expedition of his own, landed on the
Darien coast again, hidden his ships, marched over by Balboa's
route with the help of the maroons, and built a new ship in a
river on the Pacific side. Within a week or two, he had captured
one of the treasure-ships which sailed unarmed from Peru to
Panama, and had landed in the islands demanding pearls and gold

from the Spanish settlers. At that moment, Drake in the *Golden Hind* was still sailing down towards Cape Horn, so Oxenham was the first to fulfill the ambition they had shared at the top of the tree—the ambition to sail an English ship on the sea they saw from there.

Almost nothing is known about Oxenham. He was a Plymouth man, and a Spanish description says he was thick of speech and grave of demeanor, much feared, respected and obeyed by his men. But he was not a second Drake: he lacked the brilliant flair for leadership and maneuver. Let loose in the Pearl Islands, his men did one thing Drake's had never done: they entered Spanish houses. That first house, where the slave gave her memorable shriek, may well have been the first Catholic home those Plymouth sailors had ever seen, and the shock to their narrow Protestant minds overcame, for the moment, their interest in gold. They spent the night destroying Catholic images, and giving stern but crude lectures to the Spanish family on the evils of popery. Oxenham found a crucifix in a box and threw it at the owner of the house, but it missed him and broke in pieces. A man called John Butler, who was second-in-command and interpreter, read out the Ten Commandments from a lesson-book which belonged to the children, and laughed raucously when he came to "Thou shalt not steal." The ship's cook put on an alb, and cut off the skirt of it so that he could use it as a shirt. They trampled on holy pictures and broke up an altar, and when one of the children said to the others, "Boys, let's pick up Holy Mary," they called him a rascal and his sister a troublesome slut. When a Franciscan friar had the misfortune to turn up in the middle of it all, they put a chamber pot on his shaven head and made him eat his wafers. And the maroons who were with them joined in, explaining "I English, pure Lutheran."

All in all, it was a grievous bit of religious intolerance—Elizabethan sailors were a coarse lot—and it caused a solemn scandal in Panama. But there was one good thing to be said for these men: they did no physical harm to the Spanish families. And when they had as much silver and gold and pearls as they could carry, they went back to the Gulf of San Miguel and began to walk back across the isthmus by the way they had come.

But then everything went wrong. Oxenham is said, in Spanish reports, to have promised the maroons they could have all his captives to kill or keep as slaves—a thing Drake, of course, would never have done. But when it came to the point he would not let them take the Spanish captives: one account says he fell in love with a beautiful Spanish woman he captured on a ship, and that she made him change his mind. For breaking this promise, the maroons turned against him at the moment when he needed them most to guide him back through the jungle.

As soon as his depradations were known in Panama, a force of 200 men was sent to pursue him through Darien, and another went along the Caribbean coast to cut off his retreat. The pursuers, faced with a choice of rivers he might have used, picked the right one because they saw chicken feathers and bits of bacon rind floating down it. They caught up with the Englishmen, skirmishes were fought, and Oxenham's command broke up, some men being killed, some captured, some scattered in small parties and lost for ever in the jungle. The maroons, caught between the European opponents, suffered badly: the Spaniards found their hidden town of Ronconcholon and laid it waste. Of all the Plymouth men, there were no survivors, except some boys the Spaniards thought too young to execute. Oxenham was captured and taken to Panama and then to Lima in Peru. He had to admit he had no commission from the queen, and therefore was legally a pirate: and he came to a pirate's end.

The other sequel to Drake's first voyage was in 1595, when he himself came back to Darien. His exploits in the intervening twenty-three years—the voyage of the *Golden Hind,* the attack on Cadiz, the defeat of the Spanish Armada—had made him the hero of England and the terror of Spain. He came back as an admiral, as Sir Francis, with twenty-seven ships and 2,500 men, and six of the ships were the queen's. Yet over the whole of this voyage was an air of querulous argument and defeat. His com-

mand was halfhearted, indecisive, second-rate. The touch of his
genius had vanished. The change in him epitomized the pathos of
growing old.

The aim of the expedition, when it was first discussed, had
been to march across the isthmus and capture Panama—whether
simply to rob the city or to hold it had never been clearly decided.
The queen appointed Sir John Hawkins, Drake's early captain,
now sixty-five years old, to share the command with him—"a man
oulde and warie, entering into matters with so laden a foote, that
the other's meat would be eaten before his spit could come to the
fire." And in one of her most fickle moods, she postponed the journey for month after month, and only agreed to it in the end because news was heard of a Spanish treasure-ship which had been
dismasted in a storm and was lying helpless in Puerto Rico. This
ship was made the first objective, Panama the second.

Drake and Hawkins, who were both proud men and both
resentful at having to share command, disagreed as soon as the
fleet had sailed from Plymouth, and argued angrily in front of
their subordinates. Drake insisted on attacking the Canary Islands, but in the face of Spanish troops drawn up on the beaches
he withdrew. Hawkins, with no regard for secrecy, let every sailor
in the fleet know where they were bound. And as they passed
through the Virgin Islands, a small ship which had lagged behind
was captured by a Spanish fleet. Consequently, the Spaniards in
Puerto Rico knew they were coming. Just as the fleet reached the
island, Hawkins died, dictating for the queen on his deathbed a
bitter complaint against Drake, and foretelling failure for the
expedition. Drake attacked the place. Some of his officers thought
his tactics were mistaken, and believed the harbor and the treasure inside it could have been taken. But at the first repulse he
gave up trying, and sailed away again.

By the swiftness he had been master of, he might still have
surprised Panama. But he went down to the coast of South America and attacked two lesser cities, Rio de la Hacha and Santa
Marta. (His chronicler Thomas Maynarde, whose spelling was
eccentric, called the place St. Tomarto.) Both cities had been

warned. The people had hidden their property and fled. Both governors kept him bargaining while warnings were sent farther along the coast, and both in the end refused to ransom their empty towns and allowed him to set them on fire. In one, a few pearls were taken, and in the other nothing.

So he came to Nombre de Dios, the town he had taken when he was young with seventy men, by the use of surprise which now he had thrown away. "We founde small resistance," Maynarde wrote, "more than a little forte at the east side of theyr towne, in which they had left one peece of ordinance which brake at the first shotte. Certaine prisoners were taken in the flyinge, who made it knowne, that havinge intelligence, longe before, of our cominge, theyr treasure was conveyed to places of more safetie, eyther to Panama or secretly hidden; and it might very well bee, for the towne was left very bare; wherefore it was resolved that we should hasten with speed for Panama." They landed 750 men, and the next day, under their colonel-general Sir Thomas Baskerville, they started to march up the Spanish trail.

Drake waited with the fleet, and he must have reflected on the time when he made the same journey with less than a score of men and had the Spanish defenders on the run. But he must have remembered also the muddy nine-foot track, the overarching jungle, the even narrower gorges, the unpredictable river crossings, the rains and the dripping trees. He must have hoped, but could he have believed that an organized army, with all the trappings it needed, could march through there and come out fit to fight at the other end? It was an enterprise that needed a gay disregard of danger, or else the spurious courage that comes from ignorance. But Drake could not give it either. His army commanders, even before they started, were analyzing the risk, and by any cautious analysis the jungle track was impregnable.

The first day they marched nine miles, the second eighteen, and they reached a halfway house where there had been stables for several hundred mules, but it had been burned. On the third day they came to a fortified hill where the Spaniards had felled the trees to make a palisade, and there they stuck. There was not much fighting. Most of the soldiers had eaten all their rations—"seven or eight cakes of bisked or ruske for a man"—and most of their powder and match was spoiled by rain. They simply lost heart. Five days after they marched out of Nombre de Dios, they were straggling back again, "our men so wearied," Maynarde wrote, "with the ilness of the way, surbaited for want of shoes, and weake with theyr diet, that it would have bin a poor dayes service that we should have done upon an enimie had they been there to resist us." Maynarde at least had learned the lesson: he was an army officer. "Undoubtedly," he wrote, "two hundred men foreknowinge their intentions ... are able to breake or weaken the greatest force that any prince in Christendome can bring thither ... unless it might be some few goinge covertly to do som sodaine exploite before it were thought of by the enemie, and so returne unspied."

Drake's most perceptive biographers have been puzzled by the loss of his power of command: he seems to have been puzzled by it himself, as a man might be who was suddenly paralyzed. He was over fifty—about the same age as Columbus on his last voyage—and that was still an age when the powers of many men began to fail. Yet the failure was so complete, the change so pitiable, that it seems to point to something more drastic than age alone—some unrecognized sickness, a partial stroke perhaps, sclerosis, a past heart attack, or even syphilis, which was very common in the fleet. The Canary Islands, Puerto Rico, Rio de la Hacha, Santa Marta—all had been disasters and all were solely the fault of his indecision: and Nombre de Dios, the very scene of his earliest triumph, was now the scene of his final irretrievable failure.

He knew that if he went home without the victory and the treasure he had promised to the queen, he could only expect to live his last years in disgrace. But he did not know of anywhere else he could look for victory or treasure. He sat in his cabin, searching his maps and charts, seeming not to absorb the advice his officers tried to give him. "Since our return from Panama," Maynarde wrote, "he never carried mirth or joy in his face." His men were dissatisfied, and even his loyal officers were cynical about their two commanders. "Our blinded eyes began now to open, and wee found that the glorous speeches, of an hundred places that they knew in the Indies to make us rich, was but a baite to draw Her Majestie to give them honourable employments and us to adventure our lives for theyr glory." All he could suggest was to try the Bay of Honduras or the Lake of Nicaragua —a counsel of despair, for these were places he had never seen, and no Englishman knew whether either of them had riches worth the taking. Quite unlike himself, he asked his officers which they should attempt, and Baskerville said "Both, one after the other— and all too little to content us if we took them."

So they sailed, east from Nombre de Dios, past Portobello and along the cost of Veragua. With winds against them, they sheltered in the lee of a barren island where they found nothing to eat but tortoises: and there the Darien sickness began to take its victims. Drake was sickening himself, and in a phrase of hopeless resignation he resolved to "take the wind as God sent it." It blew them back to Portobello, the best of the harbors on the coast, which the Spaniards were just beginning to fortify: and there in defeat and despair Sir Francis died. They buried him at sea outside the beautiful and pestilential bay. There is a little island just to the north of its entrance which is still called by his name. If any place were haunted, this would be. It was a grave of lost hope, lost youth, lost reputation.

(*iv*)

The Buccaneers

I come not hither to hear lamentations
and cries, but to seek Moneys.

Henry Morgan at Panama, 1670

Some of the glamor of the Elizabethan adventurers has rubbed off on the buccaneers who followed them half a century later, and given them a romantic reputation they never deserved. It is true that in their own day and their own countries—England, France, and Holland—they were admired. People then were ready with admiration for any daring deeds against the Spaniards, and the deeds of the buccaneers were only known from their own descriptions. But in fact they were most unlikable people, the dregs of the seafaring world, as avaricious and cruel as the worst of the early Spaniards.

Buccaneers were a particular kind of pirate. Piracy has existed in every age and in every sea, but the buccaneers only lasted for three-quarters of a century, from 1625 to 1698, and only sailed the Caribbean and the coasts of South America. The origin of their name is very strange. About the end of the sixteenth century, the Spaniards began to abandon Hispaniola, the first of the islands they had colonized. The gold mines were worked out, the native population was dead and slaves were expensive, and there was a better chance of making a fortune on the mainland. On the deserted island, domestic cattle ran wild and increased enormously. Ships of all maritime nations put in there from time to time to hunt for food, and bands of castaways and deserters accumulated there and started to hunt the cattle as a trade, selling dried meat and hides to passing ships.

They used the same process for drying the beef that the Caribs had used for drying the human flesh they ate: the meat was hung on a wooden frame above a slow smoky fire. The Carib name for the frame was *barbecue,* and the whole hearth was known as a *boucan:* so was the finished product. Hence the hunters were called—in French at first—*boucaniers;* and it was these men who put to sea from time to time as pirates. But oddly enough, the Englishmen among them adopted the French word and anglicized it to buccaneer, while the Frenchmen preferred to call themselves *flibustiers*—a French pronunciation of the English word freebooter, which itself was borrowed from the Dutch and referred, of course, not to boots but to boats. By much later metamorphoses, *flibustier* found its way into modern American politics, and the cannibal barbecue into suburban gardens.

The buccaneers were as international as the words. Many of them, on the run from other crimes, lived under pseudonyms, and their nationalities were almost forgotten. But they were only united by having a common enemy, the Spaniards, on whom to exercise their fighting instinct. Large forces of them sometimes coalesced, under whatever man they thought would win them most booty, and some of these leaders had visions of founding a buccaneer state, independent of all the European kingdoms. But none of them lasted long enough for anything so ambitious. Most of the coalitions broke up in bloodthirsty quarrels. When loot was shared out, the men disbanded themselves to spend it on orgies in whatever port would receive them. Romanticists have given them customs and codes of honor, but there is no real evidence, even in what they wrote about themselves, of any honor among them. Their only laws were self-interest and plunder, their only pride was in raggedness and filth, and their only authentic custom was to wear breeches stiff with the blood of the animals they had killed. Like many men whom history makes into heroes, they must have been intolerably smelly.

They raided shipping mainly to provide themselves with ships, getting rid of the Spanish crews by whatever means seemed most convenient, often by throwing them overboard. Most of

their profits were made in raids on land. Their habit was to capture a Spanish town and lock up the citizens, usually in the
church, while they looted the place, drank the wine and raped
the women. When that had been done, they put it all to ransom—
so much for the town itself, under threat of burning it down,
and so much for each man's and woman's life. Their threats were
seldom empty, their tortures were as ingenious as the early Spaniards', and they learned a devilish skill in extorting all the riches
in a town and leaving it destitute.

The buccaneers' exploits came to a sudden stop at the end
of the century, because the English authorities, under the Treaty
of Ryswick of 1697, began to execute these men as pirates, and
left them no port of refuge in the Indies. But there was still
plenty of sympathy for them at home, and several out-of-work
buccaneers found they could make a living, rather like the generals of the Second World War, by writing their reminiscences.
They are racy stories, perhaps with some exaggeration here and
there, but no more than a reader can allow for. And among them
is the book of John Esquemeling, a Dutch buccaneer who marched
across the isthmus to Panama in 1671, under the leadership of
the infamous Welsh ruffian Henry Morgan.

It was just two years under a century since Drake's first
expedition, but very little had changed in Darien when Morgan's
band of rogues descended on it. During that century, Drake's
final failure and Oxenham's sordid end had discouraged adventurers, and the place had been left in peace. But Spain's policy of
making a monopoly of the entrance to the Pacific had equally
discouraged development or expansion. Of course, the city of
Panama itself had grown rich. A good part of the wealth that
flowed through it was diverted to the coffers of the merchants and
officials who lived there, and they built themselves rich men's
houses of the native mahogany and cedar. There were monas-
teries and nunneries, a huge slave market, the locked and guarded
treasure houses, a cathedral of some magnificence, and seven
churches, one of which had an altar and reredos of solid gold. But

outside the city, there was nothing—only the muddy track connecting it with home. The jungle had not been explored again since the captains of Pedrarias raged through it. It had become less menacing, however, because the Spaniards had despaired of recapturing or wiping out the maroons, and had been forced to recognize their freedom. Ronconcholon had never been rebuilt, but new negro towns had been founded, with Christian names, and the maroons had settled down in them and been converted back to the Catholic faith from their ill-digested protestantism.

The biggest change on the Caribbean coast was that Nombre de Dios had been abandoned in favor of Portobello. The change had just been started when Drake made his last voyage there. Nombre de Dios had been a bad choice to begin with: its open bay was a very poor anchorage, difficult to defend. But the bay of Portobello is long and narrow, and its mouth is dominated by steep hills on either side. Two forts were built to command the entrance, and two more inside the bay, and a town was established between them.

It is still there now, no bigger, no less miserable, and no more in touch with the civilized world than it was in the early seventeenth century. The ramparts are still intact, with elegant little watchtowers at the corners. The great guns lie rusting in rows, still pointing at the harbor. The roof of the huge stone Treasure House has fallen in. The Spanish church, which is even bigger, has a roof of corrugated iron and trees have rooted in its pediment, but it is still in use and holds sacred an effigy of a black Christ which is carried in procession once a year. Here and there among the weeds and mud are other relics of the centuries of empire: a stone bridge, and the gate through which the trail led to Panama and the treasure-trains came in. And superimposed on it all are the shacks and shanties of the Negroes who live there now—some descended from slaves or maroons, and some from laborers who were brought to Panama to dig the canal in the nineteenth century and never sent home again. An air of doom and hopeless boredom hangs over the place today. On the whole of the rain-sodden coast, this is the wettest place of all. For week

after week, month after month, it rains every single day—160
inches in a year. Negro women sit in their doorways, doing nothing; boys fish from a rickety pier, small children splash in the
lukewarm shallow water, and their shouts are the only sound. A
supercilious young Negro, home from employment in the city,
strolls down the muddy street in tight trousers and pointed shoes,
turning the knobs of his transistor radio; it does not work. Steep
jungly hills press round the shacks and ruins, and if the rain
stops, wet vapors cling in the treetops like visible wraiths of the
doom and lethargy. It was always like that. "The East side is
low and swampy," a buccaneer wrote of it in 1699, "and the Sea
at low water leaves the Shore within the Harbour bare, a great
way from the Houses; which having a black filthy Mud, it stinks
very much, and breeds noisome Vapours, thro' the Heat of the
Climate." No wonder the Spaniards hated the place. "It rains
hard most of the year," one of them wrote, "and the drops of
water after falling turn into little toads." The garrisons had to
stay there, but nothing happened for months on end except when
the fleet came in. The merchants and their families only came
when they had to, and left as soon as they could for Panama.
Mosquitoes lay like a fog in the windless hollow, and every man
who lived there was living in fear of death.

The only other innovation on the Caribbean coast, in that
century between Drake and the buccaneers, was a fort which was
built at the mouth of the Rio Chagres and dedicated to San Lorenzo. That also still exists. Unlike Portobello, it is totally deserted; so is the river mouth it was built to protect. It was never
a town, never anything more than a fort; but as forts go, it must
always have been a pleasanter place than Portobello. A small
narrow peninsula, with a flat top and sides that are almost sheer,
curves out across the river where it meets the sea, and the fort
covers the whole of the top of it. Sea breezes cool it, and surf
breaks at the foot of its cliffs. To the right, it looks out across
the pellucid sea and along the beautiful empty coast towards
Veragua; on the left, the river winds out of sight between its
jungly banks. In those days, there could hardly have been a

stronger defensive position. The cliffs were impregnable, and on the landward side a deep ditch with a stone wall behind it and a wooden palisade in front cut off the fort entirely from the jungle. In normal times, it had a garrison of 150 men.

With Portobello defending the end of the trail and San Lorenzo defending the river route, the isthmus was a tougher proposition for marauders than it had been in the time of Drake. But the strongest defence of the city of Panama was still the fifty miles of jungle.

Welshmen are not much given to enterprise at sea or to crime on the grand scale, and it was strange that a man of the highly respectable Welsh family of Morgan should have become the leader of the buccaneers. Henry Morgan's father was a yeoman farmer in Glamorganshire, but when Henry was a boy he ran away to Bristol to look for something more adventurous than farming, and he signed on aboard a ship which was bound for the Indies. It is said that in Barbados his captain sold him as a slave—perhaps he had not been a success as a cabin boy—and this harsh beginning may be some excuse for what he did when he became a man. After some years in slavery, he escaped to Jamaica, which the English had captured from Spain in 1655. Of course he was destitute, and it was for want of money that he joined a buccaneer ship that happened to be in port. But having done so, he quickly rose to the top, simply because he was even more cruel, unscrupulous and wily than the rest of the gang of cutthroats.

His portrait does not make him look a pirate, in spite of the burning ships and drowning men which the artist has used to decorate the background. He is clean, fat, double-chinned, magnificently dressed, and his waved hair hangs down to his shoulders. He wears a rather fierce expression, but it is nothing like the sheer malevolent ferocity of other buccaneers who had their portraits painted. However, the picture evidently shows him in the final stage of his detestable career; for after many years of

robbery, rape and destruction, he was rewarded with a knight-
hood and made the deputy governor of Jamaica.

In 1670, Morgan was in the ascendant as a leader. He had
distinguished himself in the eyes of the buccaneers by sacking
a good many towns. One of them was Portobello, which he attacked and captured in 1666 and held for a fortnight. By tortur-
ing the inhabitants till they confessed where their money was
hidden, and by ransoming the town itself, he came away with a
quarter of a million pieces of eight, and he added to his reputation with a stratagem which the buccaneers thought was ingenious and amusing. When one of the forts held out against him he
collected all the priests and nuns in the town and made them advance with scaling ladders while his men took cover behind them.
He thought the Spaniards would not fire on their own religious
people, but they did. Several, both priests and nuns, were killed.
But the ladders were set in place and the fort was taken.

By a paradox, it was a treaty made between England and
Spain that made Morgan think with greed of the farther, richer
hunting ground of Panama. The treaty was meant to put an end
to buccaneering. It declared that all hostilities should cease between the subjects of the two kingdoms, in America and everywhere else, and be replaced by universal peace and friendship.
Nothing could have seemed more insipid to the buccaneers. But
friendship could only have been enforced by the navies of the
two powers, and the buccaneers decided with one accord to have
a last glorious fling before anyone could stop them. The largest
fleet of them that ever came together converged on the coast of
Hispaniola, over 2,000 men in thirty-seven ships. Morgan was
elected to command them, and the captains in council fell in with
his proposal for the most dangerous and ambitious raid that any
of them had ever undertaken, the very enterprise that Drake had
tried without success—a raid across the isthmus to the city of
Panama.

Morgan started by seizing an isolated island called Santa
Catalina—it is called Old Providence now—which is nearly 300

miles north of the isthmus. The buccaneers had already used it
from time to time as a hide-out: between their visits, it was a
Spanish penal settlement. Morgan not only wanted it as a base,
but also hoped to recruit a few Spanish malefactors who would
guide him across to Panama. His attack was an easy victory. The
Spanish commander, seeing such an invincible pirate fleet, agreed
to surrender, but asked Morgan to save his face by attacking him
with blank ammunition. A noisy battle was fought, with powder
but no shot on either side, until the Spaniard's honor was satisfied
and he hauled down his flag.

Morgan's idea was to force his way to Panama up the Río
Chagres rather than try like Drake to follow the jungle trail. So
he next had to capture the fort of San Lorenzo. This was a much
stiffer proposition. He sent 400 men in four ships and a boat: but
as he expected a hard fight without any loot, he stayed behind
with the rest of his fleet at Santa Catalina.

If he had known what was happening, he might not have
tried at all. His secret was already out. News of the huge assembly of buccaneers had gone all round the Caribbean, and a few
deserters—there were always some—had warned the Spaniards he
was aiming for Panama. The isthmus was waiting for him. San
Lorenzo had been reinforced and was packed with troops, more
than double its usual complement of 150. The men of his flotilla
took one look at the cliffs and the guns on top and saw that they
could not hope to take the fortress from the sea. But they were
more afraid of him and their own companions than they were of
Spaniards. None of them dared to talk about retreat. They landed
in a cove three miles along the coast to try an attack by land.

It was one of the bloodiest, most costly battles the buccaneers
ever fought. Blundering through the jungle, the leaders came
suddenly into a space the Spaniards had cleared outside the palisade. Many fell to the Spanish muskets there and then, before
they could duck into cover of the trees again. The rest of them,
peering out from the thickets, saw they would have to cross the
open space. On its two sides, it was bounded by the tops of the

cliffs, about a hundred yards apart, and beyond it was the palisade, the ditch and the wall, with a gatehouse and a drawbridge in the middle.

It looked impossible—but so did the thought of going back to Santa Catalina and explaining why they had failed. On the edge of the jungle, they argued and wrangled, screwing up each other's courage for an assault. And at last they all dashed out together, carrying swords and fireballs. Some reached the palisade and tried to climb it, some threw the fireballs over, some tried to set the palisade alight—and the Spaniards, jeering "Come on, ye English dogs," shot them down and drove them back to cover.

At nightfall, they tried again, and the fight went no better for them until an accident gave them a sudden advantage—an accident only credible because the men who described it afterwards were so plainly astonished themselves. A pirate was shot in the back by an arrow. He pulled it out in front—it had gone right through him—wrapped some cotton wadding round it, pushed it down the barrel of his musket and fired it back at the fort. The powder set the wadding on fire. Still burning, the arrow landed on a thatched roof inside the fort and set the thatch on fire. The Spaniards, busy on the wall, did not see it in time, and the thatch set some powder on fire, and that blew up and threw the burning fragments all over the other roofs. Soon the fort was blazing. In the light of the flames and the cover of the smoke, pirates were creeping across the open ground, shooting at glimpses of the Spaniards on the wall. At daylight it was seen that bits of the palisade had fallen into the ditch and bridged it. Hand-to-hand fights broke out on the wall, the Spanish governor himself defending it bravely with muskets, pikes, swords and stones, and others throwing down burning pots full of combustible matter and odious smells. A breach was made, artillery was brought up from within the fort to seal it—but the pirates broke in and pursued the stricken garrison across the peninsula. Spanish survivors jumped over the cliff, preferring to die that way than ask for mercy. The governor defended himself to the last, and was

killed by a musket shot. Of the 300 men inside, only thirty were
found alive and hardly ten unwounded. And over a hundred
buccaneers were dead.

This fearful episode seemed to the buccaneers to have left
the way to Panama wide open. Morgan came up with the rest
of his forces and divided them again: 500 to hold the fort and rebuild the palisade, 150 to man the fleet, and no less than 1,200
to follow him up the river. But of course, isolated though San
Lorenzo was, news of its fall had escaped. The governor of Panama was warned, and his second line of defense, the jungle, was
still inviolate.

Morgan set off up the river full of confidence on January
18th, 1671, and the progress of his band of ruffians through the
jungle is one of the most macabre of Darien scenes. They went
in five boats and thirty-two canoes, and they took practically
nothing to eat because they expected to capture plenty on the
way. Their first setback was to find that the river, since this was
the middle of the dry season, was much too low for transport. The
boats soon stuck, and even the canoes progressed so slowly that
Morgan landed most of the men and tried to march up the banks.
But that was worse. The river was the highway there, the jungle
had no tracks, and to force a way through it for such an army
was almost impossible. On the third day he took to the river
again, transporting the men in relays to load the canoes more
lightly.

And to their added consternation and surprise, there was nobody there, no Spaniards, no Indians, no maroons—nobody to
fight and rob of his food supply. At every new bend, the reach
of the river ahead was empty, the banks deserted, enigmatic,
silent. Here and there they found places prepared as ambuscades,
but all of them were abandoned, and nothing was left in any of
them to eat.

The buccaneers began to starve. Hunger made them resentful and more ferocious. But not one of them thought of any
constructive action. They were hunters, or had been, but it never
entered their heads to hunt in the jungle. For all their martial

courage, the jungle scared them: they were afraid of being lost
in it or ambushed. And the noise they made, cursing, arguing,
trampling, shouting orders, must have frightened away the animals for miles around. In Esquemeling's account, which is full
of other detail, no animal is mentioned: they seem not to have
seen a monkey or a bird or even a crocodile, though crocodiles
were always plentiful in the Rio Chagres, and were easy to shoot
and possible to eat. They simply trudged on, endlessly sweating
and grumbling, and their only idea was to find a human being to
kill for the sake of whatever food he was carrying—or, as the days
went by, for the sake of his own dead body, for they all began to
talk of turning cannibal.

On the fourth day, the jailbird who was guiding them saw
another ambuscade ahead. They stormed into it, but again there
was nothing—except, this time, some empty leather bags. They
fought over those like a pack of dogs. The winners cut them in
strips, pounded them with stones, scraped off the hair and boiled
them—and with plenty of water they managed to gulp them
down.

After six days, most of the men were weak and some thought
they were dying; and still they had not found the settlement of
Venta Cruces, where the trail from Panama came down to the
river. No regular commander, responsible for his army, would
have tried to lead it on, with such a tenuous line of retreat. Even
Morgan, who was no soldier, must have seen that the Spaniards
were trying to lure him into a position he could not escape from.
But he had no sense of responsibility for his men, and pirates'
incentives were more tangible than soldiers': hope of gold did
more than hope of glory. The sixth night passed in argument and
discontent, but a majority was still for pressing forward.

On the seventh day they came to the point where the river
valley bends to the east, and they crossed it, and saw in the distance the smoke from the settlement. Encouraged, they hurried
onwards, talking about the dinners they supposed were roasting
on the fires. But it was the houses themselves that were burning.
The people had fired their homes and fled, leaving nothing behind

but some dogs and cats, which were instantly killed and devoured. The royal store houses and stables were empty, except for some jars of Peruvian wine. The men who drank it were sick—no wonder, on stomachs that had been empty for a week—and the rumor went round that even the wine was poisoned.*

Next morning, they left the river and started up the trail— and here they had their first taste of opposition. Thousands of arrows fell on them out of the blue. Eight men dropped dead, ten more were wounded, and nobody could see where the arrows had come from. Advancing cautiously, they saw some Indians running among the trees. A few boldly turned and assaulted the pirates head-on and were shot to death—and no doubt were eaten, for the pirates were far beyond caring what kind of meat they ate. This was the first recorded encounter with Indians since the massacres Pedrarias had ordered 150 years before. Since these men were on the Spanish trail, they must have been slaves, per- haps herdsmen; and like many hereditary slaves, they may have been quite content to fight to the death in loyalty to their masters.

The whole of the next night, it poured with rain. The buc- caneers found some huts and stacked their powder and muskets in them, but there was only room inside for a few of the men, and the rest spent a gloomy night in the open, with their courage at its lowest.

But on the next day, the ninth of the journey, they came out of the jungle into the grasslands: and there in the distance they saw the South Sea at last, and some ships approaching the city. And better still, they saw a herd of cattle and donkeys. A great slaughter followed, and a nauseating feast, the animals hacked into gobbets, half-roasted and gnawed so impatiently that men could be seen with blood dripping off the ends of their beards and running down to their waists.

That unguarded herd was the Spaniards' undoing. Before the

---

* This was not the same settlement that Drake fought his way through, although it had the same name. In the intervening century, it had been moved about eight miles down the river, and a new trail opened to connect it to Panama. Both trails are still there, but both settlements are under the artificial lakes of the Panama Canal.

feast, the buccaneers were in no condition to fight: the Spanish tactics had been perfectly successful. After it, they marched on again revived and soon, when the highest steeple of the city came in sight, they were shouting and leaping for joy and throwing their hats in the air. Spanish horsemen now appeared, and surrounded them just out of musket shot, calling abusive names and blowing trumpets. But as evening was falling the buccaneers made camp, put out a few sentries, stuffed themselves again with lumps of meat, and lay down to sleep it off, looking forward to a victory in the morning.

The fight on the next day, January 28th, was the biggest formal battle ever fought between European forces on the isthmus. The buccaneers were daunted when they saw the size of the Spanish army, cavalry and foot, drawn up on the approaches to the town: "few or none there were but wish't themselves at home." But even the stupidest could see they had to fight: to retreat through the jungle, starving again and pursued, was out of the question. So they marched directly at the Spaniards, putting the best of their musketmen in the lead. With shouts of *"Viva el Rey"* the Spanish cavalry charged. The ground was marshy and hindered their maneuvers; the pirate vanguard knelt and fired the first full volley. The Spaniards, discomposed, brought up a secret weapon: a huge number of wild bulls, herded by Indians and Negroes, which they drove at the enemy. But the bulls were frightened and scattered by the noise of battle: only a few broke through the pirate lines, where they tore the battle colors to pieces and the pirates shot them down, more pleased than alarmed by the sight of so much beef. The pitched battle lasted two hours. Slowly the musketry of the buccaneers wore down the Spanish cavalry and demoralized their foot. The buccaneers could not retreat: the Spaniards could. At last, with a final volley, Spaniards began to throw down their arms and run, back into the city or out to the neighboring woods. The buccaneers were too weary to chase them. The few they caught—some monks among them—were callously put to death. But still, it was not all over. In the streets of the city itself the defenders had mounted great guns which were charged with small pieces of iron or musket bullets, and blasts of this shrapnel cut swathes through the pirate ranks before the city succumbed and the looting could begin.

Before night, the whole place was burning. Who started the fire has always been a mystery. The buccaneers themselves believed Morgan had done it in person, and were angry at such stupidity—for the city was worth a fortune to them in ransom. Morgan, when he was accused, said the Spaniards did it. Whatever the truth, some Spaniards and some buccaneers, all working together, tried to put it out and even blew up some houses to stop it spreading. But it was beyond control. All the splendid mahogany and cedar houses were destroyed, and all the slaves' quarters, and most of whatever treasures the city contained were burned or melted or buried irretrievably in the ashes. Only the stone-built churches, the cathedral and public buildings were still left standing above the ruins.

For the buccaneers, the battle had been a resounding though costly success. The looting was less so. They started their usual debaucheries. Morgan, to keep them reasonably sober in case of a counterattack, spread a story that the wine in the city was poisoned, as they believed it had been at Venta Cruces. But they soon discovered by experiment that it was not. Some of the women were less reluctant than they should have been. Their husbands had told them buccaneers were monsters, and they were pleasantly surprised on the whole to find they were only men. Morgan "gave them no good example in this point, for when any beautiful woman was brought Prisoner to his presence, he used all means, both of Rigor and Mildness, to bend them to his lascivious Pleasure." But not always with success. There was one outstandingly beautiful girl whose husband was away in Peru, and Morgan claimed her as his own and wooed her first with stolen jewels and then with threats and imprisonment: but she earned the other pirates' hypocritical admiration by resisting him successfully.

While they were thus employed, the pirates learned that all

the gold plate that had been in the city, and all the nuns, had been sent to sea in a galleon at the first alarm. A boat was manned in pursuit, but too late. The galleon was never found, and Morgan himself put an end to any idea of sailing the Pacific. He came to suspect that some of the men were plotting to desert him and put to sea, and to thwart them he had the masts of all the remaining ships cut down.

With most of the treasure taken away or destroyed, the only way to make a profit was to ransom prisoners, so Morgan sent out parties through the countryside to gather in as many as they could. Some, to raise the price, were put to tortures the buccaneers had learned from the early Spaniards themselves—deeds inconceivably brutal to a modern mind, which the buccaneer writers described in gruesome detail with a hollow pretense of distaste.

The riot went on for three weeks before the pirates were sated and left the city—or the place where the city had been. In their retreat, they drove 175 beasts of burden laden with loot, and 600 prisoners, men, women and children, up the trail again to Venta Cruces. "Nothing else could be heard but Lamentations, Cries, Shrieks, and doleful Sighs. Many of the Women begged Capt. Morgan on their knees, with infinite Sighs and Tears, to let them return to Panama, there to live with their dear Husbands and Children in little Huts of Straw. It would have caused compassion in the hardest Heart, but Capt. Morgan, as a man little given to Mercy, was not mov'd in the least." It was to be ransom money, or slavery in Jamaica. For once, this was an empty threat; even in those days, Morgan could hardly have sold Spanish women and children as slaves in an English colony. But it worked. All through the journey back to the other side, desperate friends and relations came hastening up the trail to buy the prisoners' freedom.

Halfway down the river again, Morgan had all his men mustered and made them swear they had not hidden any loot. Then, "knowing those lewd fellows would not stick to swear falsely," he had them all searched, and whatever was found—mostly jewels—was added to the common booty to be shared. Back at the fort of San Lorenzo, the share-out took place: only 200 pieces of eight for each man. They were furious, accusing Morgan to his face of having kept the best of the plunder for himself. He hastily had the castle demolished—the people of Portobello refused to pay a farthing for its ransom—and secretly went aboard his ship and put to sea, leaving most of his followers hungry, defenseless and angry on the Spanish shore. The old villain went back to England, salted away his fortune and found favor at court with his own version of the exploit; and when his men next saw him he was deputy governor of Jamaica—Sir Henry, a gentleman of consequence, who took a righteous delight in hanging pirates.

They might have been angrier still, and so might he, if he had known that the greatest treasure of all in Panama had been there in front of their eyes all the time, and they had never seen it. This was the golden altar and reredos. The inhabitants had not had time to dismantle the massive structure and take it away; so they painted it and left it where it was. The trick was successfully kept a secret. Not one of the prisoners tried to buy his freedom or his life, or even the lives of the people he loved, by telling the pirates about it and burdening his own conscience with the sacrilege that would have followed: and not one of the pirates thought of scratching the paint. This magnificent relic is still in Panama today, but in a newer church. For the old city was never rebuilt: a new one was built instead, the nucleus of the present city, six miles farther to the west along the shore. The golden altar nowadays is one of the sights that tourists go to see, and so are the ruins of the city Morgan burned. They still stand, on the edge of their odorous mangrove swamp, much as they stood when he left them in 1672.

*　　*　　*

Like Drake's crossing of the isthmus, Morgan's crossing had a sequel, and the two events, a hundred years apart, were strangely similar. After Drake, Oxenham crossed by Balboa's route through the heart of Darien, and put to sea on the south side: and after Morgan, a party of 350 buccaneers did exactly the same. This was in 1680. The journey was not a disaster like Oxenham's, but it was not a great success. Five pirate captains, all English, took part in it with their crews: Bartholomew Sharp, Richard Sawkins, John Coxon, Peter Harris and Edmund Cook. So did William Dampier, who became a captain and an author afterwards. There were far too many commanders. After a few successes and some failures in the South Sea, the party was split by jealousies and rivalries. Some of the pirates sailed successfully round Cape Horn in stolen Spanish ships, and some walked back through the jungle to the coast near Acla, where they had left their own. But the expedition has a special interest: for the first time since the massacres of Pedrarias, an Indian civilization was found again in the jungle. On the way over, Indians guided the buccaneers and even went to sea with them; like the maroons a hundred years before, they were eager to help anybody who said he had come to fight the Spaniards. And on the way back, an Englishman called Lionel Wafer, who was the buccaneers' surgeon, was injured and left behind, and lived with the Indians for several months—the first literate and observant man who had ever done so.

Wafer was a young man, and perhaps not a very good surgeon—his only training was as assistant to other seagoing surgeons, who were seldom at the top of their profession—but he was a very graphic writer, and his comments on the jungle ring as true today as they did 300 years ago. Among his adventures, he was lost for a week, with four other men who had fallen out of the march. Aiming for the north sea, they followed a river which was flowing that way—a mistake that many other explorers have made since then, for all the major rivers of Darien except the Chagres, whichever way they start, turn southwards in the end. They found themselves hemmed in by rivers too deep and fast to cross, and they had to spend a night in trees to escape from a sudden flood. It was midsummer, and at that time of the

year, Wafer wrote, "for about four or six Weeks, there will be
settled continued Rains of Several Days and Nights, exceeding
vehement. It is very hot also about this time, where-ever the Sun
breaks out of a Cloud: For the Air is then very sultry, because
then usually there are no Breezes to fan and cool it, but 'tis all
glowing hot. Yet at certain intervals even in the wettest of the
Season, there will be several fair Days intermix'd, with only Tor-
nado's or Thunder-Showers; and that sometimes for a Week together. These Thunder-Showers cause usually a sensible Wind,
by the Clouds pressing the Atmosphere, which is very refreshing,
and moderates the Heat: but then this Wind shaking the Trees
of this continued Forest, their dropping is as troublesome as the
Rain itself. When the Shower is over, you shall hear for a great
way together the Croaking of Frogs and Toads, the humming of
Moskito's or Gnats, and the hissing or shrieking of Snakes and
other Insects, loud and unpleasant; some like the quacking of
Ducks. The Moskito's chiefly infest the low swampy or Mangrove lands, near the Rivers or Seas: But however, this Country
is not so pester'd with that uneasie Vermin, as many other of the
warm Countries are." This was Darien in June 1680. Apart from
the shrieking snakes it might be Darien in any June since then.

Wafer thought the Indians were not very numerous, and it
is probably true that they never recovered the numbers they had
before the Spanish massacres. But all his experience confirms the
impression one reads between the lines of the earlier Spanish reports: that they were essentially generous, gentle people who
were ready to be kind to any strangers who treated them reasonably well. They had welcomed the buccaneers as allies against
the Spaniards, whom they passionately hated, but when Wafer
was left behind, defenseless and useless, they cared for him and
his four companions out of pure compassion. He was quite un-
sentimental about them, and regarded them as savages to whom
he could break his promises as soon as it suited him; but in spite
of himself, he admired them. In his week's wandering, he went
round in a circle and came back to a village he had passed with
the buccaneers. "The Indians were all amazed to see me," he

wrote, "and began to ask many Questions; but I prevented them by falling into a Swoon, occasion'd by the Heat of the House, and the scent of Meat that was boyling over the Fire. The Indians were very officious to help me in this Extremity, and when I revived, they gave me a little to eat, and treated us all very kindly." These villagers took him to their *cacique*, whose name was Lacenta; and there he found an Indian society exactly like those which Balboa had conquered and Pedrarias had destroyed. There again were the ceremonial cotton dresses which had incensed Balboa, the gold plates on the men's noses and the rings on the women's, the peccary-hunting with spears and arrows, the solemn council meetings and the drunken parties, the modest but amiable women—all the old ways of jungle life revived after a century and a half on the edge of extinction. In all that time, the Indians had only made a single innovation: it had become a fashionable whim for their fighting leaders to use a Christian name. The two leaders who fought with the buccaneers against the Spaniards called themselves Andreas and Antonio.

Wafer easily made a reputation as a surgeon. Bloodletting was the European doctor's cure for most things, and so it was among the Indians. The Indians did it by seating the naked patient on a stone in a river and shooting large numbers of little arrows into him: "and if by chance they hit a Vein which is full of Wind, and the Blood spurts out a little, they will leap and skip about, shewing many Antick Gestures, by way of rejoycing and Triumph." Wafer watched Lacenta's wife, who had a fever, being given this alarming treatment, and suggested a better way. He lanced her arm, and by the next day she recovered; and Wafer thereafter became the court surgeon, was carried in a hammock wherever Lacenta travelled, "and lived in great Splendor and Repute, administring both Physick and Phlebotomy to those that wanted."

It seems an idyllic life as Wafer describes it, a jungle Eden in which the only serpent so far was the Spaniard. Idyllic at least for the men, who did very little work—hunting and felling trees were all that was expected of them. The women did all the

rest: digging, planting, cooking, washing, carrying all the luggage
on journeys, and tenderly reviving their husbands when they
drank too much. Nevertheless, Wafer wrote, "the young Women
are very plump and fat, well-shap'd; and have a brisk Eye. They
are little better than Slaves to their Husbands; yet they do their
Work so readily and cheerfully, that it appears to be rather their
own Choice than any Necessity laid upon them. They are in
general very good condition'd, pitiful and courteous to one another, but especially to Strangers; ready to give any just at-
tendance or assistance they can. They observe their Husbands
with a profound Respect and Duty upon all occasions; and on
the other side their Husbands are very kind and loving to them.
I never knew an Indian beat his Wife, or give her any hard
Words. They seem very fond of their Children, both Fathers and
Mothers, and I have scarce seen them use any Severity towards
them. And the Children are suffered to divert themselves which
way they will. Swimming in the rivers and catching Fish, is a
great Exercise even for the small Boys and Girls; and the Parents also use that Refreshment."

No wonder some of the older buccaneers who had glimpsed
this delightful life remembered it at the end of the century when
buccaneering was brought to a forcible stop. A number of them,
especially the French, simply walked ashore in Darien and lived
the rest of their lives among the Indians. But Wafer was young,
and he always wanted to get away, in spite of Lacenta's insistence that he should stay there as his doctor. He found his chance
at last when Lacenta had spent a whole day in a fruitless hunt
for peccary. He told the *cacique* about English ways of hunting,
and offered to go to England to bring him a pack of hounds.
After long hesitation, Lacenta agreed. He made Wafer swear he
would come back, and promised him his daughter when she was
of marriageable age. Wafer made a solemn pact to do so, although he never thought for a moment of keeping it, and Lacenta
gave him an escort across the mountains and down to the coast.
Soon a buccaneer ship came along and he went aboard, painted
and naked except for a gold plate hanging from his nose. "I was

willing to try if they would know me in this Disguise; and 'twas the better part of an hour before one of the Crew, looking more narrowly upon me, cry'd out, Here's our Doctor."

He never went back: no hounds reft away from the English shires ever gave tongue in the jungle. But the next visitors to Darien would hardly have been more incongruous if they had come in hunting pink. They were a large party of Scottish Presbyterians, earnestly led by the man who founded the Bank of England.

(V)

The Scottish Colony

To Scotland's just and never-dying fame,
We'll in Asia, Africa, and America Proclaim
Liberty! Liberty!—Nay, to the shame
    Of all that went before us.
Where'er we plant, trade shall be free;
And in three years' time (I plainly foresee)
GOD BLESS THE SCOTTISH COMPANY,
    Shall be the Indian chorus.
No brawls, no murmur, no complaint,
No cause of any discontent,
Where *Patersonian* government
    Shall once commence a footing.

From Trade's Release, or Courage to
the Scotch-Indian Company, an
excellent new ballad: 1697

THE SCOTSMEN 1,200 OF THEM in five ships, made landfall in the middle of the coast of Darien in November 1699. They came to found a colony, and to open a crossing of the isthmus free for the trade of all nations. This high-minded idea—the Darien scheme, as it was called—was the brain-child of the Scottish economist William Paterson. And he came with them.

The end of the seventeenth century was the only time when the Scots could have formed such a national project as a colony which was independent of England. In the ninety years since the death of Elizabeth they had shared the English kings but possessed their own parliament, except when Cromwell brought them under English rule. All that time, the country had been riven by religious dissent, dynastic rebellions and the feuds of rival clans. Thousands of Scotsmen were driven by poverty or persecution to emigrate to English colonies, but the country had not had enough cohesion or surplus energy to organize a colony of its own, except the Presbyterian settlements in Carolina and the short-lived attempt in Nova Scotia. In 1690, the Act which established the Presbyterian Church put an end to religious dispute—or at least to the most violent forms of it—and set the minds of Scotsmen free to think of adventure and trade. But in 1707, the Scottish and English parliaments were united; and after that, whatever colonial enterprise the Scots displayed, the results of it could never be Scottish; they were British.

William Paterson was typical of that moment of Scottish history in every way except one: he was a liberal and tolerant man in an age when bigots were commoner. He was a farmer's son from Dumfriesshire, and so far as anyone knows his only education was in one of those bleak but efficient Scottish parish schools where grammar, spelling, arithmetic and Latin were remorselessly driven into the heads of little boys. When he was seventeen, he was involved in some kind of underground Presbyterian plot against the rule of King Charles II, and he had to run away from home. He went to Bristol, because he had a relative who lived there. Bristol was a port of infectious adventure and romance, and in about 1674, when he was nineteen, he went to sea from there, like Henry Morgan, to seek his fortune, first in Amsterdam and then in the English colony of Jamaica.

So far, this was a story which could have been told of a good many Scottish boys in the seventeenth century. The distinction of William Paterson only began to show when he came back from Jamaica ten years later. Still in his twenties, he had in fact made a comfortable fortune. He had also acquired an understanding of trade and high finance which was far ahead of his time, and a collection of maps and reports of central America. And although he had never been to Darien, he brought back with him the splendid dream which stayed with him all his life: to found a peaceful trading colony on the isthmus.

Only one portrait of Paterson has been discovered. It is an amateurish pen-and-ink drawing in a manuscript copy of one of his tracts which is in the British Museum. One cannot read any character in the formal face, which is surrounded by a billowing wig and perched on a shoulder and bosom vastly too big for it. The eyes are unnaturally large, and so is the nose; the mouth is a smudge. It might be anybody, or nobody. It was drawn in 1708, when Paterson was still alive, but it may simply be an eighteenth-century clerk's idea of what a seventeenth-century financier ought to have looked like. If it is really a portrait from life of Paterson, it must be reckoned a failure. Surely no man with such a forceful character could have gone through life with such an insipid face.

His character shows a little more clearly in his writings. He wrote a great many tracts and pamphlets, mostly on banking, finance and trade. They are not very easy to read, but here and there all through them one comes across flashes of his passionate beliefs. He believed in freedom—freedom of trade and of religion—and he hated war and violence, not perhaps on any moral or compassionate grounds, but because they were the opposite of freedom. And he also believed, at a time when it was not very fashionable, in honesty. "Bribery, cheating, designed cheating, wilful bankruptcy, and fraud," he wrote emphatically, "are likewise theft, and, so far from being a lesser or inferior degree thereof, they are the worst and most heinous of all. It seems strange that those who invented the hanging of thieves did not begin with this sort first."

Like most men ahead of their times, Paterson was often impatient with people too obstinate or stupid to understand him, and when he was proved right he often said "I told you so," sometimes at enormous length. And he was nearly always right— so often right that lesser people longed to prove him wrong. But for all his puritanical ideas and his financial erudition, he was never affected or pretentious—there is often a dry humor in the convolutions of his eighteenth-century prose—and he was never vindictive. Fate, and his own contemporaries, dealt him some cruel blows. He hit back hard enough at fate, but never at other people. So although he was not, perhaps, a person who was easy to love in life, he deserved the sympathy of history.

Nobody knows what he did in the ten years he spent in Jamaica. Long afterwards, some of his critics said he had been a preacher, and others, at the opposite extreme, said he had been a buccaneer. Both seem unlikely. In later life, he never showed much taste for preaching, and certainly ten years of preaching would not have made the fortune he came home with. On the other hand, a man who detested violence would not have made much of a success of buccaneering. Most probably, he was simply a shrewd, hard-working merchant. But he must have met some buccaneers, and heard their hair-raising stories. Nobody could have lived in Jamaica then without meeting them—it was in 1674, the very year when Paterson left Bristol, that Morgan was knighted, and made the lieutenant governor—and the buccaneers were the only people who could have given him his maps and knowledge of the isthmus, for nobody else in that era, except the Spaniards, knew anything about it.

But the dream he came home with was nothing like the buccaneers', or the Spaniards' or even the Elizabethans'. It was not to possess the country, not to conquer the Indians, not to rob anyone of gold, not even to oust the Spaniards from their monopoly and substitute another monopoly for it. It was more like Columbus' dream, or Saavedra's. What he imagined was ships of every nation converging from Europe on one side and from all the far eastern countries on the other, and exchanging their goods at free peaceful ports on the isthmus—goods which would be transported across by wagon roads at first, and later by canal. To open this route, he believed, would divert two-thirds of the trade between Europe and the East from the route round the Cape of Good Hope.

"The time and expense of navigation," he wrote, "to China, Japan, the Spice Islands, and the far greatest part of the East Indies will be lessened more than half, and the consumption of European commodities and manufactories will soon be more than doubled. Trade will increase trade, and money will beget money, and the trading world shall need no more to want work for their hands, but will rather want hands for their work. Thus, this door of the seas, and the key of the universe, with anything of a sort of a reasonable management, will of course enable its proprietors to give laws to both oceans, and to become arbitrators of the commercial world, without being liable to the fatigues, expenses, and dangers, or contracting the guilt and blood, of Alexander and Caesar."

It was a splendid vision. But he had not begun to think of it then as a Scottish scheme: there was no sign at that time, in the 1680s, that his own country would ever be capable of such a grand design. He took the idea to Germany and offered it to the trading cities of Emden and Bremen, and to the Elector of Brandenburg, but all of them turned it down. So he came back to England, and put the dream in the back of his mind, and settled down in London as a merchant. And in the next few years, almost as a side line, he proposed the idea of a national bank, took the leading part in founding the Bank of England, became one of its original directors at the age of thirty-nine, and then resigned from it after some forgotten disagreement.

What revived the idea in his own mind was an Act for Encouraging Foreign Trade which was passed by the Scottish Parliament in 1693. It legalized the formation of Scottish companies to trade "with any Country not at war with their Majesties—to the East and West Indies, the Straits and Mediterranean, Africa and the Northern Parts." This roused the ambitions of Scottish merchants, and they called on Paterson for advice. He drafted a bill for constituting the kind of company they wanted, and the Scottish parliament passed it two years later. It authorized the founding of The Company of Scotland Trading to Africa and the Indies. It gave this company a monopoly in Scotland of trade with Asia, Africa and America, freedom from duties and taxes, the right to take possession of territories, plant colonies, wage war, make treaties and expect the protection of King William, the king both of Scotland and of England. In return, the company was to pay yearly to his majesty and his successors a hogshead of tobacco, if required. Not a word in it pointed to Darien. Paterson purposely drew a wide scope, including most of the known world in it, for fear that if his objective were known before he was ready, somebody else would be sure to get there first.

Nor was it yet an exclusively Scottish project. Paterson and his cofounders proposed a capital of £800,000, half to be raised in Scotland and half in London, and they started in London. Paterson shrewdly insisted that the subscription lists should only be open for a short time, "for if a thing go not on with the first heat, the raising of a Fund seldom or never succeeds, the multitude being commonly led more by example than reason." And the prospectus should not give too many details. "For reasons, we ought to give none but that it is a Fund for the African and Indian Company. For if we are not able to raise the Fund by our Reputation, we shall hardly do it by our Reasons." No wonder he wanted to be vague: he had not even told his cofounders what he firmly intended them to do.

The fund succeeded. The London subscription list was opened on November 13th, 1685, and nine days later the whole issue had been taken up. But a fortnight after that, the company was in trouble. Hitherto, trade with the East had been the monopoly of the East India Company, which was English. That company took alarm at the prospect of a Scottish rival, and petitioned the House of Commons. The Commons petitioned the king, and the king, who had been friendly, took fright and turned lukewarm. Paterson and his English colleagues were threatened with impeachment, and the whole of the London issue had to be withdrawn.

Perhaps this powerful English opposition ought to have given the company warning of trouble to come. But it was the very thing, of course, to rouse Scottish pride and determination. The directors resolved to reduce the capital to £400,000, but to raise it all in Scotland. This was an astonishing undertaking.

Scotland's population was under a million, most of it was desperately poor, and the country had not recovered yet from its
centuries of strife—the massacre of Glencoe was only four years
past. The purchasing power of £400,000 was then something like
£10,000,000 now. (The company's chief accountant was paid £120
a year, the masters of its ships £80, its able seamen £14, its mes-
sengers £10—a year.) To collect that sum from the people of
Scotland then might be compared with collecting £60,000,000 or
£80,000,000 from the people of Scotland now. But Paterson's reputation for absolute integrity was behind it. And it was an offer
which exactly seemed to fulfill the longings of the Scotsmen of
the time. Foreign trade had made England enviably rich: it
seemed the solution to Scotland's poverty. A Scottish colony, a
Presbyterian plantation, no matter where it was—a bit of Scotland overseas where any Scotsman poor or oppressed could make
a new start in life—it was the very message of hope and pride
that the country needed. And England had had the impertinence
to try to stop it! Then England be damned! Scotland would
show what she could do alone.

It took rather longer than in London. Subscriptions were
limited to a maximum of £3,000 and a minimum of £100. At
first, when the books were opened, people flocked to subscribe
from all over the country: the nobles, the landed gentry, rich
widows, merchants, ministers, shopkeepers, surgeons, lawyers.
The poor were represented by the royal burghs, which subscribed
from their common funds. In a month, three-quarters of the total
had been reached. But then the flow dwindled, for the fact was
that all the available funds in the country had been scraped together. The final £25,000 took two months to find, but at last it
was done.

It was not until he was certain of success that Paterson revealed his dream to his fellow directors, and showed them his
maps and reports of Darien. They listened entranced, and asked
him to put his proposals in writing and deliver them to the company in a packet, which was to be sealed by four directors and
only opened by special order of the court of the company. From

that day, their thoughts of trading to the East were abandoned. The directors put all their funds into fitting out an expedition to Darien. But the secret was strictly kept inside the boardroom— or at least, they thought it was. They ordered five ships to be built in Hamburg and Amsterdam, and they began to buy an enormous stock of provisions and trade goods, which they stored in a warehouse in Edinburgh.

What extraordinary things seemed necessities of life to travellers then, and what dull things they had to eat! The Scotsmen bought for their voyage 300 tons of biscuits, 200 slaughtered oxen, 70 tons of "stalled beef", 15 tons of pork, 7½ tons of suet, an inestimable quantity of stockfish and 20 tons of prunes. More enjoyable perhaps was their purchase of 20 tuns of brandy, 5 of strong claret and 7 of rum. Most of the trade goods, which they hoped their colony would barter, were ironmongery and clothing. There were carpenters', coopers', shoemakers', blacksmiths' and farmers' tools, a vast number of knives, 300 candlesticks, a thousand assorted locks. Perhaps these were not badly chosen, although the quantities were enough for armies of artisans. But who did they think, in the steaming forests of Darien, was going to buy the bolts of good thick Scotch serge cloth, whether black, blue or several sorts of reds? Who would wear the 79 dozen of worsted Aberdeen stockings, or the 36 dozen of fine loom stockings at the high price of 5/7 sterling the pair, or the 500 pairs of slippers, the 1,440 Scotch bonnets, the six dozen of kid gloves for women? Who among their Spanish or Indian neighbors would read the Bargan of Bibles and Catechisms, 1,500 in all, which they brought from a printer's widow for £50? Who would smoke the 23,000 clay pipes, or blow the hunting horns? Above all, where would they find a market for 4,000 periwigs, some long, some short? As for the gross of Meikle Hair Buttons, the six gross of gudges of sortable sizes from a straw broad to an inch, the hangers to Pattentash belts, the 50 Fish-giggs, or the 100 wombles of 3 sizes at 7½d overhead—one is content not to be quite sure what these things were, but to hope they were as useful as the forty Oyled hides for Bellowses.

Reading the orders in the company's minute book, one begins by assuming that the directors knew what they were doing,
and that the strangeness of their purchases is only due to the
passage of 270 years. But did they? Was this a reasonable list
of merchandise even then? Slowly a sad suspicion grows. These
men were worthy solid citizens, lawyers, merchants and a good
number of nobles, the backbone of respectable Edinburgh life.
They were rushing ahead with childlike enthusiasm, enjoying
every moment of it, blazing a trail for Scotland, ploughing the
seas by proxy. But they knew nothing at all about founding a
colony. Not one of them was a seaman. Not one of them, except
Paterson, had ever travelled far afield from Scotland. Not even
he had ever been to Darien—and they had not told anyone else
where their ships were bound for.

Paterson was not on the committee which ordered the stores;
perhaps if he had been the choice would have been wiser. But
the court of directors sent him to Hamburg to pay for the ships
and their equipment, and this led to disaster—a personal tragedy
which Paterson never quite recovered from. They put £25,000 in
his keeping. To get a better rate of exchange, he remitted £17,000
to a friend in London, a man called James Smyth who had been
a director before the English subscriptions were abandoned—and
Smyth disappeared with the money.

Paterson was already in Hamburg when the news was brought
to him. No shock could have been more cruel. Smyth was pursued and £9,000 was recovered, but £8,000 was irretrievably gone,
and Paterson, who had founded his whole career on financial integrity, went back to Scotland to face recriminations from the
other directors, and to defend himself against a charge of deliberate swindling—the very crime he believed was worse than ordinary theft. The whole thing, like so much of the company's
proceedings, was hushed up, but a committee of two directors
was appointed to enquire into what he had done. Their report
still exists. They concluded he had not meant to cheat the company; if he had, they said, he could just as easily have cheated
it of the whole £25,000 and never come back to Scotland. But

they held him morally responsible for the loss. He accepted the judgment, but having abandoned his business interests in London, he could not afford to pay such an enormous debt. He asked the company either to dismiss him, so that he could go back to London, earn money there and repay them by degrees, or else to retain him and deduct the debt from the value of the services he could give them. The committee recommended the second of these offers, which were certainly more than fair. But the court of directors refused it. He was told he could go on the expedition if he wished, but without any official position or authority. So they condemned him to watch in impotence while other men, much less intelligent than himself, put into practice the idea he had conceived.

At the end of 1698, the company had assembled five ships in the Firth of Forth. In March 1699, they published an advertisement: "The Court of Directors of the Indian and African Company of Scotland, having now in readiness Ships and Tenders in very good order, with Provisions and all manner of Things needful for their intended Expedition to settle a Colony in the Indies: give Notice, that for the general encouragement of all such as are willing to go upon the said Expedition—

"Everyone who goes on the first Equipage shall Receive and Possess Fifty Acres of Plantable Land and 50 foot square of ground at least in the Chief City or Town, and an ordinary House built thereupon by the Colony at the end of 3 years.

"Every Councillor shall have double. If anyone shall die, the profit shall descend to his Wife and nearest relations. The family and blood relations shall be transported at the expense of the Company."

Still no mention of Darien, no indication whether the East or West Indies were the destination: but nobody cared. Fifty acres and a house in town! Far more people volunteered than could possibly have been taken. The company chose 1,200, including 300 young men of the best Scottish families, 60 ex-army officers and a large number of demobilized soldiers. There were not many women among them. A few of the officers were allowed

to take their wives, but the married men among the rank and file
were to wait until the colony was established. On July 17th, 1699,
all the people of Edinburgh went down to Leith to see the fleet
set sail, taking all the highest hopes of Scotland with it. The
captains had been given sealed orders which they were to open
in Madeira, and not a soul on board the ships, except Paterson,
knew for certain where they were going.

> "*St Andrew,* our first tutelar was he,
> The *Unicorn* must next supporter be,
> The *Caledonia* doth bring up the rear
> Fraught with brave hardy lads devoid of fear;
> All splendidly equipt, and to the three
> The *Endeavour* and the *Dolphin* handmaids be."

These were the ships: *St. Andrew, Unicorn* and *Caledonia*
were armed merchantmen of forty-six to seventy guns, and *Endeavour* and *Dolphin* were tenders. The verse was from a ballad,
Caledonia Triumphans, a part of a spate of enthusiastic, patriotic, deplorable poetry which was printed in pamphlets and sold
in the Edinburgh bookshops. Paterson was the popular hero, and
in the public eyes the author of the great adventure, for the public had not been told of the missing money or the directors'
censure—and if they had, in their ecstatic mood, they would
certainly have taken Paterson's side. Many of the ballads, like
the extract which heads this chapter, were written in personal
praise of him.

But in spite of the adulation, Paterson was on board the
Unicorn not as the leader of the expedition or even as a member
of the council appointed to govern the colony, but simply as a
private planter. And even before the fleet had left the dock he
was given a taste of his new diminished status. He suggested to
one of the captains that a council should be called to check the
provisions for the voyage. "Give me leave," the captain replied,
"to think that I know my business." Four days after they had
sailed, however—four days too late—they discovered that the

crews of the ships, who had lived on board all winter, had eaten one third of the biscuits and beef and prunes, although they had scorned the stockfish, and everybody had to be put on short rations at once, with stockfish for dinner four days a week.

The voyage went well, by the standards of those days. The ships were separated, but a month out from Leith they all met again in Madeira, where the captains opened their orders: to proceed to a place called Golden Island on the coast of Darien. On the way across the Atlantic, there was friction between the ships' captains and the fresh-water men, the passengers, but that was not unexpected. Forty-three men and one woman died at sea. Twenty-two of them were reported to have died of fever, and twenty-one of flux. The odd man out died of decay. But as the company pointed out when it published the list of dead, it was a great mercy that in five crowded ships, on such a long and tedious journey, so few had died, for even more might have died in the same length of time if they had all stayed at home. On the morning of November 1st, 1699, they dropped anchor off Golden Island, and two days later, to the southeast of it, they found an excellent harbor, fit for a thousand of the biggest ships in the world. They named it Caledonia Bay.

There are two direct links with this faraway expedition: one is an oak press full of documents, meticulously written, in the National Library of Scotland, and the other is the bay where the expedition landed. Both of them bring the events of those years almost painfully close. Among the documents are all the minutes and accounts of the company, written in the beautiful cursive script of the Edinburgh clerks. But also, there are hundreds of letters and reports which were written in Darien itself, some signed with Paterson's educated flourish, some with the almost illiterate marks of the ships' captains, some stained by rain or sea—and many written in the most intense excitement or in the face of death. Letters like these do not lose all their force through time, perhaps because letters are always read at a distance in time and place. They still display the acutest emotions:

hope, optimism and resolution; anger, frustration and despair;
loyalty, anguish, courage, fear. In some, one can even witness
the approach of death. The writing starts boldly, neatly, confidently; and then the hand starts to tremble, the eyesight starts
to fail.

And after reading those letters, to sail nowadays into Caledonia Bay brings a very strong feeling of having been there before. For the bay lies quiet, beautiful, empty, just as it lay when
they first sailed in that morning, seeing it then as their home.
It is all familiar. There on the right are the mountains, hill beyond hill to the ridge of the continental divide, which is so close
to the coast that one can see the trees on its summit standing
against the sky. There on the left is the long hilly peninsula
which shelters the bay from the ocean. Here in the middle of the
entrance is the rock where the *Unicorn* carelessly grounded when
she was sailing in. On the end of the peninsula is the hill which
they used as a lookout, anxiously watching day after day for a
ship bringing news from home. And here, half way down on the
left-hand side of the bay, is the promontory where they landed
and built the fort they named after St. Andrew—and just beyond
it, the sloping wooded shore which they laid out in their minds'
eyes with houses and streets, and called New Edinburgh. It has
houses on it now, but not theirs—only the bamboo huts of a
little Indian village, which was not there when they came.

Ashore also, it is all the same—as they found it, not as they
left it, for only the indestructible things are still there: the
stream, rather too far from the fort for convenience, where they
went to fill their buckets every day, and the mangrove swamp
they had to skirt round to get there, and the forest on the hill
behind where their ministers held their meetings for lack of a
kirk. Of all that they did there, only one tangible relic remains:
the moat which they dug across the promontory to defend Fort
St. Andrew. Indians pole their canoes into it, not knowing what
it is, when they are harvesting coconuts, and perhaps it is that
use that has kept it open through the centuries. The fort, which
was built of wood, has rotted away and vanished. The place

where it stood is covered by stately palms. And among their roots, if anyone cared to disturb them, the bones of a thousand Scotsmen might be found.

When the first of the Scotsmen rowed into the bay in a longboat to take soundings, there was nobody there except a small group of Indians, who waved a flag of truce and unstrung their bows—signs of friendship which no doubt they had learned the hard way from the Spaniards. The shores appeared delightful. "The land on the peninsula is extraordinary good, and full of stately trees fit for all uses, and full of pleasant birds, as is also the opposite shore, and hath several small springs which we hope will hold in the dryest season." "The Air makes on the tops of the Trees a pleasant melancholy Musick, so that one of the Colony, considering the Coolness, Pleasant Murmuring of the Air, and the infinite beauty of a continued Natural Arbor, called them the *Shades of Love*." These were the comments of two of the colonists. Paterson himself wrote a letter a few weeks later: "Our situation is in one of the best and most defensible harbours, perhaps, in the world. The country is healthful to a wonder, insomuch that our own sick, that were many when we arrived, are now generally cured. The country is Exceedingly fertile, and the weather temperate. The country where we are settled is dry, and rising ground, hilly but not high; and on the sides, and quite to the tops, three, four, or five feet good fat mould, not a rock to be seen. We have but eight or nine leagues to a river, where boats may go into the South Sea."

This last, significant sentence is the only expression Paterson ever made of belief in an existing boat passage through the isthmus—the very thing the Spaniards had sought and failed to find. He did not say who told him about it—perhaps it was the Indians—and most people then or even now would have said he was wrong. But there is a possibility he was not. The river must have been the Atrato, at the head of the Gulf of Darien, whose head waters, as explorers discovered over a century later, are only a few hundred yards from streams which flow down to the

Pacific. And Paterson's single enigmatic sentence is the first appearance of a rumor which turns up so often in later centuries
that one comes to believe it was true: the rumor that some forgotten pioneer, up there in the backwoods of the Atrato, had
already dug a canal to join the oceans.

Most of the Scotsmen thought nobody had ever discovered
Caledonia Bay before, but they were wrong. Paterson must have
heard of Golden Island from the buccaneers, who had often used
it as a rendezvous because it is high and conspicuous from the
sea. But he may not have known he was on historic ground. The
bay was in what had been Comagre's territory. The lost city of
Acla was in sight of it. He had hit on a spot within a day's march
of the start of Balboa's crossing, and the wagon road he expected
to make, winding up through the hills above the bay, would
follow Balboa's route and Oxenham's.

The Indians soon came to investigate the Scotsmen—a new
breed of foreigner, neither buccaneer nor Spaniard, quite different from any they had seen before. On the very first day, some
of them came aboard the ships, and the Scots made them so
drunk on brandy that they had to sleep where they were. They
were stark naked, but they were given Scots bonnets and went
ashore in them the morning after, incongruously dressed but
happy. Two days later, a *cacique* with his retinue came to ask
the Scots what their intentions were, and they told him they
meant to settle there, if the Indians received them as friends, and
to trade at much better terms than the Spaniards. This *cacique*
said his name was Pedro, and when the Scots discovered the
Indians' liking for Christian names, they began to award them
as honors. Soon there were good Scots names, an Alexander and
a Steven for instance, among the brown Ambrosios and Antonios
in the jungle.*

A deputation with Paterson as a member was sent to visit
the highest *cacique* of all, who was camped in state among the
neighboring mountains. For some days, the deputation was en-

---

* The Cuna Indians still have this endearing taste. In 1964, the territory
around Caledonia Bay was ruled by a *cacique* named Winston Churchill.

tertained with song and dance and feasting and a peccary hunt—
days which they spent in wide-eyed wonder at the Indians' customs. Like Wafer and Balboa, they were astonished at the long
cotton dresses the leaders wore, and at the nakedness of the
lesser men, who wore only a piece of plantain leaf "which was
rolled up into the figure of an extinguisher, and but half covered
their privities." Paterson made a speech explaining his peaceful
intentions, which was translated into Spanish and then, by an
Indian who had been a slave, into the Indian language; and
while the *cacique* was listening, he twirled the gold plate in his
nose as a sign of pleasure. An offer was made at night of young
women to solace the deputies, and modestly refused.* The Scots
did not try to harm or dispossess the Indians or even, at that
stage, to convert them from their heathen ways, and they concluded a Treaty of Friendship, Union and Perpetual Confedera-
tion. This treaty, of course, was not purely altruistic—it was a
form of mutual defense in case the Spaniards were belligerent—
but it did express the peaceful tolerance which distinguished
everything Paterson had a hand in.

At the end of December, when the colonists had been two
months in Darien, a turtle-hunting ship was sighted, and they
took that chance to send their first report to the company at
home. It was the end of March before the report reached Edinburgh. All over Scotland, there was a surge of rejoicing and pride
at the news of the colonists' safe arrival, and the Indians' welcome, and the verdant beauty of the country they had found. But
the news had been on the way too long. At the very time when the
bells were ringing in Scotland, and prayers of thanksgiving were
being offered in the churches, and illuminations and bonfires were
being lit in every town, the colonists were faced with ruin.

Even in the idyllic start of the colony, the seeds of serious
trouble were sprouting, some far away outside it and others

* But this tale has been told by explorers in every century, about primitive people all over the world from Eskimos to Bedouin Arabs. One wonders
whether it was ever true, or whether inventing it fulfils some psychological
need among explorers—who always add that they refused the offer.

within. The seeds within were the most injurious, and these had
been planted by the stubborn ignorance of the company's directors. They had not only fitted the expedition out with a ludicrous
choice of goods, and not only rejected Paterson, who was far the
wisest man at their disposal: worst of all, they had appointed
councilors to rule the colony but had not appointed a president
of the council. It was to be run by a committee without a
chairman. Perhaps this was a naïve, idealistic essay in democ-
racy—there is nothing in the company's papers to explain it
—but its effect was to deprive the colony of any leadership at all.
Half of the councilors were captains of the ships. During the
crossing, Paterson and the other landsmen had put up with the
bullying of these seamen, in the hope of getting their own back
when they came ashore. But even ashore, the captains "took upon
them to know everything." They could not outvote the landsmen,
but in their double capacity as councilors and ships' captains,
they had everything their way even when they disagreed among
themselves. Yet none of them had the slightest knowledge of
lawful government, only of the crude discipline used in those
days to run a ship. Two of them could scarcely write their names.

Paterson fell foul of them from the start, and since he had
no authority he spent most of his time in giving advice to everybody—advice which was always good but nearly always scorned.
After a while the councilors co-opted him as a member, but he
still could not steer them to any intelligent decisions. One of his
early proposals was that, since the lack of a president made chaos
of the council meetings, each councilor should be president for a
month, and that the landsmen should take their turns first. He
hoped that by the time it came to the captains' turns, some stable
kind of government would exist. But he found the council had
already agreed—though it seldom agreed about anything—on a
form of government which has probably never been tried before
or since. Each councilor was to act as president for a week. As a
result of this unique arrangement, each councilor spent most of
his week of office undoing what had been done in the six weeks
before. Factions, jealousies and discord grew, and the ordinary

colonists hardly knew who was in charge. Nothing got done—or what did get done took ten times as long as it should. The captains insisted on landing the landsmen in a mangrove swamp, and two months were wasted in trying to build a settlement there before the landsmen's votes prevailed and the whole thing was started again in a better place. There was so much wrangling about the building of the fort, and the landing of guns to protect it, that the job was never finished. Above all, through sheer lack of leadership, the colonists began to starve. The councilors themselves reported that the country was full of fish and game and fruit, but they were so obsessed by their own disagreements that they never sent out detachments of men to collect the abundance of food. Seeing everything beginning to go wrong, Paterson went through the depths of frustration and dejection.

Enemies were gathering round them too. They had always expected protests from the Spaniards, but persuaded themselves that before the Spaniards could be ready to attack, the fort would be ready and able to hold them off. They never suspected they had a more subtle and dangerous enemy: England. They had only been in the bay a fortnight when a sail was sighted, and two days later a ship dropped anchor off Golden Island. She was a small English man-of-war, the *Rupert Prize,* and her captain's name was Long. The Scots made him welcome. He dined on two of their ships, and when three of the councilors went to return his call they had to spend the night with him because there was too much wind for their longboats to take them off. He said he was fishing and looking for wrecks to salvage.

Some students of Scottish history have said that Long was a spy, sent to reach Darien first and plant the English flag there, or at least to find out what the Scots were doing. But on the whole the evidence is against it: the English were given credit, as they sometimes still are, for devilish cunning when all they had was luck. It was true there were plenty of people in England who would have liked to get to Darien first, and were determined, after the Scots arrived, to get them out again. The secret of Darien had been well kept in Scotland, but the shrewd mer-

chants and politicians of England had deduced where the Scotsmen were likely to go. One way and another, they had eliminated
all the other possibilities—Chile and the Straits of Magellan were
among them. Nearly a year before the fleet set sail, the English
Board of Trade had secretly petitioned the Lords Justice to for-
bid the Scottish settlement, which they claimed would provoke
the Spaniards and injure English trade. But for English traders
to base an argument on sympathy for Spain was blatant hypoc-
risy, as they showed in a second petition a few weeks later, which
begged for an English expedition to do exactly what they feared
the Scots were doing—and to do it first.

But if that petition was the cause of Long's voyage, he did
not do much about it. Before he met the Scots, he had spent some
time at the head of the Gulf of Darien, making friends with the
Indians and trying to sail up the Atrato River. His own report
to the naval authorities shows this was his own idea: "His Majesty's instruction were so large to me as to give me leave to go
to any part of America not possess'd by Christians, to discover
gold or other treasures, upon which it bred a thought in me to
go for the Gulph of Darien." He saw himself as counteracting the
influence of the French and Spaniards, not the Scots, among the
Indians; and it was the Indians who told him the Scots had
arrived. "I next day visited them, who treated me very honorably.
About 1,200 men landed ashoar as proper as ever I saw. They are
very healthy, and in such a crabbed hold that it will be difficult
to beat them out of it.... To acquaint your Lordship with it, I
am no hater of the Scots nation, but a lover of them, as we are
all one Island and must joyn together upon occasion against the
Dragon of religion."

Whatever his motive, Long's report brought confirmation to
England of exactly what the Scots were doing and what they
hoped to do. It has no date on it, but it must have reached England two months before the councilors' first report reached Scotland. Nobody in England told the directors of the Scottish company that their people were safely ashore. On the contrary, by
the time that Scotland knew and was ringing its bells in jubila-

tion, secret instructions were on their way to the English governors of Jamaica, Barbados and New York. And in April all three governors issued proclamations denying that the Scottish settlers had the king's approval, and forbidding all English ships to trade or communicate with them.

Paterson and his colleagues, of course, knew nothing about these plots. They were more than fully occupied with their own quarrels and the impossible burdens the company had put on them. They could not sell their goods. The Indians did not want them, and the Spaniards never came near. A good many trading sloops came in from New York and Boston and the Indies, bringing the food the colony so desperately needed, but all of them refused the clothes and hardware at the Scottish prices. Most of them sailed away again to trade in Dutch or Spanish ports. What they wanted was cash, and the company had not thought of giving the colonists a cash account, or letters of credit. Once, to get a cargo of food, the councilors took 30 per cent off the prices of all their goods. But whatever they did, there was no reason in the world why traders should come from the settled colonies right down to Darien for manufactured goods they could bring as easily from Europe.

Trade might have gone better if the Scots could have taken their goods to the possible markets, but through another piece of foolish shortsightedness they were practically prisoners in their bay. Experienced seamen had warned the company's directors that weatherly ships were essential in ocean trade, but none of the Scottish ships, not even the tenders *Endeavour* and *Dolphin,* were any good to windward. The New England sloops came and went without trouble, but for month after month the winds were northerly or northeasterly. Down there in the very bottom of the Caribbean, there were lee shores for hundreds of miles in both directions, and after sailing in with the wind behind them, the Scottish ships could not sail out again.

In February, the wind seemed to be moderating, and some of the councilors decided to send the *Dolphin* to the Dutch island of Curaçao with a cargo of goods to barter for a sloop. She tried to claw her way out of the Gulf of Darien, but failed. She drifted onto a rock on the opposite shore, and had to be beached right under the walls of the Spanish fortress of Carthagena. The Spanish governor, delighted with such a prize, seized the cargo and put the crew in his prison as pirates. The captain, who was one of the council members, and two of his officers, were sent to Spain and only released after eighteen months in irons and being at first condemned to death. The rest of the men were used as slaves and never seen again. And before the council heard of this disaster, they sent the second tender, *Endeavour*, to touch at Jamaica and then to proceed to New York to barter goods. But after she had beaten to windward a month and had only made 120 miles, she had sprung so many leaks through the stress of sea that she had to return.

In spite of everything, Paterson doggedly pursued his high ideals. In April, he proposed a parliament with one delegate for every fifty men. It was elected, and set up a court of justice, and enacted a curious set of laws. In general, the colony was to be governed by the precepts of the holy scriptures, and in particular, drastic punishments were prescribed for certain crimes, which were mentioned in this revealing order: blasphemy, disrespect towards the council, correspondence with an enemy, rebellion, mutiny and sedition, disobeying a superior officer, violating safe-conduct, using provoking words or gestures or injurious names to an equal, duelling, wilful injury and assault, murder, abuse of a woman whether she belong to an enemy or not, stealing a person away from the colony, and robbery, especially from Indians. It was a primitive list, but it was an achievement to have made and agreed upon any list at all, and if there had been more time it might have grown to the Patersonian government the ballad-writer had foreseen: no brawls, no murmurs, no complaint, no cause of any discontent.

But that was in April, and by then the worst of all their disasters had hit them. It had started to rain. They had arrived by chance at the beginning of the dry season: now it was over.

Their delight in the climate, which had seemed so healthful when they came, had turned to disgust and horror. Paterson had chosen the site for the colony, in the middle of the coast of Darien, because there were no Spanish settlements there, nothing from Portobello to Carthagena. But he had never asked himself why there were none. The reason was, of course, that no Europeans had ever been able to live there: it was too sickly. Now, as the rain teemed down, and the swamps steamed, and the mosquitoes bred, the Scotsmen paid for this ignorance. After six months in Caledonia Bay, there were 300 graves along the shores. One man in four was dead, and hardly a day went by without hasty burials. The funeral rites were performed by the dead men's friends: two ministers of the church had sailed, but both had been among the first to die.

What were they dying of? Was it malaria and yellow fever—the diseases that decimated expeditions 200 years later? Did their insistence on eating biscuit and barrelled meat, much of it rotten by then, give them scurvy or food poisoning? Was there a typhoid epidemic? One can guess but never know. The meticulous lists of the names of the dead, with their curt diagnoses of fevers and fluxes, were not kept up to date. Perhaps the man who made the lists was dead.

Paterson wrote of this period: "I had then some fits of intermitting fever; but, however, I put force upon myself as much as possible to be present in the Councils, lest some rash act should be committed, or an innocent man should suffer." And through the restraint of this statement, one sees him with the mind's eye, among the gradual wrecking of his hopes and dreams, dragging himself out of bed, feeling miserably ill, dressing himself again in the elaborate clothes and the sword and wig of a Scottish gentleman, and walking out in the pouring rain on the sodden tracks among the huddle of shacks they had so bravely and prematurely named New Edinburgh. One sees him among the aimless frightened men, unable to give them an order because he knows someone else on the council will countermand it; or again, being rowed to the ships in the bay to face another day of argument, and to try to settle the flaming quarrels among the captains of the ships. Every day he must have regretted the impulse that had made him trust Smyth with the money, and so had robbed him of the power to run things as he knew they should be run. Every day he must have braced himself to cope with new disasters, and every day they came. There was a mutinous plot to steal the ship *St. Andrew*. The Indians said the Spaniards were preparing to attack, and begged the Scots to sally out against them. A sloop they chartered to trade their goods on the coast of South America came back with nothing sold, because the goods were unsuitable. One of the seafaring councilors, in a rage, imprisoned the boat's crew of a friendly trading ship. Another started a rumor that there was only enough food for three weeks. And whatever happened, it always fell to Paterson to try to make peace between angry warring factions. "Our men did not only continue daily to grow more weakly and sickly," he wrote, "but more without hope of recovery; because, about the latter end of the month of April, we found several species of the little provisions we had left in a manner utterly spoiled and rotten; but under these our very unsupportable difficulties ... every one expected with patience the arrival of good news, and the needful recruits from the mother country, to make way for happy days and glorious success to come."

It was on news from home that everything now depended. In seven months, the colonists had not had a word of advice or help from Scotland, or any answers to the dispatches they had sent. They did not even know if the people in Scotland knew where they were. They felt lost, neglected, even deserted, and rumors began to spread that something had gone disastrously wrong at home. The lookout on the hill above the fort was manned with desperate anxiety.

Then, on May 18th, a story from Jamaica exploded in the colony like a bomb. A ship came in, whose crew had heard from another ship at sea about the proclamations the colonial governors had made in the name of the king. The incredulous colonists heard that the king had disowned them, decreed that their settlement had broken the peace with his ally of Spain, and forbidden his subjects to trade with them. Did this prohibition apply to his subjects in Scotland itself? Was this why no ships had come from home? It looked as though it were, and this fearful thought was supported by a second rumor which was quite untrue: that the company had made a request to the Scottish parliament—though nobody knew what it was—which had been unanimously rejected. Every man in the colony jumped to the same conclusion—that the company had been forced to abandon them. Every man, that is, except two: one was Paterson, and the other a young army Captain called Thomas Drummond, who emerged at this moment of crisis as a loyal friend and a pillar of common sense.

The king's proclamations, of course, had been instigated by the English traders, and one must admit it was one of the dirtiest tricks the English ever played on the Scots. There was one good excuse for it, and only one: it was implicit in the Scottish parliament's act that if the company was a success, the profit would be Scotland's, but that if it got into trouble the English navy would have to get it out—and the landing in Darien was certain to get into trouble, sooner or later, with Spain. It was too much to expect the English to enjoy this one-sided bargain. And the Scottish directors, by yet another piece of foolishness, had made it easy for the English to turn the king against them. In their passion for secrecy, they had not even told the king where they were going, and that was absurdly tactless. It was true that the act had received the king's formal assent and given them authority to go almost anywhere they liked. But the assent had only been given by the king's commissioner in Scotland. He had not been told personally what was in the act until it was passed, and he had not been told at all about Darien until he heard from his English subjects that the Scots were already there. Any king would have felt annoyed. The proclamation issued in Barbados began with words which gave the clue to his displeasure: "His Majesty is unacquainted with the intentions and designs of the

Scots settling at Darien." But the insincerity of the whole plot
was shown by the fact that the proclamations, forbidding all his
Majesty's subjects whatsoever to communicate with the colony,
were in fact only issued in the colonies, and not in Scotland, as
the colonists had feared: for in Scotland, everyone would have
seen at once that the proclamations contravened the Scottish
parliament's act, and a fine constitutional crisis would have
started. The English took care that the Scottish directors should
be kept in the dark. Long after everyone in the Americas knew
what the king had done, and the story had even reached the isolated settlement itself, the directors still knew nothing about it
and were happily, though very slowly, fitting out a second expedition on the Clyde.

Nobody who knew the American colonies would have expected the proclamations to have a decisive effect. The king was
a long way off, and trading captains were in the habit of sailing
wherever profits were good, whether they thought the king would
approve or not. And in fact, plenty of sloops sailed out of New
York and Boston bound for Darien after the proclamations were
made. But the Scots in the settlement did not wait to see what
would happen, or even whether the rumor had been true. A panic
broke out. The men on shore made a rush for the boats to get
themselves and their property back on board the ships. The men
on the ships tried to make them ready for sea, and to tow them
with rowing boats out of the windlocked bay. They even wanted
to abandon the guns in the fort and sail away unarmed. Nobody
knew where to go—there was an added rumor they would be
hanged as pirates if they went home to Scotland. Their only idea
was to go, and go at once.

Paterson went round arguing and pleading. The first rumors
of things of this kind, he said, were always the most alarming. If
the colonists would only wait a little while, ships must surely
come from Scotland. If they insisted on going, they would all be
ashamed of themselves. But nobody would listen. Step by step,
he was forced to watch his colony abandoned. He had to agree

that the men ashore were too sick to man the fort and should man the ships instead, for greater safety: and then that the ships should put to sea, but come back if they met the ships from Scotland. He proposed himself to stay on the coast with twenty or thirty men, and live on turtles and fish until news or recruits came from home. And Thomas Drummond, the only man who wholly supported him, fell in with that idea, but suggested that Paterson should try to go home to Scotland to report what had happened, and he should be the one to stay. But under the worry and strain and disappointment, Paterson's health broke down: "About the 4th of June, I was taken very ill of a fever; but trouble of mind, as I afterwards found, was none of the least causes thereof." For the last week, he was left alone on shore, too weak to leave his hut, and nobody but Drummond came to see him. On the night of June 15th, 7½ months from their hopeful landfall, some men came and carried him on board the *Unicorn*, half-conscious.

The panic flight of the four remaining ships, with their unsold cargoes of rusting tools and rotting drapery, is one of the ghastliest stories of the sea. At the mouth of the bay, they were struck by a squall, and the *Unicorn*, which had not enough healthy men to man her, lost her longboat and an anchor. In trying to save the boat she lost the wind, and had to drop another anchor close under Golden Island, where she rode out the night in peril. The *Caledonia* and *Endeavour* cleared the land and disappeared. At dawn the *St. Andrew* was also out of sight. The crew of the *Unicorn*, alone and too weak to weigh their second anchor, cut it away—and the bay was left deserted, the fort and the huts of New Edinburgh still intact but empty.

Somewhere in the Caribbean, the *Unicorn* lost her foremast, fore topmast and mizzen topmast in a storm. She was leaking so fast that all the available men could scarcely keep her afloat. In that distress, she sighted the *St. Andrew*, and on a calm day which followed the storm, her captain took a boat to the *St. Andrew* to ask for help in salvaging sails and rigging. But the *St. Andrew's* captain refused, and when a fair wind sprang up he sailed away and abandoned his fellow countrymen.

There were, or had been, 250 men on board the *Unicorn*. But she could only muster five or six seamen to a watch, and twenty landsmen who could move. The landsmen were kept at the pumps. In a week, the seamen got a jury rig on her, but they had drifted past Jamaica and were forced to round the western end of Cuba. On the northern shore, the captain went in his pinnace into the Bay of Mattanzas for water, and found himself under the guns of a Spanish fort. The boat escaped under fire, but one man who had landed was captured and left behind. On the coast of Virginia, the ship grounded several times; but on August 14th, two months out of Darien, she limped into New York. Of the 250 men who embarked, 150 had died and been thrown overboard.

The *Caledonia* had reached New York before her, and her captain, who was another Drummond, wrote a dignified and tragic letter to a merchant in Glasgow: "Sir, In our sad and lamentable condition, We all embarqued upon the 19th day of June; Having equally divided our people and small stock of provisions we had: With orders from our Council to make the best of our way for new-England, or anywhere else upon the Main, where we might have provisions to get home to Scotland. I arrived heire the 3rd of August. And in our passage from Caledonia heither our sickness being so universall aboard, And mortality so great, that I hove overboard 105 Corps. The sickness and Mortallity continues still aboard, I have buried 11 since I came heire already. We have never heard so much as one silible either by word or wryting from any in Scotland since ever we came from thence. I am afraid I shall have a hard pull to gett the Ship home for my people are still dying being all weak ...

"Sir, I am not capable by wryting to give you ane account of the Meiserable condition we have undergone first before we came offe from Caledonia being starved and abandoned by the World. As also the great deficulty of getting the Ship to this place! So that I shall reffer the particulars untill meeting which is all from him Who is Sir your very humble servant Robt. Drummond. New York August 11th 1699."

As for the other two ships, the *Endeavour* had been abandoned at sea and foundered, and the *St. Andrew* had been chased by a Spanish fleet and her captain and 130 men had perished. She reached the lee of Jamaica under command of an army officer who wrote to the directors: "I know not in all the world what to doe; I am certain ye seamen will mutiny, and play ye devill, for they have nott a weeke's bread." So, of the 1,200 men who had sailed so bravely from Leith in November, at least 750 were dead by the end of the following summer, and most of the rest were scattered and lost for ever in Jamaica and North America. Of the five ships only one, the *Caledonia*, ever returned to Scotland. Paterson reached Now York alive, and several Scotsmen who saw him there wrote home about him: "He looks more like a skeleton than a man. God grant he may recover." "The grief has broke Mr. Paterson's heart and brain, and now hee's a child."

The story ought to have ended there, but it did not. It started all over again, simply because nobody on either side of the Atlantic knew what was happening on the other side. It is quite difficult to imagine the isolation of a place like Darien 270 years ago. If men were to colonize a planet now, they would be far more closely in touch with their homes than the Scotsmen in Darien were. Scotland, in that summer of 1699, was a fool's paradise. The whole country went on rejoicing at the colony's success long after it had been abandoned, and the directors went on sending reinforcements long after there was nothing left to reinforce. Even the ballads were still being written and sung when most of the men they were written in praise of were dead.

In this national euphoria, the management of the company remained as bad as ever, and its luck was even worse. The directors had in fact dispatched a ship to the colony in February, and with favorable winds it should have arrived at the very time when Paterson was most desperately looking for it. But it ran aground and was wrecked in the outer Hebrides before it had even left Scottish waters. In May, two more were sent, the *Olive Branch* and the *Hopeful Binning of Bo'ness,* with 300 new recruits on board. They reached Darien in August, and were astonished to find that everyone had gone. A few days later, a man went into the hold of the *Olive Branch* with a lighted candle to draw some brandy. The brandy caught fire, the ship burnt down to the water line, and all the men, unnerved, sailed away in the *Hopeful Binning* to Jamaica, where most of them died the same miserable deaths as their predecessors.

But those were minor reinforcements. A second expedition, even bigger than the first, was also being prepared that summer. There were four more ships: the *Rising Sun,* the *Hope,* the *Duke of Hamilton* and the *Hope of Bo'ness.* (That made three expressions of hope in the names of the sips, but it was only coincidence: the *Hopeful Binning* and the *Hope of Bo'ness* did not belong to the company, but were chartered.) There were also 1,300 more men. And there were all the old mistakes: four more councilors without a chairman to rule the expedition, unweatherly ships, and a mass of goods which were costly in Scotland where they were bought but worthless in Darien where they were meant to be sold. The councilors seem not to have known what was in their cargoes when they sailed, for they wrote peevishly to the directors afterwards: "We cannot conceive for what end so much thin gray paper, and so many little bonnets were sent here, being intirely useless, and not worth their place on a ship. It cannot be unknown to your Honours that wee have not £50 sterling of vendible gods."

The new expedition was ready in the Clyde on August 18th. That was four days after the *Unicorn,* the last of the first expedition, had crept into New York under her jury rig, and a month or so after the *St. Andrew* had drifted into Jamaica. The news of the colony's desertion was already on its way to England, and if only it had arrived in time the new ships might have been reequipped and the old mistakes put right.

The events of that autumn seem like a stock situation of melodrama. The ships in the Clyde are delayed for a whole month by contrary winds. Everything else is ready, and they are packed with men who are eager to start their adventure. The moment the wind shifts, they will sail. Meanwhile, a ship is beating across the Atlantic bearing the news of disaster. Its master and crew have no sense of urgency; they are more concerned to make port before the equinoctial gales. They reach Bristol. Somebody posts to London, and the wicked English traders show their glee. A coach called the *Flying Packet* rumbles down the Great North Road for Edinburgh. And still the fleet is storm-stayed in the Clyde. Can the stagecoach arrive in time?

On September 19th, the fleet is still waiting. On that day, the news reaches Edinburgh—and the directors, heartbreakingly foolish, refuse to believe it. They wait three days, then they write to the councilors on board the ships, telling them that a man called M'kye or Mackay is on his way from Edinburgh to join them, and asking them to wait till he arrives. He is one of the councilors of the first expedition, who has come home some months before. The same letter gives instructions about two boatloads of bread and rice which are being sent out to the fleet from Greenock; and among these trivialities the directors mention the news: "We are likewayes advised of a story made and propagate in England, viz., that the Scots hade deserted their colony of Caledonia. . . . The story is altogether malicious and false, and is contrived on purpose to discourage people to goe to oure Colony with provision, etc., since they find the proclamations in the West Indies, and all their other methods against us has not hade ye designed effect. Wee are certainly informed the story is contrived by Mr. Vernoon, one of ye Secretarys of England. McKye laughs at the story; but though there be nothing in it, yet wee think it fitt that yow keep it to yourselves while yow see M'kye, who, we hope, will be with you tomorrow night."

The letter is delivered to the ships. But that night the wind changes, and the fleet sets sail.

Paterson, still in New York, was recovering slowly from his fever and from what would probably be called a nervous break-

down nowadays. For some weeks after the dreadful voyage of
the *Unicorn,* he seemed to the people who met him to have lost
his reason; but as he revived, his old determination came back
to him. He and his friend Thomas Drummond started again to
discuss the plan they had had to abandon: that Drummond
should keep the Scottish flag flying in Darien while Paterson
went back to Scotland to report what had gone wrong. One problem which had seemed insoluble in Darien presented an easy
solution in New York: in spite of the king's proclamation, there
were plenty of merchants there who were willing, simply on
Paterson's and Drummond's words of honor, to send food to the
Scottish colony and wait for payment from Edinburgh. Accordingly, some time that autumn Drummond chartered a trading
sloop and sailed again for Darien with a cargo of food and the
best of the tools that could be salvaged from the *Unicorn,* and
Paterson took passage home in the *Caledonia.*

Drummond seems one of the most attractive of the Scotsmen. He had been a captain in the army, and he must have been
a much younger man than Paterson, who was forty-four. All his
actions suggest a boyish enthusiasm, and a letter which Paterson
wrote him the following year shows warmth and friendliness, and
is full of the kind of advice an uncle might give to a favorite
nephew. He was imbued with Paterson's aspirations for the colony, and he had all the spirit of courage and adventure by which
the English, for better or worse, were planting their colonies all
round the globe. By the middle of November, with a crew of twenty
men, he was back again in the empty bay in Darien. The fort
was in ruins, the huts of New Edinburgh burnt, the few acres of
land they had cleared were overgrown already by jungle weeds.
Yet at that moment, the future must have looked bright to him,
and the present intensely exciting. Their lessons had been learned,
a supply of provisions was assured, and Paterson was on his way
to Scotland to put everything right and organize a fresh start
for the colony. And in the meantime, the fortunes of the company
and the honor of Scotland were in his hands.

He had only been there a week when sails were sighted, and

four ships stood into the bay with their decks packed with men: the fleet which had prematurely left the Clyde in August. He eagerly rowed out towards them, and as the first, the *Rising Sun,* dropped anchor, he climbed aboard to greet his countrymen fresh from home. But his eagerness turned to dismay—for here was every one of the old mistakes repeated, and nobody was glad to see him, nobody wanted to listen.

The four new councilors were reduced to a state of helpless consternation by finding the colony gone. For a whole week, without landing a single man, they debated what to do. Three of them were totally ineffective—one was said not to care what happened as long as he had his pipe and his dram—and they were dominated by the fourth, a man called James Byres. And Byres, unluckily, proved to be strong-willed, self-seeking and autocratic, stupid, unscrupulous and cruel. He was also a liar who twisted the truth in any way that suited his purposes, and reviled the character and reputation of anyone who disagreed with him.

Confronted by this intolerable man, Drummond suffered all the frustration that Paterson had borne the year before. He knew exactly what had gone wrong with the first expedition. He knew Caledonia Bay, he knew the Indians. He had in fact been co-opted to the council shortly before the desertion. But Byres refused to admit him to council meetings, insisting that all the previous councilors had been fools or knaves or both, and that he and Paterson had been the worst of all.

The first week's argument was on the simple question of whether to stay or sail away again. Byres said they had come to reinforce a colony, not to found one, and he started a rumor that they had only six weeks' food. A rummage in the holds of the ships soon showed that there were six months' food and four months' brandy, but Byres was the sort of man who can brush unwelcome facts aside, and he still insisted he was right. Drummond tried to assure him that food was no longer a problem, since he and Paterson had established the company's credit in New York. Byres called him a liar, and implied that the credits were some kind of dishonest trick to line his own pockets. He even refused to accept the cargo of a sloop which had already arrived. And by the end of that week of bitter controversy, he announced a decision which was fatal to the colony: in order, he said, to conserve the supplies of food, he had decided to keep 500 men in Caledonia Bay, and to ship the rest away, with three weeks' provisions, and land them all in Jamaica.

That destroyed the morale of the colony at a single blow. Byres began to order men ashore to repair the fort and to build new huts, but nobody had been told who was to stay and who was to go to Jamaica, and the men worked unwillingly, grumbling that it was no use building huts if they were not to be allowed to live in them. A rumor spread that the councilors meant to sell the surplus men into slavery; and in fact, the decision was not much better than that, because 500 or 600 destitute men put ashore in Jamaica would either have starved to death or have had to take work in plantations on whatever terms they could.

Within a fortnight, mutiny was brewing. Men were being arrested for talking of overthrowing the council and seizing the ships. Byres tried to stop the rot by the typical desperate act of a weak commander—by making an example. He seized on a humble carpenter, a man called Alexander Campbell, set up a hasty court with himself as judge, and sentenced him to be hanged. Campbell had not done anything more than hundreds of other men: he had criticized the council and talked about leaving the colony. But a scaffold was built in the ruins of Fort St. Andrew. The councilors wrote vindictively: "Wee alwayes fancyed the rascall expected relief to the last minute." But there was no relief. A church minister wrote: "This poor man seemed to die very penitently, confessing ... that for some time before this, particularly since God had recovered him from a late sickness, he had left off prayer to the Lord, and therefore God had justly left him to this sad end." Both reported that on the scaffold Campbell said: "Lord forgive them that brought me to this lock," and then jumped off unaided.

Drummond had been appalled by Byres' scheme. It was not

only callous, not only unnecessary, not only destructive of morale. There was another aspect of it: 500 men were not enough to man the fort and the ships if they were attacked. A colony so small would be defenseless—and there were signs that the Spaniards had been slowly building up their forces ever since the Scots had first appeared, and were ready at last to use them. A sloop from Jamaica, trying in vain to sell the last forty of a cargo of slaves, brought news of four men-of-war which had newly come from Spain to Portobello, and of three more expected from Carthagena. All the bakers of Portobello, it was said, were busy baking bread for these ships to take on an expedition against the Scottish colony. And the Indians were telling stories of a Spanish army approaching across the hills.

Like Paterson, Drummond had always been friendly with the Indians. He had taken the trouble to learn a little of their language, and was said to have a better way with them than anybody else. So it was to him that they brought their warnings. He passed them on to Byres. But it was not in Byres' nature to be friendly with primitive people, or to let himself seem indebted to them. He laughed at the Indians, said they were no better than a parcel of monkeys, insulted the *caciques* and ordered them out of the fort. And he said he was quite ready to fight whatever force the Spaniards could send, if they could send any at all.

That was just stupid bravado. Nothing was ready, or ever likely to be ready under Byres' rule. Drummond wrote a letter to the council, asking that 150 of the men condemned to be sent to Jamaica—any who would be willing to take their fate with him—should be allowed to join him in his sloop, with nothing more than their arms and the three weeks' provisions agreed for their voyage. He promised they would not be any burden on the colony until it was able to support them. He refused to tell the council exactly what he proposed to do, but it was common knowledge that he wanted to forestall the Spanish attack, by a surprise raid on Portobello or Carthagena, and to win some Spanish hostages who could be bargained for the captured crew of the *Endeavour*. But Byres rejected his offer as chimerical, and delivered a dictum which became a byword in the colony: "We are not come for the taking of touns."

Every one of the colonists was soon discussing Drummond's offer and Byres' rejection of it. It was exactly what most of them wanted—a promise of positive, adventurous leadership. Hundreds responded to it: suddenly, Drummond found he was being acclaimed as a popular leader. He may have been flattered: he was certainly alarmed. He was sure that Byres was leading the colony to a final disaster, and he was smarting under unforgivable insults; but he had come back to Darien as a Patersonian idealist and a loyal servant of the company, and he was not the kind of man to lead a mutiny.

Byres, on the other hand, was not the kind of man to tolerate a rival. Unluckily, most of the men arrested and questioned on suspicion of mutinous thoughts told the council they would rather volunteer with Drummond than be shipped to Jamaica. And with no more excuse than that, Byres had Drummond arrested and locked in a hut under guard. Half a dozen other young officers who had liked him were imprisoned on the ships. Everyone else who approved his ideas—everyone who was "for the taking of touns"—was added to the list to be deported to Jamaica, and five or six hundred men were packed into two of the ships and given sailing orders. And there they remained for six weeks, because the winds again were contrary and the ships could not get out of the bay. Within a month of its refounding, the colony had fallen into a state of paralyzed inaction. And after reducing it to that unhappy condition, at the beginning of February, Byres bought a sloop with the company's money and sailed away to Jamaica, saying he was going to arrange for the reception of the men he was sending there—and leaving the colony without any active leader, good or bad.

Drummond may be said to have represented common sense and integrity, and Byres stupidity and chaos. But there was a third force in the colony too: three ministers sent by the General Assembly of the Church of Scotland. Some people put the blame for the colony's troubles on the harsh repressions of these clergymen, but they really had no decisive influence at all: they were hopelessly out of their depth in that buccaneering world. The Reverend Frances Borland wrote a book called *Memoirs of Darien,* the Reverend Alexander Shiels wrote some informative letters, and the Reverend Archibald Stobo contributed to their joint reports to the General Assembly; and from all their own writings, they seem to have had an uphill struggle which was often pathetic, yet sometimes had the element of comedy which is apt to attach to people who are too self-consciously good.

At that time, the God of the Scottish church was stern, and the three ministers, interpreting His ways, found an easy explanation of the colony's disasters in its sins. "The Source and Fountain Cause of all our Miseries," they wrote jointly in February, "we brought from our own Countrye with us, arising from the inconsiderate Choice that was made there of the worst of Men to go along with us, that ever were sent to command or serve in a Colony: which in the judgment of GOD, our Land hath spued out as its scum." And a tract they all wrote a week after they landed accused the colonists of a thunderous list of sins: "There have abounded and do still remain among us, such abominations (notwithstanding all the means used to restrain and suppress them) as the rudest Heathens from the Light of Nature do abhor, such as Atheistical swearing and cursing, brutish drunkeness, detestable lying and prevaricating, obscene and filthy talking, mocking of Godliness, yea and among too many of the meaner sort base thieving and pilfering, besides Sabbath breaking, contempt of all Gospel Ordinances &c which are stumbling to the very *Indians,* opprobrious to the Christian Name, and reproachful to the Church and Nation to which we belong. Many are grosly ignorant of the principals of Religion, and among the more knowing, Hypocrysie, Formality, Impenitency, Unbelief, Indifferency, security, Omission of prayer, neglecting the great Salvation, slighting of Christ offered in the Gospel and other spiritual sins, do lamentably prevail."

Perhaps it was all true: it seems a likely enough description of seafaring men and soldiers of almost any era, and the ministers must have led sheltered lives if they were surprised at it. But their threats of wrath to come had no effect whatever on the sinners. Borland's book gives glimpses of the three clerics on their daily avocations, dressed in their sombre black, Bible in hand, ever ready with a Latin tag or a biblical quotation, exhorting, admonishing, reproving, handing out tracts and seeing men throw them away. They are always in distress, and always being snubbed. Nobody has any time for them. The council declines their offer to open its meetings with prayer, the people neglect the sabbath, and nobody has time to build a hut for them—they do not think of building it themselves—so that they have to hold their meetings in the "shady, dark and silent woods, Inter densas umbrosa Cacumina Sylvas." When, after long opposition, they declare a day of prayer and preach a marathon of three sermons, one each, they are grieved that so few come to listen, and that so many absent themselves either from sloth and indifferency or from malignancy and wicked perverseness. Even an expedition to the Indians is not an unqualified success. The naked savages learn it is wrong to try to sell food on the Lord's Day, and they attend a church service. But the preaching of the Gospel is sadly hindered by the lack of any interpreter to speak either Indian or Spanish, and on the way home the ministers get lost in the jungle and Mr. Shiels is taken faint. All in all, the three appear as totally humorless men, simple and narrow-minded to a scarcely credible degree; and compassion seems to have vanished from their Christianity. In every event, whether trivial or disastrous, they look for the hand of their God. It is easily seen when Mr. Stobo is rescued from a shipwreck in which over a hundred Scottish sinners are drowned; harder perhaps when Byres is found to be another of the few survivors; and hardest of all when it pleases God to put a sudden end to Mr. Shiels' earthly pilgrimage just after he has preached on his favorite text "The Ways of the Lord are Right." One is sorry for Borland when he writes in his memoirs of "the disappointment of all our expectations, that had swelled before to too great bigness." But one's sympathy is strained when he compares the whole colony to Sodom and Gomorrah, and himself and his colleagues to Job.

In the dispute between Byres and Drummond, these moralists were on the side of Drummond. There were only three or four men in the colony, besides themselves, that they mentioned in their reports without positive disapproval, and Drummond was one of them: Mr. Shiels said he had the reputation of a most diligent and useful man. They detested Byres, who had been as rude to them as he was to everybody else, and they put his imprisonment of Drummond down to jealousy. They did not give Drummond any help, and perhaps they were right not to meddle in politics; but they thought it a sign of the Lord's deliverance when Byres took ship to Jamaica, and four days after Byres had gone, there was another sign: the arrival from Scotland of a man called Captain Alexander Campbell of Fonab, who sailed into the bay on February 11th and woke up the moribund colony with a whirlwind of common sense and energy.

Fonab was an army officer of the same regiment as Drummond—they had fought together in Flanders—and to judge him by his name and deeds alone, he must have been a typical young laird of his notoriously warlike Highland clan. He had been dispatched by the company's directors as soon as they brought themselves to believe the stories of the colony's desertion. They had appointed him a councilor and told him to catch up with the fleet if he could and re-establish the colony—if necessary, by fighting any foreign forces he found in possession. He failed to catch it up; and arriving in the bay he found the most intelligent men locked up, the 500 discarded men still in their ships, doing nothing but waiting for a favorable wind, and the whole place full of rumors that the Spaniards were coming. No useful work was being done. Some great guns which the company had sent to equip the fort were still in the hold of the *Rising Sun,* and the fort itself, which looked formidable enough on the seaward side, had not been finished on the side that faced the land. A deadly lethargy had settled on the place, through lack of leadership and through sickness: 220 men were lying in fevers and fluxes, and dying by dozens every day.

The change Fonab wrought was astonishing. Within forty-eight hours, he had sized up the whole situation, released Drummond and the other prisoners, countermanded Byres' order to send the men to Jamaica, and set them and everyone else to work on the defences. And not only that: he had found out from the Indians where the Spanish army was, and had disappeared into the jungle, leading a force of 200 enthusiastic volunteers, to take it by surprise. The Indians joyfully joined him, and after three days' march they found the Spaniards, encamped inside a stockade. Fonab in person, brandishing his sword, led a charge which put the enemy to flight. He was wounded in the shoulder, and nine of his men were killed. So were nine of the Spaniards; and among the equipment they abandoned was a trunk containing the clothes of their commander and his insignia as Knight of the Order of St. Iago. These trophies were carried back to Caledonia. But it was too late. Emerging triumphant from the woods, Fonab and his men saw eight sail of Spanish ships, which came to anchor off Golden Island and blockaded the entrance of the bay.

His exploit put new heart in the colonists: so perhaps did the sight of the Spanish ships, after so many weeks of demoralizing rumors. They expected the Spaniards to enter the bay and come to grips in a formal naval battle, and an ex-officer of the English navy who had turned up from somewhere advised them to make a fire-ship of the *Hope of Bo'ness,* and volunteered to sail it into the Spanish fleet. But the Spaniards were too wily. Instead of sailing into the windlocked bay, they started to land their men on each side of it, and the Scottish fleet, unable to sail out, could not do anything to stop them.

In the records of the siege which began then, Fonab does not seem to have played much active part. Perhaps his wound had put him out of action. Nor does Drummond—and his movements are enigmatic. Soon after the Spanish fleet was sighted, he slipped out of the bay in a sloop for Jamaica, telling the council he was going home to vindicate himself. If that was his real intention, he changed his mind in Jamaica, and it seems more likely that he went—perhaps at Fonab's suggestion—to ask for the help of the English, and especially of the celebrated Admiral Benbow, who had recently been there chasing the pirate Captain Kidd. But while Drummond was there he met Mackay, the councilor who had missed the fleet on the day it left the Clyde, and possibly Mackay assured him there was no need to go home to defend what he had done. He must also have quickly learned that Benbow and his squadron had left for New York and England, and that there were no other English forces able, even if they had been willing, to challenge the Spanish fleet. At all events, he and Mackay set sail together to return to Darien, and Byres sailed with them in another ship.

It would be hard to invent the variety of disasters, great and small, which overcame the Scots. On the way back to Darien, Mackay was fishing from the stern of the ship, and he fell overboard and was eaten by a shark. At the mouth of the bay, Drummond and Byres, in their separate ships, found the Spanish fleet still in command of the approaches. Typically, Drummond sailed safely in by night: Byres ordered his ship's captain to go about and return to Jamaica, and threatened to kill him with a billet of wood until he reluctantly agreed.

As the colonists, day after day, watched the Spanish soldiers landing from the ships, the courage Fonab had raised in them began to ebb away. The hopelessness and lethargy came back. The Spaniards were an organized army, and the Scotsmen, although there were plenty of soldiers among them, were not. A tactician might have thought the proper place to fight was on the beaches where the Spanish boats were landing. But thick jungle lay between, and when the Scotsmen sent out scouts they were picked off by snipers in the trees. The woods full of pleasant birds and murmuring airs, the beautiful natural arbor someone had called the Shades of Love, became a place of haunting fear that no one would venture into. And within the fort, the conditions of life sank down to a depth of horror worse than the stinking holds of the ships on passage. Now, there was really nothing left

to eat, except moldy biscuits full of worms, and rotting flyblown
meat. Two or three hundred men at a time were lying sick,
crammed into the huts. The fevers began to strike with terrible
speed, so that men who were active one day were sometimes dead
the next. Then fire swept through the lines of huts, and the sick
were dragged out and died more quickly in the teeming rain.
And as the sickness spread, the Spaniàrds drew nearer, advancing
very cautiously, taking their time. The moat, which should have
held them, fell without a fight; one evening, they were still beyond it—next morning, their musketeers were lurking in the
woods on the promontory itself. Men fetching water from the
stream came under fire, and the dying garrison was forced to dig
for water, and drink the filthy puddles at the bottoms of the
holes. Everyone saw his own death approaching, and the Spanish
fleet at anchor made it plain there was no escape.

It was a cat-and-mouse affair: through their own failings,
the Scotsmen never had a chance. Yet it lasted more than a
month before the Colony's officers gave up the last pretense of
hope. On March 18th they met, and this entry was made in the
council's minute book:

Fort St. Andrew, 18th March 1700

Att a meeting of the Council, Land and Sea Captains,
Capt. Wm. Veitch, Praeses.
A motion being made for capitulating on honourable
terms with the Spaniards, who have besieged us both
by sea and land:—It being putt to the vote,
Capitulate or not, caryed nemine contradicente
Capitulate; and a draught of a letter being brought
before this meeting, it was resolved a drummer should
be sent therewith to the Governor of Carthagina,
Generall of the Spanish forces.

Sixteen men signed their names to this forlorn entry—but
not Fonab. Throughout the siege, he refused to treat with the

Spaniards except by the sword, and presumably, since the vote was unanimous, he refused to attend the meeting. But next morning, two of the captains marched out of the fort, preceded by a drummer, bearing the letter which proposed a cessation of arms and declared that the Scots were willing to abandon Darien. The Spanish general, Don Juan Pimienta, received the emissaries courteously—"a little thin Man in Stature, but mighty proud, passionate, stiff and wilful." He agreed to let the colonists go, but his terms were strict. They could go in the chartered ships which were then in the bay, and could take their own clothes with them. All arms and goods, and all the company's own ships, must be surrendered. The Scottish officers could not bring themselves to accept. They went back to the fort, and finally resigned themselves to die.

A week later, the Spaniards were in musketshot of the fort, on the landward side where it was weakest. The Scots returned their fire, but they seldom saw a target, because they had neglected to fell the jungle behind the fort, and the Spaniards were still in the cover of the trees. Then, about March 28th, the Spaniards were seen to be landing heavy guns and ammunition on the shore. Against cannon fire from the land, the fort was powerless, and the defenders knew the end was very near.

It came in a way which was wholly unexpected. On March 30th, the musket fire died away, and in the silence a Spanish drummer was heard approaching through the woods. He was escorting an emissary who said that his excellency the Spanish general was ready to parley. The Scottish officers followed him to the Spanish camp, prepared for a final demand for unconditional surrender. None of them could speak Spanish, and they took a French interpreter with them; and through this language, foreign to both sides, they heard with astonishment terms that were generous—far more generous than those they had rejected a fortnight before. Don Juan Pimienta said they could board their ships with drums beating and colors flying. He would give them fourteen days to stock the ships with wood and water. Then, as soon as the wind was fair, all the ships would be allowed to

sail, with guns and ammunition to protect them on the voyage
back to Scotland. The Scots should free any prisoners they had,
and he would free all he had taken since the Colony had first
been founded. Formal articles of capitulation were drawn up
then and there. Pimienta refused to sign them in French, so they
were written in Latin. His wilfulness only showed when the three
ministers joined the negotiations to request him not to molest
the Indians who had been friendly with the Scots. To this he
replied that the Indians were the king of Spain's subjects, but
that if they kept out of his way he would not go to look for them.
And when Mr. Shiels pressed the point, he told him not to be
officious, saying in Latin *"Cura tua negotia"*—"Mind your own
business"—to which Mr. Shiels replied, rather weakly perhaps,
"Curabo."

At this sudden reprieve, the colonists hurried to board the
ships, scarcely wondering why the Spanish general had relented.
To the ministers, it appeared to be "God's wonderful, seasonable
and preventing Mercy, that had delivered them from falling a
prey to the Teeth of their bloody, Popish enemies." But this
seems ungenerous when it was by or through the Popish enemies
that the mercy had been shown. The simple fact was that Pimienta was tired of the whole affair, and was losing his own men
through sickness. All he needed to do, as a matter of policy, was
to turn the Scots out of Darien. All he could do by prolonging
the siege was humiliate them further, and seize a few ships of
doubtful seaworthiness, and a mass of trade goods as useless to
him as they had been to the Scots. There was no reason why he
should bother: he preferred to go home.

The colonists were not only too far gone to speculate, they
were too far gone to rejoice, and if they flew their colors and
beat their drums as they retreated, it was still a mournful journey. Some of the sick men died as they were being carried to the
boats, more died in the boats before they could reach the ships.
The survivors weighed anchor with difficulty: they hardly had
the strength to man the capstans. The crew of the *Rising Sun*,
the biggest and most cumbersome of the ships, had to ask the

Spaniards to help them to tow and warp her clear of the mouth of the bay. On April 12th, 1700, she came to anchor off Golden Island, in full view of the Spanish fleet: and that evening she sailed, taking away the last Scotsmen ever to settle in Darien.

But not one of the ships reached home. The *Hope* was wrecked on the coast of Cuba. The *Hope of Bo'ness* was so leaky that she had to run into Carthagena, where her captain sold her for almost nothing to the Spaniards. The *Duke of Hamilton* was wrecked by a hurricane in Charleston, Carolina. In the same hurricane, the *Rising Sun* was lying outside the harbor bar, because she had too much draught to go in. She broke up, and it was then that over a hundred men were drowned while Byres and the Reverend Mr. Stobo were saved—they had rowed ashore, with a dozen others, including Mrs. Stobo, before the hurricane struck. Stobo was doubly blessed: he found the Presbyterians of Carolina in need of a minister, and he settled there. Among his descendants, six generations later, was another man who made his mark on the isthmus: Theodore Roosevelt. But altogether, 940 men of the 1,300 of this second expedition were dead within a year of the time when it left the Clyde. Byres, Fonab and Drummond were among the very few who lived to return to Scotland. Byres was severely censured by the company: Drummond was vindicated.

As for Paterson, he reached home from New York before the second expedition was abandoned, but too late to save it. Yet even after this second disaster, he refused to give up. He still believed his idea of a peaceful crossing-place on the isthmus was sound—and so it was. He saw a mistake more fundamental than the government by committee and the foolish choice of goods: it had been wrong from the very beginning to try to found a company-owned colony, of the kind the English ran successfully in the East. In the Americas, there was too much competition. It should have been a crown colony, with all the power of England and Scotland behind it—power enough to defy the Spaniards to prove that they had a valid claim to that empty coast. And he even proposed to start again on a much bigger scale, with a company shared with the English and a capital of no less than £2,000,000. With his old persuasiveness, he convinced the king that it was still feasible and would bring enormous profit and authority to the crown. But that was in 1701. In 1702 the king died, and under Queen Anne, who succeeded him, the project was abandoned.

Paterson turned his energy then to promoting the Union of England and Scotland. Most Scotsmen blamed the English for the Darien fiasco, but a few saw the moral in it—that it was wiser to join the English than try to beat them at their own game. And union offered the only chance of recouping the £250,000 the company had lost. It was a crippling loss for Scotland alone, but the United Kingdom could afford it. The English still wanted the company dissolved: it seemed fair enough that they should pay. And so they did. In the financial settlement which accompanied the treaty of union, it was enacted that £232,884. 5s. 0⅔d. should be repaid to the company's subscribers, and in 1707, after long delays and arguments, twelve wagonloads of gold were dispatched for the purpose from London to Edinburgh, escorted by Scots dragoons.

But the man who had suffered most in the enterprise, short of losing his life, was Paterson. He had surrendered his stock in part payment of the debt caused by Smyth's defection, so none of the English gold came to him. The failure of the company left him destitute. The last session of the Scottish parliament commended him to the queen, and the first of the British parliament proposed a suitable payment for his services. But nothing was done. He was still a highly respected public figure and the leading financial expert of his day, but he was reduced to borrowing money, accepting charity and teaching arithmetic to save himself from starving. At last, when he was nearly sixty, parliament voted him the recompense of £18,000. But he only lived four years longer to enjoy it. He died in 1718: a man wise ahead of his time, yet not quite wise enough. Nobody knows where he died, or where he was buried.

Long before then, however, a final scene had been enacted in Caledonia. A single Scottish ship, sent out by the company before all hope was lost, reached the mouth of the bay. Seeing no ships inside, her captain sent a boat to reconnoiter. Fort St. Andrew was still standing, but the Spanish flag was flying over it. Mystified, the Scotsmen stood away again—and Spain was unchallenged there for over a century more.

(vi)

The Lost Canal of Raspadura

It is only by investigating an hydraulic problem in its
greatest generality, that it can be advantageously solved.

Baron von Humboldt, 1826

With Paterson, the idea of a way through the isthmus disappeared from the daydreams of Europe. For the whole of the
eighteenth century, after the Scotsmen had gone, Darien was
covered again by the Spanish cloak of secrecy. In 1702 a party of
Englishmen from Jamaica followed Balboa's route, like Oxenham
and Wafer, and seized a gold mine near the Pacific shore, but
they soon retreated, with only eighty pounds weight of gold. In
1739, San Lorenzo and Portobello were taken again, this time by
the English Admiral Vernon—"Old Grog": his nickname is immortalized in the Royal Navy's ration of rum and water, and his
battle in the London street market of Portobello Road. In the
middle of the century, a party of French Academicians soberly
crossed by the Spanish trail on their way to make some astronomical observations in Peru. But the isthmus stagnated. Under the
threat of English attacks in the Caribbean, more and more of the
Spanish traffic from the Pacific coast of South America was sent
round Cape Horn, and Panama slowly lost its power and prosperity. In the course of the century, most of the wealthy Spanish
families moved away, leaving half-castes of every proportion of
Spanish, Negro and Indian blood, who lived the sleepy, aimless
life of a tropical city whose purpose and glory are past. The
Indians survived in the jungle and kept their independence, because nobody could find them there. In the second half of the
century, an order is said to have been issued in Spain that all of

them should be converted or exterminated; but a deed which had been impossible at the height of the colony's vigor was not worth attempting by then.

But at the beginning of the nineteenth century, the old idea of a canal was suddenly revived. The Canal Age had come to its peak in Europe. The Railway Age had not begun, and the ingenuity of engineers was being applied to locks and lock gates, and various sorts of inclines up which ships could be hauled to refloat at higher levels. Telford had designed and started work on the Caledonian Canal in Scotland, which was the greatest project so far of its kind, and it occurred to a good many people that this could be a model for a Panama Canal. Its twenty-eight locks, 160 feet long and thirty-eight feet wide, were big enough for frigates of thirty-two guns, and for most of the ocean-going merchant vessels of the time. The chain of locks at its western end—Neptune's Staircase—was designed to lift ships sixty-five feet above the sea, and there seemed to be no reason why the same principle should not carry ships over any mountain divide, provided there was a supply of water at the top.

Another more immediate cause of the revival of interest in the isthmus was the journey of the Prussian Baron Alexander von Humboldt, who landed in Spanish America exactly a hundred years after Paterson, in 1799, and brought back to Europe a mass of new information. Among it he brought a renewal of the rumor Paterson had heard—the rumor that somebody, long before, had already made a canal to join the oceans.

Baron von Humboldt was a phenomenon that could only have belonged to the early nineteenth century. He was a scientist: not merely a specialist in one branch of science, but a high authority on all branches that had been created then—a botanist, geologist, biologist, astronomer and meteorologist, chemist and physicist. He lived at a time when it was still just possible for a man of outstanding brain to encompass all the scientific knowledge there was. It was also a time when science was fashionable and scientists were revered as a kind of high priests, and admired as heroes. Humboldt became the most celebrated of them all—the most famous man in Europe, it was said, after Napoleon.

Like many eminent men, Humboldt has the misfortune to be remembered, when he is remembered at all, as an old man, a grave and pompous nineteenth century savant in a frock-coat. In his old age, he was so highly respected that every opinion he expressed became a dictum, and even when he was wrong, as he sometimes was, hardly anyone dared to contradict him. He was a bachelor, and for several decades he was the lion of the Paris salons or the favorite companion of the king of Prussia, loaded with social and scientific honors. And after years of adulation, he became pontifical and vain, too dignified, too self-important, too willing to lay down the law on every subject. He was the kind of old man it is difficult to imagine as anything so undignified as a youth: yet at the time when he went to America, he was young and gay, brave and adventurous.

A portrait exists of him at the age of twenty-six, and a description on a passport issued when he was twenty-eight: height five feet eight inches, light brown hair, gray eyes, large nose, rather large mouth, well-formed chin, open forehead, marked with the small pox. On the cover of the passport Humboldt had written, in a mixture of languages, *"Grosses Maul, dicke Nase, aber menton bien fait."* It suggests a sense of humor, and to judge by the portrait the description might have included a distinct twinkle in the eyes and a flicker of a mischievous smile. It is an ugly but attractive and merry face. One can hardly believe it belongs to the person he became when he was old.

The use that Humboldt made of his journey might be a lesson to explorers who write a single meager book about each expedition. The journey lasted five years, and he spent the next twenty-one years in writing thirty-three books about it. It was not that he wrote about trivial daily details: it was simply that he was incredibly industrious and observant. Wherever he went, he was never inactive, never sick, and apparently never too tired to be absorbed in everything he saw. All the way, he recorded temperatures, barometric pressures, the earth's magnetism, latitude and longitude, the heights of mountains, widths of rivers and depths of lakes and seas. With one companion, he collected, classified and drew meticulously 5,000 plants. He learned Indian languages, explored the craters of volcanoes, loaded trains of mules with samples of rock, and climbed mountains far higher than anyone had ever climbed before—and to judge by his own sketches he did it all in a top hat. He made friends with all kinds of people, including the Indians and the Spanish colonists. Everything interested him: everything from tables of magnetic dip to the case of a man who suckled his children, and whose he-goats, taking after their master, suckled their kids; everything from the temperature of the ocean to a hat invented by a friend of his which opened, when one pulled a string, to form an umbrella three feet wide.

Most of the books were on single scientific aspects of the journey, but in 1814 he started publication of his *Personal Narrative,* and it was this that caught the public imagination and drew the attention of Europe again to the long forgotten problem of the isthmus. By the time this was written, the excessive dignity of his old age had begun to set in. The story ran to seven volumes and was still unfinished, because he could never resist being sidetracked into dissertations, sometimes hundreds of pages long, into the scientific meaning of anything he saw or was told. It is written as though the mere telling of adventures were beneath him. He never admits he was surprised by the most exotic sights, or alarmed by discomfort or danger. The scraps of adventure are embedded in great wedges of solemn thought on science, politics and history. Yet it remains a splendid adventure story, and suggests that he really revelled in adventure, as much as the heroes of Jules Verne, whom he rather resembled—for whom, in fact, he could have been a model. And this is confirmed by the letters he wrote in the course of the journey. They are totally different from the books, full of a youthful wonder and excitement which his later self-importance made him suppress.

It was only by a series of chances that Humboldt went to America. As a young man in Prussia, he simply wanted to travel,

and it did not matter where. In his early twenties, he thought
about Lapland. In 1797, when he was twenty-eight, he was invited by Frederick Hervey, Earl of Bristol, to join an expedition
up the Nile. Lord Bristol was the archetype of the rich English
lords whose eccentricities as travellers are still remembered in
remote parts of Europe. He was a bishop, among other things;
and he was also a notorious freethinker and libertine—in the
phrase of those days, a votary of pleasure. Humboldt had no
illusions about him—"the mad old Lord," he called him—but he
eagerly accepted the invitation. The expedition, led by Bristol's
yacht, "with a kitchen and a well-provided cellar," and "equipped
with every appliance for securing an amount of comfort truly
prince-like," was to include archeologists, artists to draw the
ruins, and an armed crew, in addition to the Countess Lichtenau,
the mistress of the king of Prussia, with whom Bristol, who was
nearly seventy, had fallen in love. But the whole thing had to be
abandoned before it had started, for in 1789 Napoleon opened
his campaign in Egypt and Bristol was arrested in Milan and
imprisoned by the French. Next Humboldt was invited to join
a French voyage round the world which, it was hoped, would
visit the South Pole. He wrote with splendid insouciance to a
friend: "As I was just then occupied with magnetic investiga-
tions, it occurred to me that an expedition to the South Pole
might prove more useful than a journey to Egypt." But that also
was cancelled, for lack of funds, as a result of Napoleon's war.

After that disappointment, Humboldt set off to walk with a
young botanist called Aime Bonpland, from Marseilles to Madrid. They studied botany, meteorology, geology and magnetism
as they went along, and fixed the latitude and longitude of every
town by sextant—although in Valencia, when he was taking
sights of the sun, Humboldt "suffered greatly from the hooting
of the rabble." In Madrid, these unusual travellers were granted
an audience of the king. With nothing to lose, they asked his
permission to visit the New World, and to their delight and
astonishment, he agreed.

So in June they sailed together, in a Spanish ship from Co-
runna, on the voyage which changed the central Spanish colonies

from one of the least known to one of the best known parts of America. They landed, bursting with excitement, at the small port of Cumana, on the north coast of South America. "We are truly in a wonderland of fertility and luxuriance," Humboldt wrote to his brother. "We have on all sides of us extraordinary plants, electric eels, tigers, armadillos, apes, and parrots, besides numbers of genuine Indians—half wild—a very handsome and interesting race. Hitherto we have been running about like a couple of fools; for the first three days we could settle to nothing, as we were always leaving one object to lay hold of another. Bonpland declares he should lose his senses if this state of ecstasy were to continue."

But it did continue, all through a journey on foot and by canoe to the headwaters of the Orinoco, which they proved were joined to those of the Amazon. "During four months of this journey we passed the nights in forests, surrounded by crocodiles, boa constrictors, and tigers, which are here bold enough to attack a canoe, while for food we had nothing better than rice, ants, maniocs, bananas, and occasionally the flesh of monkeys. In Guiana the mosquitoes abound in such clouds as to darken the air. In Higuerote the people are accustomed at night to lie buried three or four inches deep in sand, with only the head exposed. If we had not seen it, we should have considered the account fabulous. The Indians ... still bear about them the evidence of ancient Peruvian civilization. And yet these nations, while possessing considerable knowledge of agriculture and exercising the rites of hospitality, combine a mild and gentle aspect with the savage custom of cannibalism. Wherever we went through the wild districts of South America, we scarcely ever entered a hut without encountering the horrible remains of repasts on human flesh!! My health and spirits have decidedly improved since I left Spain."

After the Orinoco, they sailed to Cuba, in a small ship with a cargo of meat which caught fire during the voyage, and then back to the mainland at Carthagena. From there, they had meant to cross the isthmus from Portobello to Panama, but they changed their minds and embarked by canoe again right up the river

Magdalena, crossed the Andes on foot and reached the coast of
Peru. Then they went by sea to Mexico, and after a year there,
on to Philadelphia and Washington, where they were received by
President Jefferson. Even now, it would be an adventurous journey. At that time, they were almost incredibly lucky not to be
eaten by animals or cannibals, bitten by snakes, imprisoned by
Spaniards, or lost, or even robbed. There is something that pro-
tects enthusiasts—perhaps their own blindness. Confronted alone
by an angry jaguar, a man is more likely to escape if he is
interested in its protective coloring, rather than in his own fate.
Confronted by cannibals with spears dipped in curare, he can
disarm suspicion by asking, with genuine interest, for the recipe
of the deadly poison. Humboldt was always too inquisitive to be
afraid. When he was almost shipwrecked off Carthagena, and the
crew had given themselves up for lost, he had recovered enough
by the same evening to row ashore to observe an eclipse of the
moon. But that was a day of misfortune. "I had scarcely landed
with my assistants," he wrote in another letter, "when we were
startled by the clanking of chains, and a party of powerful Negroes
(*cimarrones*), escaped from the prisons of Carthagena, rushed
out upon us from the thicket, brandishing their daggers, intent
apparently on seizing our boat, as they saw we were unarmed.
We fled at once to the water, and had barely time to embark."
That was his youthful version. When he described the same incident in his book, there was only one Negro—the rest were hiding
in the thicket—the retreat was more dignified and circumspect,
and he had to moralize about it: "We thought it most prudent to
return on board our vessel. The aspect of a naked man, wandering on an uninhabited beach, without being able to unrivet the
chains fastened round his neck and the upper part of his arm,
left us the most painful impressions. In climates where slavery
exists, the mind is familiarized with suffering, and that instinct
of pity is stifled which characterizes and ennobles our nature."

The blend of adventure and a high-minded search for scientific truth had a strong appeal for the educated public of Hum-

boldt's time, and probably many of his readers, delving for the nuggets of adventure, absorbed more of the matrix of science than they expected. So they read, in Volume VII of the *Personal Narrative,* about the problems of an isthmian canal. Humboldt never went to the isthmus; he went all round it. His nearest approach was to drift becalmed into the Gulf of Darien "owing to the captain's incredulity as to the correctness of my chronometer." (He was an irritating passenger at sea, always correcting his captains' navigation.) But that did not stop him writing seventy pages about it: he was always ready to use other people's observations if he had not made any of his own. And with his passion for detail, he produced a far more thorough analysis of the canal idea than anyone before him.

At the time when he wrote, between 1800 and 1820, a canal through the isthmus was an easier problem, from most points of view, than ever before or since. Steam had arrived, but the use of iron in building ships had hardly started, and the average ocean-going merchant ships were no bigger than they had been for centuries. It was feasible, therefore, to plan to use rivers for navigation: ships were still small enough to enter them, and the problem of sailing up them had been solved—steam tugs could be used for towing. Indeed, one of the first steamboats ever built, the *Charlotte Dundas* in 1802, had already been used as a tug on the Forth and Clyde Canal in Scotland. Steam dredgers had also been invented. All that was needed, therefore, was a canal to join the upper waters of two rivers. As for its size, Humboldt concluded that the Caledonian Canal, which now looks a charming and miniature relic, was unnecessarily deep: something more modest would do in Panama.

Looking at the problem from this point of view Humboldt suggested five places where a canal might be built. Three of them had already occurred to everybody else, from Saavedra to Paterson: the isthmus of Tehuantepec in Mexico, the Lake of Nicaragua, and the route of the Spanish trail at Panama itself. On Panama, he had to admit that although the trail had been in use for 300 years nobody knew the height of the pass it crossed. If the Spaniards had ever made an accurate measurement, they had kept it to themselves. On the whole of Darien, indeed, the Spaniards' secrecy had been so strict and successful that he had to refer to the book of old Lionel Wafer, the buccaneer, to find a description of the country.

In any case, he preferred Nicaragua. The river San Juan, which runs out of the Lake of Nicaragua to the Caribbean, had been reported navigable by brigs and sloops for most of its length. The lake itself was deep, and the winds on it "blew with sufficient force to render it unnecessary to tow the ships by means of steam-boats." The land between the lake and the Pacific was said to be low, and only twelve to fifteen miles across—less than the artificial part of the Caledonian Canal. He remarked that the lake had hitherto been regarded as an obstacle, because it was feared that if a canal were cut towards the Pacific, the water would all run out of the lake and leave the river San Juan high and dry. But "the art of engineering is sufficiently improved in our days to have no apprehension of such dangers. The lake of Nicaragua may serve as an upper basin, like the lake Oich in the Caledonian Canal, and regulating sluices will furnish only as much water for the canal as it requires." This route did indeed seem to suit the needs of the times, and many people, especially Americans, continued to argue in its favor long after the route of the present canal had been chosen.

The other two of the five routes Humboldt suggested were both on the river Atrato. He had heard that forty-five miles upstream from its mouth in the Gulf of Darien, a tributary called the Naipi joined it from the west. The head waters of the Naipi were said to be very close to the port of Cupica on the Pacific coast, and the land was said to be perfectly flat in between. But this, even more than Panama and Nicaragua, was an unknown land. The position of Cupica had never been fixed on a map, and nobody had tried to take a sea-going ship up the Atrato since Captain Long in the *Rupert Prize* in 1699.

But the most startling piece of news that Humboldt published was about the canal which he said had already been built.

This was on the last of the routes he proposed. He had been told—as Paterson must have been told—that the topmost tributaries of the Atrato are very close to those of another river San Juan, which flows to the Pacific. And he reported that in 1788, a monk who was the curate of the village of Novita, on the upper waters of the San Juan, had persuaded the Indians of his parish to dig a canal which joined his river to another called the Raspadura, which flowed into the Atrato. It was called the Raspadura Canal. It was only big enough for small boats, but it had been regularly used to carry cocoa from Ecuador to Carthagena—from the Pacific, up the San Juan, through the canal, and down the Raspadura and Atrato to the Caribbean.

Whether this precursor of the Panama Canal ever really existed is a small but rather fascinating problem. Humboldt had never seen it: his account was circumstantial. He had read of it in Spanish reports, and it was shown on a map which was sent to him from the district of Raspadura itself. People who traded in gold dust on the Atrato had also told him about it. He continued to believe in it all his life, and even seemed to take a proprietary interest in it, claiming that he "gave the first intimation of it in Europe." (He had not heard of Paterson's single enigmatic sentence a hundred years before.) But this was one subject on which some other explorers dared to disagree with him. An English traveller named Davis Robertson claimed, in 1821, that the canal had indeed been dug long ago, but had been filled up again on orders from Madrid, in case it became a rival to the Portobello trail. But Humboldt denied this; and Robertson, like Humboldt, had never been there.

The first European, other than Spanish officials, who crossed the divide from the San Juan to the Atrato was probably an English naval captain called Charles Cochrane, in 1824. He made a journey which rivaled Humboldt's in extent, but he travelled mainly for fun, without any learned pretensions, and he wrote a modest and chatty book about it. Like every other explorer of the isthmus, he was thinking about canals as he went along, but he had never heard of the Raspadura Canal, and nobody told him of it. Coming up the San Juan to the sordid little town of Novita, he was directed by the local mayor to a route a few miles west of the place where the canal was supposed to have been. From one of the river systems to the other, he rode a donkey which had to cross bridges made of a single log. "After an hour's travelling" he wrote, "I came to the rising ground that divides this stream from the one on the Citera (Atrato) side. I particularly inspected it, and found the distance to be about four hundred yards, and the height of the ground necessary to cut through about seventy feet; but after digging a very few feet you come to solid rock, which would make the undertaking expensive; besides it would be necessary to deepen each stream for about a league."

Humboldt had admitted that the canal was only suitable for small boats, and this at least was confirmed by Cochrane's experience of the rivers which led up to it on each side. "I had first to embark in a very small canoe, poled by a man and his daughter, a fine, young black girl, who had a handkerchief tied across her shoulders, covering one breast and leaving the other bare. She had the complete appearance of a black Amazon, evincing much strength and quickness in the use of her pole, and considerable agility in occasionally springing out of the canoe to bear it from a rock, and jumping in again when it was rapidly moving on." Going down the other side towards the Atrato was just as bad, with another canoe and a less distracting crew: "Embarking my baggage, by half-past one we set off, the stream very shallow and narrow—the Indians every moment obliged to get out and drag the canoe along. Having descended for two hours, we came to the influx of another stream, called Raspadura, coming from the north east ..." He had just missed solving the mystery: it was up this other stream that the canal was supposed to be. An oddity of Cochrane's story is that he had evidently still never heard of the canal when he wrote his narrative; yet it is shown on the map which was published in his book.

The next expedition to pass that way was American in 1852. It was one of a series organized by a New York businessman called Frederick Kelley, with the specific purpose of finding a route for a canal, and it was led by John S. Trautwine, an engineer who was already concerned by then with the building of the railroad at Panama. He did not find the Raspadura Canal: perhaps, like Cochrane, he did not know where to look. A paper written by Kelley and read at the Royal Geographical Society in London in 1856 poured scorn on the whole idea: "It is quite possible that a curate interested in the boating-business, may have excercised sufficient influence over some of the gold-hunting members of his flock, to induce them to cut down a few bushes, and to hollow out a short gutter, between two streams flowing in contrary directions from the summit. Such a ditch may have been used as part of a canoe slide from one stream to the other; and precisely the same kind of canal could now be made, by a dozen expert laborers, in a few days."

Such sarcasm is enough to make anyone want to believe in Raspadura: it is too much like the pique of an engineer, pioneering a route for a canal, who finds the job has been done by a simple priest a couple of generations before him. At any rate, Humboldt, who was eighty-six by then, still believed in it, and wrote to Kelley to tell him so. And possibly the canal was very much more ancient than Humboldt believed, and had only been reopened by the curate—for there was the sentence Paterson wrote in Caledonia Bay: "We have only eight or nine leagues to a river where boats may go into the South Sea." Somebody had told Paterson, and in those early days it was not a story that anyone would have invented.

On the whole, it seems likely there was a canal, or had been. Possibly it was built by the Indians in an earlier epoch: they had been quite capable of it. Or possibly it was a Spanish smuggling route: not only cocoa but gold and silver might have been taken that way to avoid the duties—and perhaps the awkward questions —of officials at Panama. And it is not surprising that nobody saw it in the nineteenth century. In the twenty-four years between Humboldt's journey and Cochrane's, the country had gone through a revolution, and whether the canal was filled in on orders from

Spain or not, it might well have been disused by the time when Cochrane passed it. Perhaps it was almost forgotten: perhaps the mayor of Novita, under the new regime, had scarcely heard of it. And in the next twenty-eight years, before Trautwine took his supercilious look at it, the little canal, if it was abandoned, would certainly have been so overgrown that it was hardly visible. At any rate, it is a romantic thought that the curate of Novita had joined the oceans 150 years before the Panama Canal was opened, and that Indians perhaps had done so at least a century before him. The problem awaits an explorer.

The dissolution of the Spanish empire in the early part of the nineteenth century gave an entirely new chance for exploration of the isthmus. Imperial monopoly had kept the place secret for over 300 years; but when the descendants of the early settlers had thrown off the dominion of Spain and formed a series of small impoverished republics, all their governments were eager to earn an honest fee by selling concessions to anyone who asked. Darien, Panama and Veragua became a part of the republic of New Grenada, and from the 1820's to the 1850's innumerable people went to its capital, Bogota, and came away with exclusive permission to build a canal in whatever particular crossing-place they fancied. Most of them were American, French or British. Some were genuine explorers, naval officers or civil engineers: a good many were visionaries, cranks or charlatans. Between them, they produced a wonderful crop of outlandish, impractical schemes.

The people who proposed to build canals were of two kinds: one kind believed or pretended they had found a route with no mountains to cross, and the other admitted there were mountains and thought of ingenious schemes to cross them. Most of the latter suggested huge tunnels—big enough to accommodate the full-rigged masts which all ocean-going ships still carried, whether they had steam engines or not. The most ingenious of all was the ship railway invented by an American engineer called Ead. His idea was to raise ships on an enormous cradle inside a kind of floating dock. The cradle was to have over a thousand wheels, and be towed across the Isthmus of Tehuantepec in Mexico on three sets of parallel railroad tracks by three very powerful locomotives. Among the difficulties inherent in this plan was that the solid cradle would certainly be too big to go round curves in the track, and the only feasible route required a great many curves. To solve that problem, Ead invented a floating turntable, on which the cradle, ship and all would be swivelled round and set off in a new direction. But nineteenth century engineering cunning had far outrun the limits of possibility: the railroad never came anywhere near being built.

Among the explorers who claimed to have found a flat route, the most notable was an Irish doctor named Cullen, who turned up in England in the early 1850's saying he had sailed up a navigable river called the Sabana, which flows into the Gulf of San Miguel, and then walked across with no trouble at all to the Caribbean coast at Caledonia Bay. It was Balboa's route in reverse. In the next two years, he wrote, he had "crossed and re-crossed, at several times and by several tracks, the route from the Sabana to Port Escosces and Caledonia Bay, notching the bark of the trees as I went along, with a macheta or cutlass, always alone and unaided, and always in the season of the heaviest rains." He swore the highest summits in the range behind Caledonia Bay were only 350 feet, and that he had found a pass of 150 feet. He was very reticent about his walks, but he described the country convincingly enough to interest a syndicate of British engineers. In 1852, they sent a technician called Lionel Gisborne to confirm Dr. Cullen's observations. He arranged to meet the doctor in Carthagena and sail with him to Caledonia Bay. But the doctor did not turn up—he was busy in Bogota, making sure of his concession—and Gisborne sailed on alone.

Equipped with two Scotch plaids and five days' rations, he went ashore in Caledonia Bay with four companions. After three hours of cutting a way through the jungle, he reached a hill top 275 feet high and saw a plain beyond it: he hoped he was on top of the continental divide and was looking down towards the Pacific. Descending, he found a river which ran in the right direction, and he "lunched off a tongue and some biscuits." In the afternoon, he camped beside the river, and "did justice to some boiled beef and biscuits and a strong cup of tea." That night, he thought he heard the sound of surf: "it might be the Pacific tide running up the Sabana to within six or seven miles of where we lay. . . . The novelty of our position, the uncertainty of whether the watch-fire would attract or scare away an Indian, a tiger or an alligator; and our speculations on the various noises we heard in the woods from time to time, made sleep out of the question." Next morning, he followed the river down, and by ten o'clock he had reached the sea—but not, alas, the Pacific; it was the Caribbean again, within five miles of where he started. There he was accosted by Indians who took him back to his ship and told him very firmly not to trespass in their woods again.

It was an example of the total confusion the jungle can cause in an educated but inexperienced man. All Gisborne had done was to cross the first foothills of the formidable range of mountains— it was exactly the same Sunday walk that the three Scottish ministers had taken when they preached to the Indians in 1700— but he thought he had gone much farther than he had, and he did not even see the thousand foot ridge which was only five miles inland.

Fearing another encounter with the Indians, he sailed away and crossed the isthmus by the Spanish trail to Panama, in order to try again from the other side. He hired a boat which took him, like Dr. Cullen, up the Sabana River. From there, he took another morning's walk inland and found a river running north, which he convinced himself was the same that he had found from Caledonia Bay. At lunch-time, a "heavy fall of rain during the time we were discussing some biscuits and a pot of preserved meat, drenched the graduated cards of the compasses, so that the needles stuck to them, rendering it almost impossible to fix any course." Consequently, he got lost on the way back to his boat and had to spend a night in the open, seriously contemplating starvation. A flooded river washed away his teapot.

It was on guesswork and wishful thinking like this that

canal companies were founded and concessions bought and sold. In fact, Gisborne had only penetrated two miles on the Caribbean side and seven on the other. The two rivers he thought were the same were twenty miles apart, and between them was not only the impenetrable ridge, but also the huge marshy valley of the longest river in the whole of Darien, the Chucunaque. Dr. Cullen had done even less. But both of them persuaded themselves, and even persuaded governments, that they had walked in a day across the route that had taken Balboa over a month, and had taken the Elizabethans and the buccaneers a matter of weeks. And two years later, in 1854, an international expedition was launched, with British, United States, French and New Grenadian warships, to make a detailed survey of what seemed a perfect route.

This massive force was supposed to assemble in Caledonia Bay, but a corvette of the U.S. Navy, called the *Cyane,* arrived there first, and put a naval exploring party ashore without waiting for the rest. Its commander was Lt. Isaac G. Strain, and he had twenty-seven officers and men with him. It was January, the classic month for crossings of the isthmus, and from Cullen's and Gisborne's reports, Strain naturally expected an easy walk. The beginning was not auspicious: some of the stores were lost in landing through the surf, and the local Indians refused to act as guides. And Strain very soon discovered there was something wrong with the previous explorations, for the crossing of the divide took him up to a height of 1,300 feet. On the third day's march, two officers and three men lost the rest of the party in the jungle, and turned back to the coast again. On the sixth day, Strain found an Indian village: its inhabitants, seeing him coming, had abandoned it and set it on fire. Soon after, he came to a very large river flowing east, and met five Indians there. They told him it was the Chucunaque, and offered to guide him to the Sabana, which they truthfully said was farther on. But a larger party of Indians emerged from the jungle, and told the five to have nothing to do with the foreigners.

Poor Strain: neither Cullen nor Gisborne, who claimed they

had walked that way, had mentioned the Chucunaque. Yet they could not have crossed such a large river without thinking it was worth mentioning. So he concluded that the Indians had been trying to deceive him, and that it was the Sabana after all. And he started with his twenty-two remaining men to try to march down it.

It was a fatal decision, an example of the folly of trusting anyone's judgment in the jungle, except the Indians'. The Sabana is short and straight: the Chucunaque must be the most tortuous major river in the world. To follow all its bends to the Gulf of San Miguel was at least 200 miles instead of twenty.

His young American sailors caught fever and starved. They had rifles, but finding no game to shoot they used their ammunition to bring down nuts from palm trees: whatever kind of nut it was they shot, it was so acid that it burned the enamel off their teeth. The rifles rusted in the hot wet air till they were useless. They tried to build rafts, but one sank, one broke in pieces, and those which floated never took them far because the river was choked with rocks and treetrunks. Strain kept up a naval discipline: every night, separate camp fires were lit for officers and men. The officers, to their credit, kept their nerve and even a macabre sense of humor. A midshipman was seen to catch a toad, bite off the head and spit it out, and swallow the squirming body. "Well," said another, seeing the wasted head, "you're getting quite particular." But some men died, some grew too weak to move, and some became mad or delirious. One had to be stopped by force from digging up the body of another they had buried: he meant to eat it.

After a week or two, Strain despaired of getting any of them through to safety without food, and he went on ahead with one or two of the fittest to try to find help. It took him no less than forty-seven days to reach a settlement in the Gulf—and then, exhausted and emaciated as he was, he turned round without even waiting to sleep and went up the river again, taking Indians and provisions in canoes. He found his men, but five were already dead of starvation and two more died before they reached civilization. Strain himself, it was said, never recovered from the experience and he died a few years later. Dr. Cullen wisely disappeared. Lionel Gisborne, however, really walked across soon after Strain, with Indian guides, and had the grace to admit his mistake and express his remorse for the disaster he had caused.

Strain's journey proved that even in that age of scientific, industrial confidence, the jungle of Darien still deserved respect. It proved also that even if a feasible route for a canal were ever found, there would still be enormous problems in putting ashore an army of men to build it. But nobody was much deterred. Visionary plans were still discussed in Europe and the United States, and concessions were still bought and sold. But while Strain's men were dying on the Chucunaque, the Spanish trail, 120 miles away to the eastward, was busier than it had ever been in the three centuries it had existed: and there, on the route Pedrarias had chosen, one concession was actively being exploited. It belonged to two American shipowners called William Henry Aspinwall and George Law. What they had bought from New Grenada was not permission to build a canal, but to build a railroad.

(vii)

The Railroad

Despite all obstacles, the dim glimpses of
which had, at a previous time, caused
European capitalists to shrink back with
fear, our bold operators at once, and
earnestly, pushed forward this stupendous
enterprise.

F.N. Otis, *History of the
Panama Railroad,* 1855

A NEW LIFE BEGAN on the isthmus on a morning in December
1848, when a steamer called the *Falcon* anchored off the mouth
of the Rio Chagres, where Morgan's fleet had lain below the cliffs
of the Fort of San Lorenzo. At that time, there was a village of
bamboo huts at the river mouth, and its sleepy inhabitants were
startled to see two hundred North Americans swarming ashore,
armed with rifles, revolvers, bowie knives, shovels and picks, and
demanding instant transport across to the other side. These were
the first of the forty-niners, hell-bent for California to make their
fortunes in the gold rush.

It was odd that the passion for gold, which had been the
reason for Panama's existence and the source of all its strife,
should have been the cause of its reawakening. But so it was.
The old madness which had driven the Spaniards, the Elizabethans and the buccaneers had now infected the citizens of the
United States. With the news of the Californian gold strike, thousands and thousands of them dropped everything to join the rush.
Some went by the overland trails across the continent, some round
Cape Horn, and some—an increasing proportion—across the

isthmus; and every one of them was half-crazy with impatience to get there before the gold was gone. Their impatience and their northern energy collided headlong on the isthmus with the tropical lassitude of the people who lived there, and the result was five years of supreme confusion.

It began at the mouth of the river. All of them were taken there and disembarked: not one, for some reason which is now obscure, thought of stealing a march on the rest by going to Portobello and riding the whole length of the trail. The Chagres was the only route they had heard of. Some of the people in the village at its mouth possessed canoes, and they were besieged by these foreigners, who bid against each other for a trip upriver to Las Cruces. The boatmen started by asking what was probably the highest price they could think of—$10 a head; but more and more ships came in, and soon they were being offered $50—far more cash for a few days' work than they had ever earned, or ever needed, in a year. It was a situation that brought out the worst in both races. Yankees shouted, threatened, bullied, argued and fought: Isthmians swindled. They hired canoes to one party and then, when the first had gone to fetch its baggage, hired them to another and disappeared—or after starting up the river they stopped half way in the heart of the jungle and demanded double pay.

Nothing like it had happened on the Chagres, or anywhere else in Darien, since the buccaneers. At night, the river banks all the way from the mouth to Las Cruces were dotted with improvised camps, some gloomy, some convivial. Most of the goldseekers—or Argonauts, as the newspapers called them—dosed themselves with alcohol, which was supposed to be a safeguard against the jungle fevers, so that some of the journeys upriver became hilarious, and the jungle rang with shouts and drunken songs, and the shots of happy marksmen at logs they thought were alligators.

At Las Cruces the pandemonium was worse. Every day for the first few months of 1849, more and more canoe-loads of strangers appeared round the bends of the river and settled like locusts on the derelict little settlement. All of them had to spend a night there, and bargain in the morning for mules to carry themselves and their baggage over the eighteen miles of trail to Panama. On busy days, the natives managed to charge them $20 to hire a riding mule—enough to have bought a mule a year before. And after the river trip, they willingly paid a dollar for space to lie down on one of the wooden bunks that ingenious natives fixed up in the disused stables and storehouses.

The last part of the crossing, the mule-track, was the worst of it all in the eyes of most of these travellers: they wrote hair-raising stories about it in their diaries and letters home. One would have supposed that any American in that era could have ridden a mule without any notable hardship. But what impressed them was not the exotic jungle they were riding through, it was the mud and roughness and narrowness of the track, the discomfort of the saddles and the animals' jolting gait. Few of them knew they were on historic ground, or that the primitive nature of the track had been a piece of tactical wisdom. Few of them would have cared. After the chaos on the river it just seemed one more annoying bit of foreign inefficiency. They all arrived in Panama City angry, dirty, saddle-sore and tired, and more often than not wet through with the Darien rain.

And there they stuck. Ship after ship was coming in on the Caribbean side: far fewer were leaving on the Pacific side for the last lap north to California. Some men had bought through tickets, but even they found the ships which were supposed to take them on had not arrived or, if they had, were already crowded by earlier comers who refused to get off again. The city filled up with men in a frenzy of impatience and frustration—impatience made even worse by the occasional sight of somebody coming back with a fortune in gold dust and nuggets. At one time, 4,000 men were stranded in the place: some of them had been there for months. The most sordid kinds of doss-houses, brothels, saloons and gambling dens were improvised to extract what was left of their savings, and some were left destitute. All those who could not find a bunk in the city itself lived in camps round its outskirts: and inevitably, what they called the Panama fever began to rage among them—malaria, yellow fever, dysentery, and finally cholera.

The invasion not only woke up the moldering city, it also put new life in an enterprise that was hanging fire: the plan for a railroad. Hitherto, that had seemed a project of unforeseeable difficulties and dubious profit—at its best, a long-term investment. But the gold rush entirely changed its prospects. The Argonauts were paying a total of nearly a hundred dollars each to get across by canoe and mule; obviously, if the railroad could be built before the rush subsided, its profits would be quick.

Close behind the first of the gold-seekers, therefore, engineers began a survey of the isthmus, on the orders of Law and Aspinwall, the shipowners who had bought the railroad concession from New Grenada. There was no time for extensive exploration. They followed the route of the ancient trail, simply because the trail was there and gave access to the interior of the country. But mapping it thoroughly now for the first time since it was built, they found a pass a few miles to the west of it which was only 287 feet above sea level. It was the lowest pass, as it happened, in the whole of Darien—and the credit for that must be given to Pedrarias, who built his city there so long before. Panama was still the obvious place for the southern end of the railroad. But for the northern end, the surveyors rejected the mouth of the Chagres because it had no adequate harbor, and they also rejected Portobello because—it was said at the time—George Law had bought all the land around it and held out for a price his colleagues refused to pay.

Instead of these ancient harbors, they chose a large open bay in between them: Limon Bay. It was the bay where Columbus had sheltered from the storm on Christmas Day, 1502, but nobody had used it much since then because its shores were marshy. There, in May 1850, two American engineers and six natives landed in a mangrove swamp, and began to cut a way through it.

There has always been a story that a laborer was buried for

every sleeper or tie on the Panama Railroad: some versions specify a Chinese laborer. Of course, it was not strictly true—it was probably never meant to be more than a graphic expression —and the promoters and engineers denied it angrily. But their denials were always a little too shrill, as if they had something on their consciences. Whatever the truth was, they hid it successfully. Precisely how many thousands died has never been discovered. Probably the promoting company never counted them. The figures they published were so low that nobody could believe them. It is certainly true, however, that the death rate was very high, and that often their workers were dying faster than they could replace them.

The spot where they chose to begin was on an island, Manzanilla Island, where the town of Colon now stands at the mouth of the Panama Canal. When they began, it was only an island in so far as it was a little more solid than the bogs which lay behind it. "It was a virgin swamp," they wrote, "covered with a dense growth of the tortuous, water-loving mangrove, and interlaced with huge vines and thorny shrubs, defying entrance even to the wild beasts common to the country. In the black, slimy mud of its surface alligators and other reptiles abounded, while the air was laden with pestilential vapors, and swarming with sand-flies and mosquitoes." Farther inland, they found "a deep morass covered with the densest jungle, reeking with malaria, and abounding with almost every species of wild beasts, noxious reptiles, and venomous insects known in the tropics." There was nowhere dry enough to build a hut ashore, and the mosquitoes and flies were unbearable. The first pioneers worked in veils, and spent the whole of each day up to their waists in mud and water, carrying their lunches in their hats. At night, they retreated to the hulk of an old brig they had moored in the bay. "Below decks, the vessel was alive with mosquitoes and sand-flies, which were a source of such annoyance and suffering that almost all preferred to sleep upon the deck, exposed to the drenching rains. In addition to this, most of their number were kept nauseated by the ceaseless motion of the vessel." Of course, they all went down with fevers. Fifty laborers had been brought from Carthagena, and all of them died or deserted for the gold trail, where they could earn more money and live in comparative comfort. Fifty more were imported, and so it went on: there was only room for fifty on the brig, but each time the labor force died out it was replenished. The Americans, who must have been exceptionally tough, survived this grim existence. They took turns, each working while the other was sweating out the fever on the brig. It is pathetic to think how near they were to discovering the source of the fevers. They wore their veils simply to avoid the annoyance of mosquitoes. They noticed also that men who wore veils were less subject to fever than those who did not. But they concluded that the veils kept out some of the miasma, the pestilential vapor of the swamps. Nobody for another thirty years put two and two together.

Little by little, they managed to improve the conditions of life in the bay. They replaced the hulk with a derelict steamer which was brought from the mouth of the Chagres. Later, they filled in enough of the swamp to build a few huts on land. As the jungle was cleared, the insects diminished a little. A doctor was brought in. Nevertheless, the first year of labor and suffering produced only four or five miles of track, and that was a temporary affair laid on wooden trestles through the marshes. And in those marshes, whatever the engineers and promoters said, a great many human bodies were buried by then, or sunk. In the second year, the labor force sometimes rose to over a thousand men: once at least it was reduced again so far by sickness and desertion that the work had to stop altogether. Whether one should admire the perseverance of the promoters or deplore their callousness is a matter of opinion; but that was an era when the life of a laborer counted very little if profits were in sight. A time came, however, when even the profits seemed to be receding. In New York, the promoters began to lose heart. The company's stock fell in value. The project came near to the dismal end of so many Darien ventures; defeat by the jungle.

It was revived by chance. In October 1851, the track reached as far as the bank of the Rio Chagres at a place called Gatun, eight miles by rail from the beginning in Limon Bay, and about ten up the river from its mouth. In December, two ships full of passengers, bound for the Chagres, were driven into Limon Bay by bad weather. The passengers, impatient as ever, piled ashore and demanded a journey by rail. Nobody, it seems, had thought of that before, but they were taken in trains of work cars as far as Gatun, and began their river journey there, and saved a day on the crossing. After that, everyone insisted on going that way: eight miles of rail was better than none, even though it meant two changes on the fifty-mile journey, from train to canoe and then from canoe to mule. The railroad began to earn money before its completion was even in sight, and its stock took an upward turn. For the next two years, as the end of the rail was slowly pushed up the Chagres valley, passengers went further and further by train, and a shorter and shorter distance by canoe. The village at the river mouth sank back into its torpor, and finally disappeared: there is nothing there now, except the indestructible walls of San Lorenzo. In its stead, a new town began slowly to grow at the railroad terminus on Manzanilla Island— a town entirely built on earth and rock brought from farther up the track and dumped in the swamp. The president of the railroad company named it Aspinwall, after the company's founder, but the government of New Grenada, which had not been consulted, refused to recognize this alien name and called it Colon, after Columbus. For a long time, both names were marked on maps and charts, and there was a story of a ship which sailed in, passed the town and ran firmly aground at the head of the bay: its captain explained that he had seen Aspinwall when he passed it, but was looking for Colon. In the end, the American name was allowed to fade away.

In December 1851, a newspaper in the English language, the Panama *Star,* which had recently been founded in Panama City, discovered it was possible at last to cross the isthmus in a single day: "Eating one's breakfast in Panama and supper at Aspinwall—a palpable, tangible reality—to be seen and felt, and appreciated." But it was still an exceptional feat, and impossible in the opposite direction, for the boat trip on the river section took very much longer upstream than down. Ordinary travellers still took at least two days, and all spent a night at Las Cruces: the same paper, a few months earlier, had advised every traveller to provide himself with dried beef, boiled ham, sea biscuits, sardines and a dozen or so bottles of claret.

At that stage the railroad met its greatest obstacle: halfway across the isthmus it had to cross the Chagres itself, at a point where the river was 300 feet wide and subject to floods which sometimes raised it forty feet in a night. The work so far had cost far more than the company expected, and they put the rest out to contract in the hope of getting it done more cheaply. But the result was that it did not get done at all. A bridge was built, but one span of it fell down before it was finished. The contractor brought in a force of several hundred Irishmen, the "navvies" who had done the spade work of the railways and canals of England; but they were "unable to bear the effects of the climate, and, being also badly cared for, their numbers were soon so thinned by sickness and death that the contractor found himself unable to accomplish any part of the contract for the price agreed upon. The work faltered, and at last stopped almost entirely."

The crossing, although it was quicker by then, was still chaotic. The first flood of the forty-niners had subsided, but a stream of emigrants was still passing through. Among them was no less a personage than the newly appointed Bishop of California, the Right Reverend William Ingraham Kip, who left Aspinwall by train at nine o'clock one morning in December 1853. As the train puffed gently through the jungle, he and his wife and his son Willie saw groups of the Irish workmen. "They looked pale and miserable," he wrote afterwards. "It is almost certain death to them to be employed here, and we were told"—an early appearance of the famous story—"that every foot of the road, so far as it had been finished, had cost the life of a labourer."

At the end of the rail, the Bishop and his party got out "at the top of a high, steep bank of the Chagres River. This was 'confusion worse confounded,' and passengers, trunks, express bales and all, were tumbled down to the river in a miscellaneous mass." There were nine miles of river to navigate up to Las Cruces, and it took five hours. They reached the settlement about six o'clock, but found that in addition to their own shipload of several hundred people, it was crowded with returning Californians. "At one end of the town," he wrote, "a wooden tavern has been hastily run up. We found it filled with hundreds of ruffians, and with great trouble secured for the ladies a place upstairs containing half a dozen beds. The lower story was filled with long tables, which were spread again and again for a succession of dinners, where very many, with oaths and imprecations, as they struggled for their places, got what they could at $1 each. The only chance for the decent portion was to get together at one end, and procure something to eat, if possible. I have taken my meals in many queer places when travelling, but I confess never before under such repulsive circumstances.

"But the worst was to come. At bedtime the gentlemen of the party were shown to a large garret. The walls were covered with wooden bunks three tiers high, two more rows through the centre and the intervals filled with cots. Here we were to sleep with some two hundred others, of the class we saw downstairs ... There were not only the most awful blasphemies that human ingenuity could devise, but the most foul-mouthed ribaldry that could be conceived by a perverted imagination. A party would rise from their beds, and, under the dim lanterns which hung from the beams, produce their brandy-bottles, and with oaths drink until they reeled again to their bunks. To make matters worse, next to us was a pen (I can call it nothing else) of boards about ten feet high, intended to afford a private room for females. This happened to be occupied by some 'women of the baser sort,' whose loud ribaldry infinitely amused the kindred spirits on our side of the partition, who accordingly replied to them in the same terms. Altogether, I set down that scene as more like Pandemonium than anything I had ever before witnessed. It was enough to convince one of the doctrine of total depravity." At midnight, the Bishop took Willie downstairs and they sat there in chairs till the morning.

The selection of mules was another scene of confusion. "Not being wise in the subject of mules, it proved to me a matter of chance. Those I received for Mrs. Kip and my son Willie were good; mine was miserable. The passengers set out from Cruces, and struggled across the Isthmus for the twenty-three miles as their mules' speed and bottom allowed. With a first-rate mule, it may be pleasant, and those who had one enjoyed it. The distance is thus passed sometimes in four or five hours; but to whip an obstinate mule, as I did, for eleven hours, is quite a different matter.... My party soon outrode me, and most of the day I was alone. On one occasion I came up with Mrs. Kip and our party, resting at a native hut. I passed on, as my mule went so slowly. I had hired a native to accompany me as guide, to prevent my getting off the path; but after going with me for a couple of miles, he deserted, and went back. Reaching the native hut, he was recognised by Mrs. Kip and questioned as to why he had left me. He stated, in reply, that I had got into a by-path and been murdered. As such things do happen on the isthmus and she knew I was alone and unarmed, it can be imagined what an excitement was produced. Fortunately, just at that time, some returning Californians who were crossing towards Cruces came up. They remembered me by the description my party gave, and having seen me after the native had left, assured them that I must be safe. I subsequently found that this travelling alone was a foolish risk. The natives, once harmless, have become so civilized as every month to be growing more dangerous and untrustworthy. One of our passengers, who was alone, was knocked senseless and stripped ... I reached Panama alone, at six, perfectly wearied out. It was the hardest day's ride I have ever had, worse than the ascent of Vesuvius."

That might have been counted a lucky crossing: six months before, 800 men of the 4th Infantry, U.S. Army, had tried it and fared much worse. There was cholera among the railroad workers —the army medical officer heard that forty out of a hundred had

died at one station—and the army caught it. The main body of
the troops disembarked from the river boats at a place called
Gorgona, a few miles below Las Cruces, and marched by a secondary
trail to Panama, spending three nights in the open on the
way. The sick, the women, the baggage and one company were
sent to Las Cruces to travel by mule; and among that detachment
was a future commander-in-chief and President of the
United States, Capt. Ulysses S. Grant. They were stuck for five
days in Las Cruces. A mule-owner had contracted to hire them
baggage-mules for 11 cents a pound of baggage, but the place
was full of civilian travellers who were offering 16 or 20 cents.
"We had the vexation," the medical officer reported, "of seeing
hundreds of citizens forwarded, with scarcely an hour's detention,
while our men were kept at the most unhealthy place on the
isthmus." A dozen men died while they waited. At last Captain
Grant succeeded in making a new bargain for the mules. The
medical officer "recommended that the whole detachment should
be furnished with mules, lest the fatigue of marching over so
desperate a road should excite the disease in men predisposed to
it, and they should perish. This was done, but notwithstanding
every precaution on our part, three fatal cases did occur on the
road." As it happened, Lionel Gisborne met this party on the
trail: he was coming up it in the opposite direction on the way
back from his exploration of the Sabana River. According to him
there was still a shortage of mules, even for the army wives. "I
had often been told," he wrote in his facetious way, "that 'ladies
have no legs,' when I committed myself by applying that term
to them. I never got a better opportunity of contradicting this
assertion. Modesty gave way to necessity; some had most wisely
put on trowsers, and discarded the petticoat, but most of them
tucked this feminine garment to above the knee, and tramped
along through mud and over rocks with greater spirit than the
men."

So they reached Panama, and embarked on their transports,
which were lying twelve miles off shore; and it was only then
that they were really stricken. The same thing had often hap-

pened to the forty-niners: at sea again in the Pacific, they began to congratulate themselves on having crossed the notorious isthmus safely, but it was on the ships sailing north that the epidemics began to break out. In those army transports of 1853, there were scenes almost as grim as those in the Scottish fleet of 1700; and like the Scottish captains, the medical officer, conscientious though he was, could not do very much more than heave the corpses overboard. "One evening," he wrote, "a small steamer brought about a dozen knapsacks that had been lying and moulding somewhere on the isthmus. The men to whom they belonged seized upon them with great eagerness, and opened them to get a change of clothing. I was afterwards informed that some of these men fell sick while in the act. Be this as it may, in about 20 hours afterwards they were all taken ill of cholera in its worst form, and within an hour of each other, and most of them died. With regard to the treatment of the cholera... all the usual means were tried, and with the usual want of success. The first cases were nearly all fatal. I think the free exhibition of brandy with capsicum and chloride of sodium was about as successful as anything. Mustard and bottles of hot water with frictions of the surface externally, camphor, calomel and quinine internally, were freely used. But... in this epidemic, we lost about eighty men."

By then no railroad, profitable or not, was ever more urgently needed. The isthmus had become one of the major passenger routes of the world, and much the most dangerous. Nobody who was not acclimatized could cross it without a risk of his life, but the quicker he could cross and get away again the better his chance.

But among the people who lived there and had survived the diseases and become immune, quite a gay social life, a mixture of American and Spanish, had developed in the first few years after the gold rush. Money was flowing again in Panama City, and Aspinwall—or Colon—had grown to a point where it had a newspaper of its own, the Aspinwall *Courier,* to rival the Panama

Star. This paper, in November 1853, reported at last the opening of the railroad bridge over the Chagres. A train was sent delicately across with five passenger cars of invited guests. "The motion of the train upon the bridge was smooth with scarcely any jarring, and the bridge fully sustained the character for firmness and strength which those who had constructed and enacted it had claimed." A picnic dinner was held beside the track. "After the removal of the cloth, and the uncorking of the Champagne, a large number of sentiments were proposed and drunk with enthusiasm and warmth of feeling." The rival *Star* reported: "An account of the proceedings on this occasion was printed in the Aspinwall *Courier,* but from the sickness of the Editor, or from other causes, it was so marred by printers' errors as to deprive it of much of the interest that it would otherwise have possessed." The *Star* reporter went on to recollect at random thirteen of the toasts.

After its contractor's failure, the company had started to pour new laborers into the bottomless well of disease, in the hope of pushing the track through the last twenty miles to Panama by sheer force of numbers. Of course, the company knew by then what would happen to the men it employed: it was common knowledge in the United States, and they did not recruit any more North American workers. But it was not so well known elsewhere, and they rounded up no less than 7,000 men, more Irishmen fresh from Ireland, coolies from India, English, French, Germans and Austrians from Europe, and 1,000 Chinese imported direct from China. For the Chinese, the official history of the project said peevishly, "every possible care was taken which could conduce to their health and comfort. Their hill-rice, their tea, and opium, in sufficient quantity to last for several months, had been imported with them—they were carefully housed and attended to—and it was expected they would prove efficient and valuable men. But they had been engaged upon the work scarcely a month before almost the entire body became afflicted with a melancholic, suicidal tendency, and scores of them ended their unhappy existence by their own hands. Disease broke out among them, and raged so fiercely that in a few weeks scarcely two hundred remained. The freshly imported Irishmen and Frenchmen also suffered severely, and there was found no other resource but to reship them as soon as possible, and replenish from the neighbouring provinces and Jamaica, the natives of which (with the exception of the Northmen of America) were found best able to resist the influence of the climate. Notwithstanding these discouragements ... the work continued to advance." With its usual reticence, the company never revealed how many, if any, of the remnants of this ghastly experiment were in fact reshipped alive. But the tactics succeeded. At midnight on January 27th, 1855, after five years' work, the last rail was laid in darkness and pouring rain, and the next morning a locomotive steamed from coast to coast. Three weeks later, a passenger train left Panama for a celebration breakfast in Aspinwall. This time, it was the reporter of the Panama *Star* who was overcome. "Judging from what we saw," he wrote, "we feel safe in stating that never on this isthmus did a pleasure party enjoy themselves better. The tables groaned beneath the weight of delicacies ... Several toasts were given on this occasion, which we would gladly publish did we remember them."

Not counting the cost in lives, it was said to be the most expensive railroad ever built: $8,000,000 had been spent for forty-five miles of track. But it was also the most profitable. By taking goods and passengers part of the way across, it had earned $2,000,000 before it was finished, and in seven years from the day when its first passengers travelled from the shore of Limon Bay to the river at Gatun, it made a net profit of nearly $6,000,000. No wonder: it was a perfect monopoly. As soon as it was finished, the Chagres was deserted again, Las Cruces atrophied, the historic trail fell at last into disuse. The single passenger fare was fixed at the enormous sum of $25—more than 50 cents a mile—and travellers had no option but to pay it. Freight was comparatively cheap. Coal was transported at $5 a ton, cattle at $5 each—though a horse on a passenger train cost $100. First class freight was 50 cents a cubic foot, and the classes of goods in this category were very curious. The list of them, in its entirety, read as follows:

Bonnets, Books, Boots
Caps, Cards (playing,) Cassia lignea, Cigars, Cinnamon, Clothing
Drugs, Dry Goods not elsewhere enumerated
Eau de Cologne, Essences, Essential Oils
Feathers, Fireworks, Flannel, Furs not otherwise enumerated
Glass shades and Looking Glasses; Glassware, fine stained
     and plate; Gloves
Harness; Hats, fur or felt, and of Guayaquil or Panama
     straw; Hosiery
Light goods, not elsewhere specified
Matches, Medicines, Millinery, Musical Instruments
Oil-cloth, Organs
Paintings and engravings; Paper hangings, Paper,
     writing and printing, Peltry, not elsewhere specified.
Percussion Caps, Perfumery, Pianos, Porcelain and
     Chinaware, fine.
Saddlery, Shoes, Silks, Stationery; Statuary, at
     owner's risk
Toys and Fancy Goods.

With this motley cargo, the little railroad prospered for fifteen years, until the first transcontinental railroad of the United States began to take away its traffic. But by then, much more grandiose schemes were being discussed in Darien.

(viii)

The French Canal

Panama will be easier to build, easier to finish
and easier to maintain than the Suez Canal.

Ferdinand de Lesseps, 1879

WHEN CALIFORNIA WAS ADDED to the United States, it did
more than encourage the building of the railroad: it also made
the government take a new interest in the canal idea. Hitherto,
it had mainly been a hobby for rich men or cranks. Frederick
Kelley had spent $75,000 on his explorations, and Cornelius Van-
derbilt had organized a crossing by river and lake through Nicaragua as a rival to the Panama trail, and had gone on from there
to try to finance a Nicaraguan Canal. But even for him it was
too big an undertaking.

Between 1870 and 1875, however, official surveys were made
of all the known possible routes, mostly by officers of the U.S.
Navy. Their surveys were only superficial: the simple difficulty
of seeing through the trees was still the despair of any conscientious surveyor. But at least they were neither prejudiced nor
crazy. They proved that most of the lines that hopeful prospec-
tors said they had found were impossible. Inland from Caledonia
Bay, where Dr. Cullen and Lionel Gisborne had said there was
a crossing at 150 feet, the naval surveyors found no passes lower
than 700. On the Atrato, Humboldt's and Kelley's proposals were
demolished one by one: the best of them needed not only locks
but a tunnel three miles long. At Panama, close to the railroad
track, they planned a route with twenty-four locks and a huge
aqueduct to carry the canal over the Rio Chagres. In Nicaragua,
they found one they thought would need only eleven locks, five

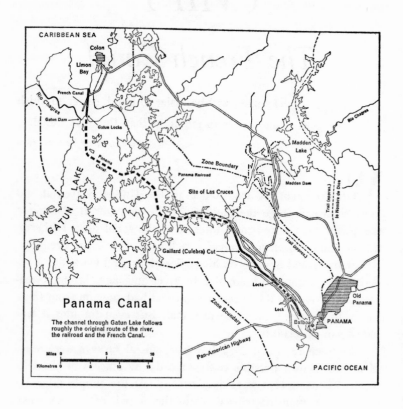

Panama Canal

The channel through Gatun Lake follows roughly the original route of the river, the railroad and the French Canal.

on the way up from the Caribbean to the lake and six down on the other side. A high-powered military and naval commission was appointed to sum up all these explorers' findings, and in 1876 it reported unanimously in favor of Nicaragua.

But in that same year, the last of the commercial adventurers was taking a hasty look at the fringe of the jungle of Darien. He was French, and his name was Lucien Napoleon Bonaparte Wyse. He represented yet another mushroom company, and like all his predecessors, his aim was to find a plausible place to build a canal, get a concession to do so from the government of New Grenada (which had now changed its name to Colombia) and then sell the concession and the discovery to anyone who would bid for them. His explorations were minimal, but he did make one important discovery: that the railroad company had only bought a concession to build a railroad. Among all the canal concessions for all the conceivable routes, nobody at that moment possessed a valid concession to build a canal on the ancient route at Panama itself. So he posted off at full speed for Bogota, and obtained a concession which was subject to the railroad company's consent. And like all the predecessors, he would have stuck at that point and been forgotten, had it not been for a single unfortunate turn of chance: that Count Ferdinand de Lesseps, the hero of Suez, was at home in France with nothing much to occupy his old age. So began the most extraordinary commercial enterprise there has ever been: an enterprise pathetic, heroic, foolish, dishonest and still, to this day, mysterious.

De Lesseps was seventy-five, and like Humboldt a generation before him, he was the most celebrated man in Europe: the man who, to the glory of France, had built the Suez Canal. He was not an engineer, an administrator or a financier. Nowadays, he might be called a fixer: until he was over forty, he had been a diplomat. Suez had been a genuine triumph, the greatest of its age. For fifteen years, five in the preparation and ten in the building, he had personally overcome every kind of difficulty, by

sheer determination and by a naturally optimistic outlook which
always made him pretend that difficulties did not exist. He had
charmed the savings out of the pockets of thousands of Frenchmen, and thousands of Frenchwomen too, by a self-confidence
and enthusiasm which were infectious—and also by flamboyance
and showmanship, an inborn knack for advertising himself and
whatever cause he believed in. And when the canal was successfully opened, in 1869, his fame was so wide that it could only be
expressed by understatement: he was simply known as the Great
Frenchman.

Of course, such fame and the flattery that goes with it are
dangerous for any man, and they were especially dangerous for
de Lesseps, because he adored them. He loved to be popular, the
center of admiration, the oracle that everyone turned to for advice. It was not an unpleasant failing. Unlike Humboldt, he
never grew pompous. On the contrary, he was always jovial,
humorous, gallant with ladies and avuncular with children: people not only admired him, they genuinely loved him. His first
wife died when he was still in his forties, but when he was sixty-
five—a week after the Suez Canal was opened—he married a girl
of twenty, and had twelve children, the last when he was very
nearly eighty. All through his seventies, therefore, he was surrounded by his own offspring, from the middle-aged ones of his
first marriage down to the babies in arms. He still seemed to
have the energy and alertness of a boy—and also a boy's capacity for sudden overwhelming uncritical enthusiasm. But his self-
confidence by then had grown too far. The thought no longer
entered his head that he might be wrong, that he might not be
able to carry other men's opinions with him, or that anyone
might deceive him. Genius though he undoubtedly was, he had
grown conceited.

De Lesseps became involved with Panama because he was
president of the Geographical Society of Paris. In 1879, that institution called an international congress to study the academic
problems of an isthmian canal. Most of the delegates were personally invited by de Lesseps, and more than half of them were

Frenchmen. The meeting lasted a fortnight. A committee was appointed to consider the possible routes and decide which was best. It listened to the advocates of several rival propositions, and narrowed them down, like everybody else, to Panama and Nicaragua. The American delegates recommended Nicaragua: Lucien Wyse was called, and strongly recommended Panama. The Nicaraguan route was agreed to be the cheaper, but it inevitably needed locks, because it made use of the lake. Wyse, on the other hand, said confidently that a canal could be cut at Panama at sea level, without any locks.

De Lesseps himself was never in any doubt which to choose. Wyse's report delighted him. He had built the Suez Canal without locks, and that, he believed, was the only kind of ship canal worth building. And there was another consideration. The concession at Panama belonged to Wyse and his company, who were French: the rights in Nicaragua were American. The Panama route seemed to offer an intoxicating vision of another French triumph, an even grander Suez—an "oceanic Bosphorus," he called it. Difficulties were only there to be overcome: there could be no difficulties worse than he had overcome at Suez. The 300-foot ridge? It was only a matter of digging. The floods of the Rio Chagres? They could be diverted. The climate? "It lends itself admirably to cultivation and industry, by means of which it would soon be completely transformed."

His optimism, with his fame and prestige behind it, was enough to infect even a scientific congress and make it lose sight of logic. His charm and confidence did make the difficulties seem to disappear. A few of the foreign delegates protested that the data were not enough for a final decision, but de Lesseps insisted that the public expected a final decision. And he got it. His committee approved the Panama route by a minority vote, at a moment when more than half the members were absent. In the general assembly, he put a resolution that "this Congress believes that to cut an inter-oceanic canal at sea level is possible, and would be in the interests of commerce and navigation. It also believes the canal should be built from Limon Bay to the Bay of Panama." Of the 138 delegates, seventy-eight were in favor, twelve against, eight abstained and forty were absent. Those who voted against the resolution were booed. Of those who voted for it, only twenty were engineers.

All through the conference, people were pressing de Lesseps not just to preside at this academic meeting, but himself to put the glorious plan into practice. He was told again and again that he was the only man alive who could do it. His own family, who saw him being tempted, tried to dissuade him; they would rather have seen him spend his old age in honored peace. His son Charles, who had been his right-hand man at Suez, wrote to him: "What do you want to find at Panama? Money? You will not bother any more about money at Panama than you did at Suez. Is it glory? You have had enough glory: why not leave that to someone else? And as for us who have worked with you, are we to have no rest? You succeeded at Suez by a miracle. Be content with performing one miracle in your lifetime, and do not hope for a second." But he went on to offer loyal support. "If you decide to take this step, and if you want me to join you, I shall do so with the best will in the world. I shall not complain whatever happens. All that I am I owe to you. What you have given me you have the right to take away."

But the old man could not resist the flattery and homage. "Well," he said at the end of the conference, "if a general who has just won his first victory is asked if he wants to win another, will he refuse?"

Long afterwards, de Lesseps' critics said this conference was loaded or packed by the shareholders of Wyse's company, and was simply a plan to unload their concession. Nobody now can possibly say if this was true, or partly true; such commercial maneuvers, if it was one, have to be thoroughly hidden to succeed. Certainly, the concession was worthless unless somebody could be persuaded to float a company to build the canal—and to do it before the Americans got to work in Nicaragua. Certainly, nothing of the kind could be done in France without de Lesseps' blessing. And certainly the ruse, if it was a ruse, succeeded—probably beyond the company's wildest expectations. For the first thing de Lesseps did was to sign a contract to buy the concession, and the fruits of Wyse's exploration, for the sum of 10,000,000 francs (two-and-a-half million nineteenth-century dollars).

Why in the world did he do it? It was the first of many things he did which set a psychological puzzle. Was he blinded by his own enthusiasm? Was he so self-confident that he never dreamed financiers might trick him? Was it that he was getting old and losing his judgment? For his first 10,000,000 francs, he bought nothing of any value. The concession had not cost the company a cent, except the expense of going to Colombia to get it, and perhaps a little bribery. The Colombian government's price was a percentage of the canal's earnings, and de Lesseps had to undertake to pay it. The concession, moreover, was subject to the approval of the railroad company, which was American. And as for the exploration, Wyse had never been over the route at all except as a passenger in the train. He had an assistant named Armand Reclus, who had spent a fortnight touring the railroad route and then had given it up because he had an earache. The map they presented to the congress was not their own work, it was a reduction of the survey made for the railroad thirty years before. Anyone could have bought or borrowed a copy in America.

After making its phenomenal bargain, the company ceased to exist. But the bargain had an even more costly sequel: in order to get the railroad company's consent, de Lesseps found at a later stage that he had to buy the railroad. This gave him his first experience of a Wall Street holdup. The $100 shares of the railroad company had been standing for some years at par, or near it. He paid $250 for them—a total of $25,000,000 for the track which had cost $8,000,000.

As soon as he bought the concession, he set about floating a company to build the canal. He gave it the grandiose name of *Compagnie Universelle du Canale Interocéanique:* but his first attempt was a failure. Scorning the help of the government or the banks, he tried to appeal in person to the thousands of small investors who had been the backbone of the Suez company. He asked for 400,000,000 francs, but only 30,000,000 were subscribed —so little that he had to return the subscriptions and try a more subtle approach. In order to educate the public, he decided to go to Panama, with a committee of experts to verify Wyse's survey.

That visit gave an example of his showmanship, and also of his charm and reputation. To prove that the climate was healthy, he took his young wife and three of their children with him. He was greeted by banquets, bands, triumphal arches and fireworks, for the people of Colon and Panama looked on the canal as a promise of future prosperity. He delighted everyone, gaily flattering local officials' wives and becoming the godfather of several of their children. In spite of his age, one witness wrote, "he would ride all day over the rough country through which the canal had been or was being located, would then dance all night like a boy, and be ready for the next day's excursion, 'fresh as a daisy.' " "Mme. de Lesseps," the same man said, "was at that time a woman of striking beauty. Her form was voluptuous, and her raven hair, without luster, contrasted well with the rich pallor of her Eastern features"—for she came from Martinique. The French children caused some speculation in Panama society, because they all seemed to be dressed like girls but behaved like boys, and it was a week or so before everyone was satisfied that two in fact were boys and one a girl.

The party was there in the dry season, which was fortunate for de Lesseps' family in their function as guinea pigs, but most misleading for him and his technical committee. All through the visit, the skies were blue and the weather delightful. One Frenchman who lived there is said to have told him that if he persisted in his plan, there would not be trees enough in the jungle to make the crosses for his laborers' graves. But the local people in general were only too glad to agree with him that reports of the evil climate were exaggerated. His committee spent a month inspecting the route, and another fortnight in Panama City writing its report. Its excursions had a picnic air, and its reports confirmed what Wyse had claimed—and took no account at all of the three most important features of work on the isthmus: fever, rain and mud.

Before he left France, he had promised to dig the first spadeful of earth on the first of January 1880, and he had brought a ceremonial pick and shovel with him. On that day, therefore, he embarked in Panama City in a steamboat with all his party and the leading citizens, bound for the mouth of a river three miles away, which was the Pacific end of the canal on Wyse's plan. There are two versions of the events of that day, his own and his critics', as there are of so many of the events he was involved in. He said he formally inaugurated the work with the solemn words: "Under the authority of the Republic of the United States of Colombia; with the blessing of His Grace the Bishop of Panama; in the presence of representatives of the general government and of those of the United States of Colombia; with the assistance of the members of the Technical Commission for the Definitive Studies of the Universal Interoceanic Maritime Canal: there will be given today, the first of January 1880, by Mlle. Ferdinande de Lesseps, the first stroke of the pickaxe, on the point which will mark the entrance of the maritime canal on the coast of the Pacific Ocean." But his critics said that the boat was late and missed the tide and could not get near the shore, so that Ferdinande, who was seven, had to strike the blow with the pickaxe in a champagne crate which some resourceful person had filled with earth. A few days later, another performance was arranged: the firing of the first explosive charge on the top of the continental divide where the canal, it was hoped, would cross it. Again there were two versions. De Lesseps described the successful explosion, and so did the local paper. But a man called Tracey Robinson, who claimed to have been an eyewitness, wrote in his reminiscences: "The blessing had been pronounced, and the champagne, duly iced, was waiting to cool the swelter of that tropic sun, as soon as the explosion 'went off.' There the crowd stood, breathless, ears stopped, eyes blinking. But there was no explo-

sion! It wouldn't go! Then a humorous sense of relief stole upon
the crowd. With one accord everybody exclaimed 'Good gra-
cious!' and hurried away." Perhaps it does not matter much
which tale was true; but to many people afterwards it looked
like a symbol.

From Panama, de Lesseps went to the United States, where
he was received with the hospitality due to a foreign celebrity,
and had a conversation with President Hayes. And then he went
home to offer a new prospectus to French investors.

Anybody else would have been discouraged by the journey.
It had given glimpses of troubles that nobody had foreseen; but
his chronic optimism transformed them all. In his reports, the
traditional hospitality of the United States became a great demonstration of support for his scheme—although in fact he had
found no Americans willing to invest in it. A message President
Hayes sent to Congress became a promise of American protection
for the canal—although the core of the message was the words
"The policy of this country is a canal under American control."
And his technical committee's brief excursions became a final
confirmation of the plan. His optimism could even alter figures.
The international congress, on the basis of Wyse's bogus exploration, had made estimates of the number of cubic meters that
would have to be excavated, and of the total cost: 46,000,000 cubic meters, and 765,000,000 francs. The technical committee increased both these guesses, to 75,000,000 cubic meters and 843,-
000,000 francs. But de Lesseps, alone in his cabin on board the
ship on the way to New York, cut down the figure of cost, without any explanation, to 658,000,000 francs; and he clung to this
estimate long after events had proved that all three of them were
ludicrously low. It was not dishonesty in any crude sense: it was
more like the blindness of love. He had fallen in love with the
idea, and he could not or would not see any fault in it, nor bear
to hear anyone criticize it. On the results of this expedition, he
announced that a canal at sea level could and would be built, and
finished by 1888. This time, his appeal for funds was a splendid
success. He asked for 600,000,000 francs, and the French public

offered double that amount—solely because the Great Frenchman had been to Panama and said the sea-level canal was feasible. No other such enterprise has ever been launched with so little preparation. Wyse had chosen the Panama route largely because the railroad made it easy to explore, and de Lesseps never considered any other. The Panama Canal, indeed, stands where it does today because the railroad was there before it, and the railroad was there because the Spanish trail was there. The choice belonged to Pedrarias, not de Lesseps.

Hundreds of thousands of pages were written about de Lesseps' project, and most of them, one way or the other, were contentious and prejudiced. But remarkably little was ever told about what happened on the isthmus when the work began. At the heart of the storm of argument that his canal provoked, there is an area of darkness and of silence. One can read the statistics of what his men achieved, but not much of what they suffered to achieve it. The reason is simply that most of them died before they could tell their stories, while those who survived were caught up in a scandal which made the simple facts of their life on the isthmus seem hardly worth telling. Yet in eight years from 1881 to 1889, Frenchmen performed prodigious feats of endurance and bravery there in a cause they thought was noble.

It was like a battlefield. De Lesseps' claim that the climate was healthy was very soon disproved. Malaria and yellow fever struck the French with more awful severity than anyone before. Nobody knows exactly how many died. American medical officers afterwards put the total at somewhere between 16,500 and 22,000, of whom perhaps 2,000 were French technicians and the rest humble laborers from all over the world. But a total figure was not what really mattered. What mattered was that two out of every three Frenchmen who went to the isthmus died there. There were never more than a few hundred there at one time; yet as they died off, there were always more who volunteered to come from home, because they looked on the task as a battle, and themselves as soldiers fighting it for France.

It was not carelessness or inefficiency that made the deaths
so high: they built the finest hospitals in Colon and Panama, and
good housing for themselves and their laborers all along the
route. It was simply ignorance—the ignorance of the world at
that time. Nobody yet had seen the connection of malaria and
yellow fever with mosquitoes—the connection that seemed so
pathetically obvious once it was seen. The houses had windows
without any glass or screens. The huge excavations they made
were full of pools of stagnant water, and nobody knew they were
dangerous. The hospital at Panama was staffed by nuns, who laid
out a beautiful garden round it with ornamental ponds. It is said
that they stood the feet of the hospital beds in bowls of water
to stop ants climbing up them, and that mosquitoes bred in the
bowls. Twenty-one of the twenty-four nursing sisters died. Of
four successive chief engineers, two died on the isthmus, and one
in France after going home because his wife and son-in-law and
daughter had died. The fourth, who took over because there was
nobody else, was a young man of twenty-six called Philippe
Bunau-Varilla: he caught yellow fever and was one of the very
few who recovered from it, and he lived to play an important
part in political events on the isthmus twenty years later. The
most shocking thing about yellow fever was its quickness. It
seldom took more than four days, and sometimes one. Every
Frenchman, every morning, knew he might feel the symptoms before the night and be lying in one of the spreading cemeteries
before a week was out.

Beyond the danger of death, their life was harsh. Most of
them lived in camps along the railroad, surrounded by jungle
except where they had cleared it. The laborers worked a ten-hour
day, and the technicians worked through all the twelve hours of
tropical daylight, and through all the tropical rain. After dark,
in the steaming breathless heat, it was difficult even to read or
write or play a game of cards, because a lamp or candle attracted
such hordes of insects. And there was nothing else to do. If they
had a day off, they could only take the train in one direction or
the other, to Colon or Panama. Both towns were described as

sinks of iniquity: one traveller, passing through, used the phrase "a hideous dung heap of moral and physical abomination." The towns had bars, roulette rooms and brothels, and the billiard saloons which played such a part in nineteenth-century debauchery. Some of the Frenchmen, with death so imminent, plunged into these sordid delights like soldiers released from the front line. Some, of course, drank nothing but wine and spirits because there was no water fit to drink. But there was also a widespread belief that yellow fever could be avoided by living a blameless life, and although the theory could not have stood up to a test, there was always a good proportion of men who were puritanical in behavior and devoted themselves entirely to their work. As time went on, however, the work itself took on the quality of a nightmare.

It was in January 1881, a year after Ferdinande's blow of the pickaxe, that the first of the French engineers arrived at Colon. Four days later in France de Lesseps published a telegram he said they had sent him: *"Travail commencé"*—a message which, as he said, was eloquent in its brevity. But of course it did not refer to the work of excavation: there was a whole year of preliminary work before the first hole was dug. They began by cutting a swathe a hundred yards wide through the jungle, surveying the route again, and marking out the center-line with stakes. That clearance gave them the first comprehensive view of what they were up against. The route followed closely beside the railroad. From the Caribbean end in Limon Bay, the first few miles led through the mangrove swamps that the railroad engineers had crossed with such hardship thirty years before. Then it followed the valley of the Chagres, crossing the winding bed of the river fourteen times. Rather more than half way across the isthmus, where the valley bent round to the east just below the deserted site of Las Cruces, the canal route took a southerly turn up a tributary called the Obispo. At the head of that stream, at a spot called Culebra, it crossed the main divide and then, for another ten miles, led down the valley of the little river called

Rio Grande to the sea on the western edge of Panama City. The
two most formidable problems were to dig through the hills at
Culebra, and to control the Rio Chagres.

Everybody since the earliest Spanish days had known the
Chagres, like every river in Darien, was subject to sudden floods.
One year while the French were at work, it showed what it could
do by flooding the railroad track to a depth of fifteen feet—and
the chief engineer of the moment, Bunau-Varilla, paddling along
the railroad in a canoe, observed that the branches of the trees for
a yard above the water line were black instead of green: they
were covered by millions of tarantulas flooded out of their holes.
The problem was that at the last of the fourteen points where the
canal was to cross the river, the bed of the river was fifty feet above
sea level, and its depth was said to vary from three feet in the dry
season to forty feet in the floods. Evidently, if the floods were
allowed to pour into the sea-level canal over a waterfall ninety
feet high, they would wash it away or fill it with debris. Wyse
had proposed rather glibly to dam the river above the point where
it met the canal, and dig a new bed for it all the way to the sea.
But nobody had found a place with bedrock solid enough for such
a big dam. Nobody much liked the idea of ships sailing through
the canal with the flood-waters held precariously ninety feet above
them. And nobody, in fact, ever solved this problem. What to do
with the Chagres remained an enigma and a threat all through
de Lesseps' operations. Whenever he was asked, he confidently
said he would divert it, but he never precisely said how.

But the problem of cutting through the divide was one that
every engineer could see and understand. The highest point on
the route, at Culebra, was 330 feet above sea level. Between the
Rio Obispo and the Rio Grande there was a mile at an average
height of 277 feet. The water in the canal was to be thirty feet
deep. So what was needed at this point was a ditch a mile long
with an average depth of 307 feet and a maximum of 360. On
either side of Culebra, the depth of cut was progressively less
until, near the sea at each end, it was merely a matter of dredging
the coastal swamps.

It was no small task by any standards: with the equipment of the 1880s it was huge. The French brought to it steam power and man power: steam shovels and bucket dredges, steam locomotives to haul away the trains of spoil, and a labor force, with a backbone of Caribbean Negroes, which grew to nearly 20,000 men. But the machines of that era were small and their uses were limited: anything awkward still had to be done by pick and shovel.

The work was begun by a large firm of contractors which had undertaken to do it all for an even smaller sum than de Lesseps had estimated—for he was not the only optimist. But the contract had an escape clause, and two years after the firm began, it gave up again in despair. It had made a fairly convincing start in the low-lying land, but around Culebra it had hardly scraped off the surface. In 1883, de Lesseps' company undertook the organization itself, letting out stretches of the route to small contractors, some of whom were American. The work began to gather momentum, but desperately slowly; for in the cut at Culebra, every evil quality of the isthmus combined against it.

Culebra proved to be covered by layers of clay from thirty to sixty feet thick. Below that, there was hard rock in some places, and in others more layers of alternate clay and shale. And when the clay was exposed in the sides of the cut and the teeming rain fell on it, it dissolved into heavy sticky mud that moved and crept inexorably down and filled the excavations, covered the rail tracks, overturned and sometimes buried the trains and machines at the bottom. At the height of the rains, the cut was inaccessible: men could not walk through the mud. And the dumps of excavated material would never stand still. The clay was tipped on them in lumps from the railroad wagons, and the lumps disintegrated in the rain and subsided until the whole heap slid away in lakes of liquid mud and took the tracks with it. Sometimes for weeks on end no progress was made at all. It was all they could do to clear out the mud from the excavations they had made.

Indeed it was even worse than that: the work went backwards. The more they dug out, the more they had to dig. The

estimates of the millions of cubic meters had assumed that the
sides of the cut at Culebra would be almost vertical. De Lesseps,
and everyone with him, had imagined a neat narrow cut like the
Corinth Canal in Greece, which has walls of sheer rock. De
Lesseps spoke of the vertical sides of quarries at home in France.
But nothing much had been done to find out if that were possible
in the isthmus: the technical committtee had made a few boreholes here and there, but the deepest of them was only seventy
feet. Now, the sides of the cut were for ever being dug back
farther and farther, to try to stop them sliding. In some places
they were cut to a slope of one in four, and even then when they
seemed at last to be stable, a sudden storm of rain would start
them moving. A ditch 360 feet deep with sides of one in four
would be more than a half a mile across, and that was wider than
the pass at Culebra. Before they reached sea level, whole hills on
each side of the pass would have to be taken away. Wyse's estimate had been 46,000,000 cubic meters. The technical committee
had raised it to 75,000,000. De Lesseps, with a ludicrous air of
exactitude, had made it 72,986,016. By 1884, after three years'
work, they had only dug out 5,250,000, but the estimate had gone
up to 125,000,000. By 1886, they had learned many lessons and
were digging about a million a month, but the estimate had gone
up again to 150,000,000. The end was always further away than
it had seemed when the work began.

De Lesseps was not in Panama. After his first visit, he only
went there once again, in 1886, for a ceremonial inspection which
lasted a fortnight. His role was as figurehead and promoter: his
son Charles, who had promised to support him whatever happened, was the practical director of the company. The old gentleman's time was occupied in raising money, for more and more
money was always needed. Many subscribers believed that his
estimate of 658,000,000 francs had been a total, but it was not. It
was only a guess at the cost of the actual work, and it did not
include expenses in France—advertising, management, salaries,
interest, commissions on the sale of stock—nor the cost of Wyse's

concession and the railroad. And as the work dragged on, expenses of every kind were multiplied. The first subscriptions were soon used up, and every year from 1881 to 1886 he raised more. His own reputation and personality were always the strongest magnets for money, and he used them to the full. But he also published a bulletin every fortnight, which offered a consistently optimistic view of the way things were going, and he gave large sums to newspaper editors and reporters who promised favorable stories, and to people in the financial world who could help, or who said they could help, in each issue of shares and bonds. In the beginning, this was a legitimate and necessary part of his campaign. But it was always a dangerous practice. So long as all went well, it worked and would have gone on working. It had worked at Suez. But at any breath of trouble, it was only too easy for payments once freely offered to be demanded, not as the price of help but as the price of silence.

There was always one easy way out of the trouble on the isthmus: to abandon the idea of a sea-level canal, and build a canal with locks. A simple scheme for a lock canal had been proposed at the Geographical Society's congress, but de Lesseps had overruled it. Lionel Gisborne had made the same kind of proposal for his canal at Caledonia Bay; indeed it was a scheme that was obvious to any canal engineer. It was to dam both the valleys, the Chagres and Rio Grande, near the sea, to form two artificial lakes which could be joined by a comparatively shallow cut at Culebra, and to build the locks in the dams or alongside them. This would have brought the volume of digging within reasonable bounds, and would also have solved the problem of the Chagres, for the river could safely have been used to fill the lakes. It is the plan, in essence, of the present canal. By 1885, some of the engineers on the isthmus had certainly come to believe that this was the only solution. Perhaps if de Lesseps had been there he would have seen it himself. But he was not, and if anyone dared to suggest it to him he took no notice. He had promised the people of France he would build a sea-level canal, and staked his vast reputation on it. To him, it had become a matter of honor—his own and France's. He still said and seemed to believe that nothing was impossible, given the will to achieve it. If he had ever been asked he would probably have used an argument familiar at the time: that a lock canal would never pay because its running expenses would be higher and fewer ships could use it. And it was true that the canal at sea level was the whole point of the Panama route, its only virtue; if a lock canal was all that could be done, it could have been done better in Nicaragua. So the digging went on. The farther it went, the more nearly impossible it became for the engineers to believe in success—but the more nearly impossible also for de Lesseps to admit defeat, for the fortunes of tens of thousands of Frenchmen, the honor of France, the lives of thousands of men, had all been entrusted to him and committed to the task.

In such an affair, there is always a point of no return. It came in 1886. There was a limit to the funds which even he could raise in France, and he was approaching it. The cost of conversion to a lock canal could have been estimated fairly accurately. But while he postponed the decision, money was being thrown away, for much of the excavation for a sea-level canal was useless for a lock canal. When the moment came, he could have made and announced the change of plan and still raised enough money to complete it. But if he saw the choice he had to make, he showed no sign of it: he remained as jaunty, apparently as confident as ever. If he saw he was wrong, he could not bring himself to say so. He let the moment pass—and from that moment, the French canal was doomed, and so was he.

Yet the work went on for another two years. De Lesseps' persistence all that time is the most remarkable of all the psychological puzzles he set historians. Not only his own engineers but other people all over the world could see what was happening. A whole book was written and published in England to prove that the sea-level canal could never be completed. France itself was full of rumors and the press was full of hints. But none of the criticism, none of the warnings, seemed to penetrate his armor of self-confidence. He never admitted doubt. He treated critics simply as enemies who for some inexplicable reason wanted to bring the grand design to ruin. His wife and his son Charles protected him so far as they were able, and the hosts of friends who had loved and admired him so long surrounded him with a loyal barrier. But it hardly seems possible he was living in happy ignorance, like a man whose doctor will not tell him he is dying. There must have been a secret dread in his heart—a dread of a disaster so shocking and so devastating that he could not bear to think of it or speak of it, even among the people who loved him best.

Charles de Lesseps certainly knew of the danger, if not of the certainty, of a disastrous end. But he had an added incentive to try to stave it off. He himself had never risen to such a height of fame, and therefore he had not so far to fall. But he was devoted to his father. He had worked for him all his life, and had been content to let him take the glory. And everything he did suggests that one fear tormented him more than any other, that his father, now over eighty, might end his triumphant life in misery.

So they both toiled on together, touring France, giving lectures, encouraging, exhorting and still charming the country's middle-class investors. But all the time it was growing harder, not only because of the growing doubts and rumors, but also because—like Paterson in Scotland—de Lesseps had gathered in almost all the spare cash in the country. To attract more subscribers, he decided to promote a lottery. That was a well-established way of raising money in France, and he had used it when the Suez company, in just the same way, had looked like failing for lack of funds. But a lottery had to have the government's approval; and so the company, which so far had been independent, began to be drawn into the complicated meshes of French political life.

It was not until 1887, after six years of labor on the sea-level canal, that de Lesseps agreed at last to make a change of plan. His own engineers led him up to it by a face-saving ruse. After all those years of trying to keep the water out of the cut at Culebra, they had decided it was cheaper to let it in, and to dig underwater with dredgers floating in pools. Bunau-Varilla, accord-

ing to his own account, had perfected a method of dredging not
only mud but rock: he broke it up first by underwater explosions.
This opened a new possibility: to build a temporary canal with
locks, and then go on dredging it while it was in use, eliminating
the locks two by two until the whole thing was finally brought
to sea level. They designed a canal with five locks on each side
of Culebra, and a summit level of 170 feet. That was an attain-
able objective, an end that could really be said to be in sight The
cut at Culebra would only be half as deep: 167 feet instead of
337. And the great thing about it was that they could put it to
de Lesseps as a merely provisional canal, a practical step on the
was to the sea-level strait he had set his heart on. In that light,
he was persuaded to accept it—still saying he had not given up,
and would never consent to give up, the original sea-level plan.
And he made a new contract at once, with M. Eiffel who built
the Eiffel Tower, to construct and supply the lock gates.

Now at last it could really be said that the lessons of the
isthmus had been learned and the solutions of its problems—excepting the fevers—had been found. Only one more effort was
needed: another three years' work, another 600,000,000 francs,
and ships could be sailing through. But the lottery was meeting
opposition in the government and the Chamber of Deputies: a
committee had been appointed to consider it, and after a long
delay had decided against it by six votes to five. That decision
made de Lesseps very angry: that six deputies should try to rob
France of her glory! "As always," he announced, "when people
try to stop me, I go on."

He was not a politician: he had always regarded himself—
and been generally regarded—as far above politics. Nobody
would have dared to go to him with any political proposal which
was even slightly shady. But Charles found himself pursued by
people who said that they could help, that no political decision
was ever final, that they knew somebody who had influence. All
of them said it would need money—not for themselves, they
would explain, but it was always expensive to influence opinion.
A somewhat sinister person called Baron von Reinach, who had

been a financial adviser from the beginning—and had also been a member of Wyse's profitable company—claimed bluntly that he had many deputies in his pocket. And the Minister of Works himself sent a go-between to suggest that in his position a million francs could be put to good use.

Charles was no more a politician than his father. He did not really understand such things: he preferred not to understand. He was being assured, by people who did understand them, that this was how politics were run, how political decisions were always reached; and at that time, in France, this was unfortunately true. He only saw two alternatives, to buy political approval of the lottery, or else—the unthinkable thing—to see the whole thing abandoned, the investors' money lost, and his father, of all people, disgraced and discredited. The company had always been liberal with its gratuities to newspaper men and others. Now, on a rapidly rising scale, Charles began to give in to what was no better than blackmail. Baron von Reinach was given millions, and nobody could ask what he did with it. The minister himself got 375,000 francs. And without any explanation, one of the members of the committee who had voted against the lottery changed his mind. The vote had been six to five against. Now it was six to five in favor.

With that permission, 2,000,000 lottery bonds at 360 francs each were issued in June 1888. It was another huge sum of money, but it was reckoned—and with some reason by then—to be all that the company would need: 600,000,000 francs to finish the lock canal and 120,000,000 to provide the lottery prizes. But by then the company had many powerful enemies, those who sincerely believed the canal was impossible, and those in politics who felt that they had to oppose it for any of the complex motives of politicians. For three days before the issue, deliberate selling of company stock brought a fall in its value of 25 per cent. On the day itself, somebody sent telegrams to every town in France to announce that de Lesseps was dead. The issue was a total failure. Only two fifths of the bonds were subscribed. In the terms of the lottery, twenty francs for each bond was payable on the day of

issue. But on the next day, the company was obliged by law
to establish the whole of the prize fund. It had to pay out more
than it received.

That was the end, except for a ghastly six months of the
company's death throes, when even de Lesseps' closest friends
had given up hope, but he would not give in. He dragged Charles
round the country on another lecture tour, and tried to create a
new company to refloat the one that was sinking. But at the end
of the year, at the age of eighty-three, he was forced to admit
he was beaten. He sent an order to Panama that work must stop.
The company went into liquidation. Eight years of grinding labor,
perhaps 20,000 deaths, 1,200,000,000 francs—and it was over.

On the isthmus, thousands of men were left unemployed and
largely destitute, and the economic life of the place fell into chaos.
The British consul rose to the crisis by feeding armies of laborers
and sending shiploads home—for a large proportion came from
the British West Indian islands. But others with nobody to care
for them stayed where they were, and simply sank into easy-going
tropical poverty among the descendants of the maroons and the
liberated Spanish Indian slaves. And the jungle, as virile as ever,
began to heal its scars.

In France, de Lesseps' energy and brilliance were instantly
extinguished by the blow. Some people said he had a stroke when
he ordered the work to stop. Certainly, within a matter of weeks,
he was a doddering old man, absorbed in thoughts of his own and
out of touch with all reality.

For about a year, the liquidation went calmly enough, and a
new company was set up to administer what assets were left:
the concession, the railroad, the buildings and machinery and—
for what it was worth—the enormous hole in the ground. Most
people, at that stage, expected the government to save the situation and finish the canal. But the government hesitated. The risk
of another failure was alarming, and so was the risk of American
opposition. The United States had tolerated the canal because it
was being built by a company: they would certainly not have

placidly watched a European government take it over. As this
hope diminished, an outcry grew against the company's directors,
including de Lesseps, and people demanded prosecution and revenge. That embarrassed the government even more. Ministers
and deputies all suspected each other. Ever since the lottery,
rumors of shady dealings had been spreading. Nobody knew where
the mud might stick if they began to stir it. Yet if they refused,
they might be suspected of guilty consciences. At last, one deputy
flatly said that 150 of his colleagues in the chamber had taken
bribes from the company or its agents. That was too much: an
enquiry had to be ordered. A year earlier, a full enquiry might
have been a safety valve, but the government waited too long. The
scandal exploded with a bang that echoed all over the world.

Of all the wildly slanderous things that were uttered, not
many were strictly true. France grew hysterical, ready to say or
believe almost anything. The canal was forgotten, except in so
far as 'Panamiste' was a term of abuse—an eloquent one when
an angry Frenchman spat it out. People behaved as if the company had not done anything in the isthmus, but had squandered
and embezzled all the millions through sheer wickedness. Some
even said that none of the engineers had ever left Paris. Fraud,
swindling, greed for money, even greed for personal power and
glory—these were all things that the crudest of critics could understand. But few people understood the subtle contradictions of
de Lesseps' character, and the uniquely awful conditions of work
on the isthmus, which together were the causes of the ruin. Most
of the attacks were therefore indiscriminate: men who had sac-
rificed health and comfort to what had seemed an ideal were
blamed, and guilty men escaped. Furious accusations were made
of extravagance on the isthmus—the salaries of the senior engineers, their houses, carriages, servants and private coaches on the
railroad—and of theft and duplicity there. In discussions of the
French canal, these accusations are sometimes still repeated. But
they were never proved or even discussed in a court, and they
were probably vastly exaggerated. No doubt there was petty theft

and waste: there often is in such enterprises. But all in all, the French effort on the isthmus was magnificent. The men who went there were the finest of the civil engineers of France. To attract them to a job where the expectancy of life became a matter of weeks, the company had been right to offer good pay and whatever amenities it could. And their perseverance in the face of death is hard to reconcile with any systematic swindling.

It was at home in France that foolishness and wickedness flourished. The foolishness was de Lesseps' and his sons. The wickedness belonged to some of the men who surrounded them. And the crux of the scandal was not simply that the company had failed and 1,200,000,000 francs had been lost, although that was bad enough: it was that the failure exposed a state of chronic corruption in the business and political life of France. Besides the parliamentary enquiry, there were two separate prosecutions, one for fraud and one for bribery; and for month after month, Frenchmen opened their newspapers every morning to find new revelations.

During the parliamentary enquiry, there were often scenes of uproar in the chamber: deputies challenged each other to duels, were carried out struggling, and hurled accusations across the floor. Among many other people, the Ministers of Finance and Justice both came under suspicion, and both of them resigned. The Minister of Public Works confessed he had accepted a bribe from Charles: he resigned and was prosecuted. In the investigation of the payments the company had made to newspaper men, the fact came out that successive French governments had been in the habit of paying the press for support: at least two former Premiers had used secret service funds for the purpose. Baron von Reinach was found to have received 9,000,000 francs from the company for what was called publicity. At the crucial moment when he was summoned to explain what he had done with it, he died. His doctor said it was apoplexy. Most people took it for granted it was suicide; some spread a story of murder, or even of a coffin filled with stones and a secret flight across the frontier. And feelings were running so high that the government was outvoted and forced to resign on the trivial question of whether the baron's body should be exhumed.

Enquiries into Reinach's affairs led into insoluble mazes of more or less mysterious transactions. His checks were traced through banks all over Europe. Of his 9,000,000 francs 2,000,000 had gone without any explanation to an even shadier person called Dr. Cornelius Herz, who had fled the country and taken refuge, too ill to be extradited, in a hotel in Bournemouth. Some of the company's money had been paid to people who seemed to have nothing to do with the case at all; and indeed, the cause of the baron's suicide, if it was suicide, might have been that he had not used the money for bribery, but had used half of it to pay his own debts. The enquiry never came anywhere near the bottom of all the mysteries. But it dug up, among other things, a used check book in which the counterfoils were marked with initials: and the initials were those of senators and deputies. Some of these men gave convincing explanations, some less convincing. The man whose change of vote in committee had legalized the lottery was called Sans Leroy. A counterfoil marked S. L. showed a sum of 300,000 francs. He was proved to have recently paid off a mortgage of 200,000, but when he was asked where he got the money he said it was his wife's dowry—and on this he was acquitted. And in a final climax of excitement, parliamentary privilege was withdrawn from five senators and five deputies in order that they could be prosecuted—and among them were one ex-Premier, two ex-Ministers of Justice, one ex-Minister of Commerce and one ex-Minister of Fine Arts.

Throughout it all, the central figure was an aged invalid, bedridden and failing in mind. Early in the proceedings, de Lesseps was summoned before an examining magistrate. Charles went to his bedroom to break this news to him, and to his surprise his father understood at once what was needed, got up and dressed himself and put on the Grand Cordon of the Legion of Honor. The interview, which was private, lasted three hours. Charles said afterwards: "My father came out with his face full

of geniality and vitality, just as it used to be in his fighting days.
But the reaction was not long delayed, and it was terrible." The
old gentleman went back to bed, and the next morning he told
his wife he had a dreadful nightmare. "I dreamed I was summoned before the magistrate," he said. "It was atrocious." For
three weeks after that, he did not speak at all, and he never
mentioned Panama again.

Whatever he said at that interview—and he was certainly
quite unfit to defend himself—the state brought charges of fraud
against him and Charles, two other directors of the company,
and M. Eiffel, the contractor for the lock gates. De Lesseps, of
course, was far too ill to be brought to court. Charles—who had
advised his father fourteen years before to rest on the glory of
Suez and not to hope for a second miracle—now had to bear the
whole humiliation. He could have put most of the blame on his
father, who was too near death to pay any penalty for it. But on
the contrary, he and his fellow-directors refused to say a single
word against the old man. The basis of the prosecution was that
the company's directors could not possibly have believed in 1888
that the canal would be finished, as they said, in 1891, and that
in all their fund raising after that they had deceived the investors. Defending counsel tried to make the point that faith and
pertinacity are the springs of any great endeavor. De Lesseps, he
admitted, had sinned in being too optimistic, but it was only
optimists who succeeded; pessimists were never anything but
idle spectators. Nevertheless, in the disillusioned light of court,
the blinding enthusiasm which had led de Lesseps on could not
be recreated: it did look as though no honest intelligent man
could have failed to see in time that the task was impossible.
De Lesseps and Charles were both found guilty and given the
maximum sentences: five years' imprisonment and a nominal fine
of 3,000 francs. The other directors had lesser sentences. Eiffel
was found guilty of taking a profit of 7,000,000 francs for work
he had hardly started, and concealing the fact from the liqui-
dators.

The sentences shocked and sobered France. Nobody really

believed the Great Frenchman could ever have stooped to fraud. People at last remembered his achievements and felt ashamed of the witch hunt that had brought him down. The thought of hauling him off to die in gaol was unbearable. His wife refused to let anyone even tell him what had happened, and no Frenchman could bring himself to insist. Even his sternest critics were thankful when a legal means was discovered, through the laws of limitation, to annul the sentences.

For Charles, however, the ordeal was not over: there was still the trial for bribery. This charge was not brought against de Lesseps, but Charles was put in the dock again, together with the Minister of Public Works, who had confessed he had taken a bribe, and five of the other senators and deputies who had denied it. By then, everyone was growing sick of the whole affair: the public wanted to get it over and forget it. Those who were in court felt themselves humiliated by the abject confession of the minister. Charles insisted he had been forced to pay out millions to defend his shareholders' interests. Every organization in France, he insisted, made the same sort of payments: even the government encouraged it. And of course, by then, all France knew this had been true. He was found guilty "with extenuating circumstances" and sentenced again to a year's imprisonment. The minister's sentence was harsher; the rest were all acquitted. And at last, the scandal was allowed to simmer down.

It was hard to tell whether de Lesseps ever knew of his disgrace. He would sit all day at his fireside, propped in an armchair, staring into the flames, and not even his wife could penetrate his thoughts. Once when Charles could not come home to the family for Christmas, he seemed to have guessed that his son was in prison. But his memory was going, and if the knowledge distressed him, he seemed to forget it. His wife protected him fiercely from intrusions, and always insisted on his innocence and greatness. When the last sentence was pronounced, she said: "God's will be done. Posterity will judge us."

But posterity judged him more harshly, on the whole, than

he deserved, especially in America and England, where people could gloat over the failure, scandal and humiliation because they were French. De Lesseps was portrayed too often and too long as a comically foolish Frenchman who tried to do something absurd and impossible. That was wholly untrue and unjust. He was a man of visions, and in the end his visions dazzled him. Where corruption is common, anyone who passionately wants something lays himself open to exploitation, and de Lesseps wanted the canal too passionately. And yet it was exactly the same qualities in him that made Suez a triumph and Panama a disaster: the single-mindedness, the optimism, the refusal to look at difficulties—these were admirable when they made the difficulties vanish, but fatal when the difficulties were really insuperable. A lesser man would never have inspired his countrymen to start the enterprise, and work and die for it: an even greater one would have seen it was impossible before it was too late.

There was one final scene, pathetic and macabre. Shortly before he died, de Lesseps complained that Charles was neglecting him, and Charles was given leave from prison to visit his father, accompanied by two prison warders. The old man recognized his son. "Ah, Charles," he said, "It is you. Is there nothing new in Paris?" That was all he was able to say. At luncheon, he took his usual place at the family table. One of the warders insisted on sitting there with Charles. De Lesseps ate a good luncheon, but often fell half asleep, resting his chin on a cane which he always carried. Once he smiled at Charles and opened his mouth as if he were about to speak, but he said nothing. And nobody told him who the stranger was at his dining-room table. After luncheon he settled down with a newspaper which his wife had brought him. It was three years old.

(ix)

The Revolution

I took the Canal Zone and let Congress debate.

President Theodore Roosevelt

TEN YEARS AFTER de Lesseps' company crashed, its successors began in earnest to try to sell its remaining assets to the government of the United States. The company's life had been remarkable and scandalous: the attempts to sell it were certainly no less remarkable, and if there was no open scandal at the time, suspicions and hints of scandal lasted for years and led to a celebrated libel action. Much of this chapter in the story of the isthmus was furtive, secretive and mysterious; and if this telling of it must still be incomplete, it is as near the truth as a conscientious history can go.

All through the period of de Lesseps' work, the United States —its government and its people—stuck to their preference for the Nicaraguan route: the same route that Humboldt had preferred in 1820. In 1880, there was still some engineering logic in the choice. It was an easier route for a lock canal big enough for the shipping of the day. If the existence of Wyse's French concession, and the dream of a sea-level canal, had not made de Lesseps favor Panama, he or somebody else would probably have succeeded in Nicaragua well before the end of the century. A canal there could have finished sooner—and would also have become obsolete sooner.

Nicaragua had a special advantage for the United States: it was farther north, and therefore, although the canal itself would be much longer, the distance from eastern to western North American ports would be shorter. But above all, it had an emotional advantage. Americans had never liked the idea of a crowd

of foreigners building the canal: it was too near home. It was
just the sort of job they knew they were good at, and they felt
affronted that somebody else was doing it. And as the French had
beaten them to the Colombian concession, it was only human for
them to favor Nicaragua even more than it deserved, and to persuade themselves that Panama was no good anyhow.

Even while de Lesseps was hard at work and his success was
still a possibility, the American government made a treaty with
Nicaragua to build a rival all-American canal. The two canals
could not have been an economic success, and like so many
projects before, it came to nothing. But a private enterprise, the
Nicaraguan Canal Association, was founded in New York in 1886,
and in 1889, within three months of the crash in France, it started
digging. At the mouth of the Rio San Juan, the river which flows
from the Lake of Nicaragua into the Caribbean, it cleared the
timber for twenty miles along the projected route, built a railroad eleven miles inland, and actually dug a canal which was
280 feet wide and seventeen feet deep—but only half a mile in
length when the company went bankrupt. The crash was much
less spectacular than de Lesseps', but even more emphatically
final, and this hole in the ground was added to other isthmian
monuments of lost endeavors.

After that, through the rest of the 1890s, the whole idea of
building a canal stagnated. Panama and Colon sank back yet
again into tropical torpor. The little trains on the Panama Railroad puffed slowly to and fro, and their passengers, looking out
of the windows, repeated the popular stories of de Lesseps' follies
and pointed out the abandoned workings and rusting machines,
some draped already with vines and almost hidden by the jungle's virile growth.

But these symbols of failure were not quite so hopeless as
they looked. There was still a dim spark of life in the enterprise.
The new French company, which had taken over the assets of the
old, was doing its best to look after them. It had persuaded
Colombia to extend its concession. Under the terms of the concession, it had to carry on the work, and therefore it always em-

ployed a token force of men, who went on aimlessly digging in the Culebra cut. It was at least trying to keep its useful machines in working order: most of the relics seen from the railroad track had been worn out or broken or obsolete before they were abandoned. It also, at last, made a thorough and efficient survey of the whole problem. And most important of all, it had two skilful, cunning, energetic advocates, one amateur and one professional. The amateur was Philippe Bunau-Varilla, the man who acted as chief engineer under de Lesseps when he was twenty-six. The professional was an eminent New York lawyer named William Nelson Cromwell. Both of these men devoted most of a decade of hard work to selling the idea of Panama, and the French company's assets, in the United States. And while they were doing it, the two of them despised each other, worked independently and were seldom on speaking terms.

Bunau-Varilla was like an Anglo-Saxon caricature of a nineteenth century Frenchman: dapper, bravely moustached, excitable in argument, and unself-consciously patriotic and vain. He wrote enormous books about Panama—or rather about himself and Panama—and filled them with ringing clichés of national honor, national glory and the national genius of France. One sees him as he undoubtedly saw himself, a symbolic soldier bearing the Tricolor against implacable foes, and always alert to spring to attention at the first note of the Marseillaise. And what foes he met! Anyone who disagreed with his ideas about the canal— and from time to time, that was almost everyone concerned— was ignorant, corrupt, futile, incomprehensible, perfidious, inane, mendacious, extortionate, or at best gravely mistaken. As for himself, he wrote that he had "consecrated his life" to the Panama Canal: and there was indeed, in his mind, something holy about this large but mundane excavation.

But at the turn of the century, of course, flag-waving patriots in any country were not the figures of fun they have become since then. Bunau-Varilla, if one reads his books today, inevitably seems a silly little man. But he was a crusader, a man with one idea, and single-mindedness has always been effective. He was critical of de Lesseps, as of almost everybody else, but he had inherited de Lesseps' blind enthusiasm. Panama was right. It was the flower of French genius—and especially of his own, for it was he, as he often explained, who had given the world the solution of the problem by his invention of dredging rock under water. If Panama were abandoned and Nicaragua built instead, the world would always believe that France—and Bunau-Varilla—had been ridiculously wrong. For ten years he had been consumed with resentment against all the people, all over the world, who had said the French idea was impossible and the French company incompetent. French honor demanded revenge, and the only possible revenge was that the Nicaragua canal should be stopped and the Panama Canal successfully completed. The new French company, which was understandably cautious in its policy, disowned him, and the French government had had more than enough of Panama and did nothing about it at all. But Bunau-Varilla appointed himself to the noble task, and was happy to carry the banner single-handed.

William Nelson Cromwell, who fought the same battle for totally different reasons, was also a rather flamboyant character with a taste for theatrical effect, but that was all he had in common with Bunau-Varilla. He was the cofounder of the great New York law partnership of Sullivan and Cromwell, in which John Foster Dulles was a later partner—Cromwell, indeed, gave Dulles his first job. Cromwell had risen from poverty in the best American tradition after his father was killed in the Civil War; but by the end of the century, at the age of forty-six, he was already an institution, a distinguished autocrat in his office, whose juniors lived in awe of him but told stories, with a certain pride and affection, of his eccentricity and strictness. He was a small man, but strikingly handsome, with aquiline features and a mane of white wavy hair which added to his air of authority and made him conspicuous in any company, and he was on terms of formal friendship with many influential politicians and a host of businessmen who were his clients. He enjoyed his authority, but he was always the kind of man who likes to be a power behind the throne, not on it: he loved to be regarded as a mystery man. The combination of all these qualities made him a most convincing lobbyist. In 1896, the new French company retained him as its counsel in America. It was a costly decision, for his fees were enormous, but it was probably the wisest the company ever made. Bunau-Varilla always said, as explicitly as he dared, that Cromwell was only interested in Panama for what he could get out of it, while Cromwell, with no reservations at all, thought Bunau-Varilla was an unprincipled adventurer and a meddlesome intruder. Both stories stuck.

All through the doldrums of the 1890s, Bunau-Varilla was in France, living with his dreams of glory and trying without success to make his own people redeem what he thought was their honor. In 1889, while the scandal in France was still boiling up, he stood for election to the Chamber of Deputies, so that he could defend Panama in debates. He was given 6,000 votes, "but unfortunately," he wrote, "my competitor received about 7,200." Then after a chance meeting with a Russian prince in a train, he tried to interest the Russian government in the project. He got as far as the czar's Minister of Finance, and for a while there seemed to be a good chance that the Panama Canal would be Russian, which might have led to a rather bizarre situation half a century later. But the French government fell at the crucial moment, and the plan fell with it.

After that, he had to admit to himself that there was only one country which could conceivably finish his canal. The two commercial failures had shown that any isthmian canal was too big a job for private industry. It needed a government's resources. But the government of Colombia—or of Nicaragua—was quite incompetent, and no European government would have cared to stir up the Monroe Doctrine by taking it on. The government of the United States was left as the only possible successor to de Lesseps. So Bunau-Varilla began to use what American friends he had to try to influence American opinion.

Cromwell had understood from the first that if his client,

the French company, was ever to sell its assets, his own government was the only purchaser. But there had been a recession in
the middle of the '90s and nobody in government was thinking
far ahead. A dramatic event was needed to revive the languish-
ing project; and it was provided fortuitously by the Spanish-
American War of 1898. The famous voyage of the battleship
Oregon, which was despatched from Pacific waters to join the
fighting off Cuba and took ninety days to round Cape Horn,
abruptly brought home to every American the importance of a
canal. But nobody thought of Panama. That was only remembered as a piece of foreign folly. In the election of 1896, a Nicaraguan canal had been a plank of the Republican party platform.
In 1900, the Democrats adopted it too. And between those two
elections, Senator John T. Morgan of Alabama pushed a bill
through the Senate, by a vote of 48 to 6, to authorize the work
in Nicaragua. That was the weight of opinion that Cromwell and
Bunau-Varilla separately set themselves to overcome.

Bunau-Varilla claimed afterwards that it was his own unaided effort that slowly changed the American choice away from
Nicaragua. Cromwell claimed the same. Bunau-Varilla claimed it
simply through his own vanity: Cromwell did so to justify an
account of over $800,000 for "fees and disbursements" which he
rendered to the company in 1907. But of course the effect of
lobbying can never be accurately measured—it is too much a
matter of verbal persuasion and verbal promises, not all of them
sincere—and nobody now can say how much was due to either.
Probably most of the effective persuasion, at that stage, was
Cromwell's: Bunau-Varilla's turn came later. Cromwell, at all
events, bombarded the press and politicians with pamphlets and
statistics in favor of Panama, and he and his employees hung
around the gates of power in Washington for month after month.
He also subscribed to party funds, at his client's expense. And in
the minds of a few influential senators, he sowed a small seed of
doubt. Its consequence was that in 1899 the Nicaraguan bill was
shelved. Instead, yet another commission was appointed to com-
pare the merits of the routes; and when the commission went to

Paris to investigate the French company's plans and claims, both Bunau-Varilla and Cromwell followed like wolves on its trail.

The members of the commission, mostly innocent admirals, generals and engineers, might not have been any match for this double attack. But Cromwell was moving too fast for his client. His lobbying scared the French company. It is very unlikely that as a distinguished lawyer he was doing anything illegal; but what he was doing smelt to the French alarmingly like what Charles de Lesseps had done. The French shareholders also disliked a scheme of his under which their company would have sold out to an American company he had founded. The commission put a valuation of $40,000,000 on the company's assets, including the Panama Railroad, and Cromwell strongly advised the company to accept it. But the company took offense. It dismissed him and rejected the valuation, proposing instead a figure of over $100,000,000 subject to arbitration. At that price, it was going to be more expensive to finish the Panama Canal than to make a fresh start in Nicaragua, and at the end of 1901, the commission reported in favor of Nicaragua. Soon after, a Nicaraguan bill passed the House by a majority of no less than 309 to 2.

The French company saw at last that the game was almost lost, and hastily cabled that it was willing after all to sell for $40,000,000. That made Panama the cheaper of the two, and three weeks after its first report, the commission issued a second in which it reversed its decision and declared that Panama was "the most practicable and feasible route." Cromwell, proved right, was re-engaged, and a bitter debate began in Congress, for which he supplied the briefs and statistics and even, he claimed, wrote some of the speeches, for the supporters of Panama.

Bunau-Varilla was also in Washington, shrewdly sniping at senators from the outskirts of the battle; and he and Cromwell had a stroke of pure luck which probably gave them the last ounce of argument to tip the balance towards them. One of the minor points against Nicaragua had always been the existence of more or less active volcanoes near the lake. Neither of them had ever made much use of this argument: even they hardly thought

it was convincing. But in May 1902, a few days before the debate
was due to begin, Mont Pelée in the French West Indian island
of Martinique exploded, killed 40,000 people and destroyed the
town of St. Pierre. It was one of the most dramatic and destructive eruptions there had ever been. Volcanic disaster was therefore in the news, and in everybody's mind. And a week later,
there was a lesser eruption in Nicaragua itself.

Both Cromwell and Bunau-Varilla seized the chance. Volcanoes were a change from tedious engineering statistics, something that everyone could understand and fear. Lurid pictures
were drawn in debate of a Nicaraguan Canal destroyed overnight
by eruptions. The government of Nicaragua, to counter the argument, said the reports of the eruption there were false, and there
was some suggestion that the Panama faction had invented them.
But Bunau-Varilla dashed round to all the philatelists in Washington and succeeded in buying ninety recent Nicaraguan postage stamps, which he mailed, three days before the vote was due,
to the ninety Senators: for the stamps had a picture on them of
a volcano with smoke unmistakably coming out of the top. And
when the vote was cast, Panama had replaced Nicaragua by a
margin of only eight votes.

The whole business had distressed a good many Americans,
especially, of course, the advocates of Nicaragua. America had
never intended to build the Panama Canal, and nobody liked to
think that a firm intention of Congress could be reversed by a
process of deliberate lobbying with a suspiciously foreign flavor.
Yet that had certainly been done, and done by two men, one im-
pelled by fanatical patriotism for France, and the other by his
French client's wish to unload its otherwise useless property. But
of course it could not have been done if there had not been some
solid substance in the propaganda. Cromwell was not only making a case, he sincerely believed that Panama was the better
choice for his own country, as well as for his client. And there
cannot be any doubt that he was right. Times were changing. In
1880, Nicaragua had probably been the better: by 1900, Panama

certainly was. Within those twenty years, the size of ships had begun to increase very quickly, and was clearly going to continue to increase. The eight or ten locks of Nicaragua, and the long winding canal, would soon have become an encumbrance. The Nicaraguan faction had been living in the past, and Cromwell and Bunau-Varilla, whatever their merits and methods, had saved the United States from a very expensive mistake. At least, they had saved it so far. There were much worse troubles to come.

The new bill authorized President Roosevelt to acquire the rights and property of the French company for not more than $40,000,000, to acquire from the government of Colombia a strip of land six miles wide along the route of the canal, and then to proceed to build the canal. But in case the French could not give a satisfactory title, or Colombia would not give control of the land, it also authorized him to go ahead in Nicaragua. Proving the title was easy: the next hurdle was to make a treaty with Colombia. It was negotiated by John Hay, the Secretary of State, and Dr. Tomas Herran, who was Colombian chargé d'affaires in Washington, and it was known therefore as the Hay-Herran treaty; but Cromwell and Bunau-Varilla were still in the thick of it, Cromwell advising both parties and Bunau-Varilla sending long letters and expensive telegrams to everyone concerned—and claiming the credit when anyone happened to do what he suggested.

It was a good, straightforward treaty. It authorized the French company to sell out to the United States, and granted the United States administrative control for a period of 100 years over the land it needed. Sovereignty over the zone remained Colombia's. For control of the land, the United States was to pay $10,000,000 in gold, plus $250,000 annually beginning nine years after the date of the treaty. It was signed by the two negotiators, and ratified by the Senate without any alteration.

But then it went to the Colombian Senate, and the trouble started. Some Colombians opposed the grant of land through genuine patriotism. A great many, being Latin, felt there had not been nearly enough bargaining: a country that had willingly offered $10,000,000, they believed, could surely be persuaded to offer more. Some thought the French company ought to pay another $10,000,000 for the privilege of selling its concession. And the most ingenious queried the concession itself. This had been extended several times. The final extension ran until 1910, but there was some idea that it might be invalidated. The previous one was due to expire in 1904, and it was a tempting thought that if the whole business could be stalled until then, the uncompleted canal would revert to Colombia and most if not all of the $40,-000,000 the Americans had agreed to pay the French would be paid to Colombia instead. The Colombian Senate debated all these ideas for six months, and adjourned on August 1st, and again on November 2nd, 1903, without having ratified the treaty. And between these crucial dates, the history of Panama assumed a cloak-and-dagger air, full of amateurish codes and alibis, mysterious journeys and totally contradictory statements.

Colombia's tactics seemed an outrage to everyone who wanted to build the canal—to the French, to Cromwell and Bunau-Varilla, to the majority of the United States Senate who voted for it, and to President Roosevelt himself, who had been converted from scepticism to a growing enthusiasm for the project. They also enraged the leading citizens of Panama, to whom the canal had always been a promise of prosperity.

The ties of Panama to Colombia were not very strong. Geographically, Panama was out on a limb, cut off by the jungle of Darien from the main body of the country. The journey to Bogota, the Colombian capital, still took two or three weeks. Panama had often felt neglected by its national government, and in the tradition of frequent revolution which Spain had left in South America, it had often tried to declare itself independent, but always rejoined Colombia when its temper cooled. And while the Colombian Senate was still debating, a stream of warnings came from Panama that the province would revolt again if the treaty were rejected. Secretary Hay heard the rumors, and told President Roosevelt he would have to decide whether to wait for the result of the impending revolution, or "take a hand in rescuing the Isthmus from anarchy," or give it up and treat with Nicaragua. Bunau-Varilla heard them in France, and Cromwell undoubtedly knew more about them than anyone else, for he was counsel and effective head of the Panama Railroad, which still belonged to the French company, and the railroad was in the thick of anything that happened on the isthmus. To everyone who wanted the Panama Canal, a revolution began to appear as the last hope of getting it. If the Colombian government would not ratify the treaty, the only thing was to make a new government which would.

It was a chance in a lifetime for anyone in Panama who happened to be in a revolutionary frame of mind. If they could declare their independence and quickly sign the treaty, they would get the glorious prize of $10,000,000 for the rights the Americans wanted, and that was enough to set a revolutionary government on its feet. Undoubtedly this had occurred to a good many Panamanians. But it has been said, without any absolute proof, that it was the senior railroad staff, with many Americans among them, who gave the first push towards revolution: and that could only have meant that Cromwell started it—not because he cared who ruled in Panama, but because it seemed to be worth $40,000,-000 to his client. Certainly railroad officials were deeply involved, and certainly the railroad's medical officer, Dr. Manuel Amador, was the spokesman of the revolutionaries.

The conspirators in Panama said afterwards that they first sent a man called Capt. James R. Beers, who was an American and the railroad's freight agent, to see Cromwell in New York and discover what help the United States would give a revolution —for all of them feared that without support they would be defeated by Colombian troops. Beers came back well satisfied with Cromwell's answer. Then Dr. Amador was sent to take the request for help to a further stage. He had two meetings with Cromwell, who received him cordially, he said, and promised him every help, but insisted that nothing active should be done unless the Hay-Herran treaty was finally rejected by Colombia.

During Dr. Amador's visit, however, something evidently

happened to make Cromwell think he was going too far and treading on dangerous ground. Clearly, if Colombia did reject the
treaty, a revolution was the last chance for the French to sell their
assets. But equally clearly, if the revolution was tried and failed,
and if the French company or the railroad was implicated in it,
Colombia would have an excellent excuse to seize the assets and
annul the concessions—and the company then would have nothing
left to sell. The conspirators believed that Dr. Herran, the Colombian diplomat, had heard about Amador's mission and put detec-
tives on his trail, and had also told his government the railroad
was involved and warned Cromwell of the consequences. Possibly
Cromwell had asked the United States government whether they
would support the revolution, and been rebuffed. At all events,
he suddenly refused to see Amador again, and sent a telegram to
the railroad superintendent to tell him to be careful that no employees took part in any hostilities. And then, leaving Amador
friendless and lost in New York, he escaped the whole situation
by taking ship for France.

But by a coincidence, somebody more than willing to be-
friend the doctor had just arrived in the city: Bunau-Varilla. He
had come over from France with the innocent intention—so he
said—of taking his wife to visit their son, who was spending the
summer on the coast of Maine to avoid an attack of hay fever. But
Amador came to see him, and this domestic mission went by the
board. The doctor (this was Bunau-Varilla's account) was almost
hysterical with distress and spoke of killing Cromwell, who he
said had encouraged them all to plot the revolt and then left them
stranded, so that his fellow conspirators still in Panama were in
danger of being discovered and executed by Colombia. Bunau-
Varilla asked him what he needed. He replied that the revolution
would be able to defend itself on land, because the Colombian
troops already in Panama would join the side of the revolutionaries; but they must have $6,000,000 to buy themselves armed
ships to prevent an attack from the sea. Bunau-Varilla calmed
him, and promised to go to Washington to see what he could do.

One cannot help being sorry for Dr. Amador. He was no

match for Bunau-Varilla, and he was out of his depth in the hustle of New York. Nobody could have looked less like a redhot revolutionary: he looked exactly what he evidently was, a dear old kindly, fusty family doctor, rather past his prime. In his portraits, a thin, scraggy, pathetic neck rises out of a high wing collar much too big for it, and in all his features is an air of bewilderment and apology: in the sad, drooping walrus moustache—so unlike Bunau-Varilla's, aggressively waxed and upstanding—in the thinning hair, the startled eyes, and even the crooked pince-nez. "This is not really me," he seems to say, "I ought not to be sitting here posing as a rebel leader." And indeed, he ought to have been at home, taking a pulse, sympathetically patting a wan hand, trying to amuse a sick child by letting it listen to the ticking of his watch—not involving himself in desperate talk of warships and coups d'état in the bedrooms of foreign hotels. One wonders whatever made him leave his practice for such a dangerous uncongenial mission. It is said he was chosen for it because his son was in the United States, which gave him an alibi that none of his fellow conspirators possessed. And the reason why he accepted may have been that he was devoted to his wife, who was said to be charming, resolute and politically conscious. Perhaps—and again, he looked it—he was henpecked. He might have been one of those men who like to be henpecked, because it is the only way they can show their love.

In Washington, under a pretext nothing to do with Panama, Bunau-Varilla contrived an invitation to meet the President. He was cunning enough not to ask what the President's opinions or intentions were on Panama, but he steered the conversation round in that direction, and came away with a firm impression that the President was still in favor of Panama, rather than Nicaragua, and was very angry with Colombia for its obstruction. He told the President he must expect a revolution, at which, he said, the President seemed surprised. A few days later, he met Secretary Hay and told him the same: and Hay was not at all surprised. "Yes," he said, according to Bunau-Varilla's recollection, "but we shall not be caught napping. Orders have been given to naval forces in the Pacific to sail towards the isthmus."

This was what Bunau-Varilla hoped for and expected. Half a century before, in 1846, the United States had made a treaty with New Grenada, as Colombia was then called. Under the treaty, New Grenada guaranteed that the crossing of the isthmus would always be open to citizens of the United States, while the United States guaranteed New Grenada's sovereignty over Panama. Several times since then, the U.S. Navy had been sent to keep the peace when revolutions or civil disturbances threatened to interrupt the crossing. At this important moment, the United States was sure to exercise its accepted right again. The only question was, which side would the navy be on? On the face of it, the treaty obliged it to help Colombia to maintain its sovereignty and suppress the revolution. But Roosevelt's show of anger against Colombia made Bunau-Varilla confident the navy's orders would allow it to stop any landing of Colombian troops.

According to Bunau-Varilla, it was pure guesswork; but, back in New York, he sent for Dr. Amador again (Bunau-Varilla stayed in the Waldorf Astoria, and the doctor in a much cheaper and less fashionable place on 86th Street.) He told him he would not need his $6,000,000 to buy the ships at all. He could promise him that within forty-eight hours of the proclamation of a new republic, the U.S. Navy would be there to protect it. Dr. Amador was unhappy about it. He had come to America in the hope of getting the $6,000,000 and a formal guarantee of protection before the revolution began. All he was being offered was a verbal promise that naval ships would arrive afterwards. But he believed, and never doubted, that Bunau-Varilla was a genuine representative from the White House. He understood that the President might have been embarrassed to make the promise in person. Bunau-Varilla knew he had given Amador this impression, and did not disabuse him.

But the revolution, Amador insisted, would still need money. To make sure of the allegiance of the Colombian troops already in Panama—500 men—they would have to pay the arrears of wages that Colombia owed them. Bunau-Varilla laughed at such a paltry sum. Twenty dollars, a hundred dollars a man? He would pay it out of his own pocket. He would lend $100,000 to the cause. That confirmed Dr. Amador's belief that the promise was official: he thought the money must be coming from secret service funds. But then Bunau-Varilla made one condition—and this, in his cunning one-track mind, was the point of the whole conspiracy. He would hand over the $100,000 when, and only when, the revolution had taken place and he had received a telegram from the new republic appointing him its minister in Washington, and giving him full powers to make the canal treaty.

Bunau-Varilla, in those days of intrigue, was on top of the world. Luck suddenly seemed to have dealt him every trump in the pack. Cromwell had gone, the revolution depended on a sum of money so small he could pay it himself, and the spokesman of Panama was a meek and frightened man: writing about it years afterwards, he still showed a repulsive glee at his success in bullying Dr. Amador. He had seen a chance of a singlehanded coup, a revenge on every critic who had ever made fun of France's noble task: to make the treaty himself, to have it named after him, was a glory he had never dared to dream of. He cared no more than Cromwell who ruled Panama: all he cared about was the canal, the concept he had "consecrated" his life to twenty years before. It has been said that he held a large block of shares in the French company, and so stood to make a fortune if the sale went through. Perhaps he did, but he was the kind of fanatic who does not seem to need such a commonplace incentive. Revenge, conceit, and his own peculiarly French idea of honor—these were what drove him on.

Dr. Amador was even more unhappy at the thought of going back to Panama and telling his colleagues that the new republic's first ambassador would have to be a Frenchman. He very reasonably said it would offend their national pride. He agreed that Bunau-Varilla's expert knowledge of canals would be needed to draft the treaty, but he suggested a Panamanian should be appointed and Bunau-Varilla should tell him what to do. But Bunau-

Varilla, who could be extremely dense, refused to see the point, and concluded that Amador had wanted the job and the honor of signing the treaty for himself. He made the bargain perfectly plain. Amador could either go home penniless, which meant the revolution could not even begin, or else he could go and arrange to send the telegram of appointment. It was straightforward blackmail. At last Amador, in distress, was forced to agree that he would try to carry the point with his colleagues. Bunau-Varilla then drafted a proclamation of independence, invented a code for Amador to use, wrote out in full the telegram announcing his own appointment, and had his wife design and make a Panamanian flag. Two days later, on October 20th, he packed Amador off in the mailboat to Colon, arranged for his bank in France to telegraph a credit of $100,000 to himself in New York, and settled down to wait.

Amador reached home on October 27th, and told his fellow conspirators, of whom there were half a dozen, what had happened —how Cromwell, in his opinion, had let them down, and how Bunau-Varilla had taken his place. They were disappointed. Naturally, they asked what authority Bunau-Varilla had. Amador could only say he understood he was acting for the United States government. Some of them plainly thought it was too risky to start the revolution on the mere promise that money and ships would be coming afterwards. And while they were arguing, they heard that a gunboat carrying Colombian troops was about to leave Carthagena and was coming to Colon. They made the only decision they could: to ask Bunau-Varilla to have the American ships dispatched at once. Amador put the message, as best he could, in the code that Bunau-Varilla had given him. It read: "Fate news bad powerful tiger. Urge vapor Colon."

Bunau-Varilla, waiting in New York, decoded the first sentence: "Colombian troops arriving—on Atlantic side—in five days —more than 200." The second sentence was not in the code, but he read it rightly as a demand for a warship. It amused him, as confirmation that these simple people believed he was an American agent. And he did not believe the news of the troops: he thought it was simply a stratagem to test his authority. Nevertheless, he hurried off to Washington again and told everyone there who would listen, including the first assistant secretary of state, that fighting would start on the isthmus in five days' time—on November 3rd. Again, nobody told him anything definite, but the assistant secretary's answer made him sure that the nearest naval vessel had already been ordered to Colon, or very soon would be. In the past few days, he had been reading the New York papers and had learned from them that the cruiser *Nashville* had recently arrived in Jamaica. That was 500 miles from Colon, and the *Nashville's* speed was ten knots. On these scraps of evidence he made another guess, and staked everything on a promise to Dr. Amador. Going back to New York, he stopped off at Baltimore and sent a cable: "All right. Will reach in two days and a half." Next day, he read in the New York *Times* that the *Nashville* had left Jamaica under sealed orders.

If Bunau-Varilla's guess had been wrong, the revolution would never have started, or would quickly have been defeated by the Colombian troops. But it was right. The *Nashville* steamed into Colon on the evening of November 2nd, only twelve hours later than he had predicted. The Colombian troops, 500 of them, arrived during that night. Everyone involved in the plot put two and two together and made much more than four. They had asked Bunau-Varilla to send a warship, he had promised it, and it had come. Therefore, it seemed to them all, Dr. Amador was right and Bunau-Varilla was a powerful representative of the United States government. And what was more, since the ship had come at their request, it must have come to help them.

In fact, however, the commander of the *Nashville* had not yet received any orders, and therefore did not try to stop the landing of the Colombian troops. It was the American officials of the railroad company who saved the situation. In league with the revolutionaries, they had sent all their trains across to Panama—and without a train there was no possible way for the troops to cross the isthmus. Two Colombian generals landed, and demanded instant transport for their men. The railroad spokesmen promised to arrange it, and meanwhile hustled the generals into a special coach with an engine which steamed off at once for Panama, so that the generals and their troops were separated. In Panama, the revolution was declared. Its leaders raised enough money from the local banks to pay $25 each to the soldiers of the permanent garrison, with more according to rank for the officers. Cash inspired these gallant fellows with revolutionary joy, and they arrested the two new generals.

During the same day, orders arrived by cable for the *Nashville's* comander: "Maintain free and uninterrupted transit. If interruption is threatened by armed force, occupy the line of railroad. Prevent landing of any armed force, either government or insurgent, at any point within fifty miles of Panama. Government force reported approaching isthmus in vessels. Prevent their landing if, in your judgment, the landing would precipitate a conflict." On the strength of this, the commander landed forty-two marines and forbade the passage of troops of either side in either direction on the railroad. For two days, there were confrontations and threats in Colon, alternating with expressions of undying friendship. Then the revolutionaries offered the senior remaining officer, a colonel, $8,000 to take his troops away, and he agreed. It is said that the revolutionaries had run out of credit by then, and that the railroad superintendent provided the cash from his company's safe in Colon. The gunboat that had brought the troops had already gone, but a Royal Mail steamer was lying in port, and there were plenty of people happy to guarantee the fares of 500 men. A formal declaration of independence was read in Panama City, and the revolution was over. Only five shots had been fired, from a gunboat lying off the city. The government was put in the hands of a junta of three men, and two days afterwards the United States gave de facto recognition to the new republic.

From the first moment, the revolutionaries had sent a stream of telegrams to Bunau-Varilla demanding his $100,000. He answered them all by demanding his appointment as minister. His homemade code was not up to the strain, and he received one message from Dr. Amador which seemed to read: "Enthusiasm cable ships Atlantic help need rabbish thousand dollars Pacific little coal took to flight Padilla pursues rest department with us." He asked for a repetition of the word rabbish, and fearing the revolution was failing for lack of money, he sent them $25,000 on account. They tried to satisfy him with the minor appointment of confidential agent. But he was adamant, and on November 6th they gave up arguing. Desperate for money, they sent the telegram he had demanded, appointing him Envoy Extraordinary and Minister Plenipotentiary. He went at once to Washington, and while the going was good he had himself photographed in diplomatic dress. On the 13th, he presented his credentials to President Roosevelt.

Roosevelt was accused, then and for years afterwards, of fomenting the revolution and conspiring with the revolutionaries. The accusations came from Colombia, from his political opponents, from the remaining supporters of Nicaragua, and also from many conscientious Americans who felt there was something indecent in the speed of it all, especially in the United States government's recognition. Many sleuths, with many motives, delved in the history of the whole affair to try to prove that he promised support for the revolution before it happened. But no positive proof was ever found.

Of course, he knew a revolution was likely: everyone did, it was in the papers. But on October 10th, three weeks before it happened, he wrote in a personal letter: "I cast aside the proposition at this time to foment the secession of Panama. Whatever other governments can do, the United States can not go into the securing, by such underhand means, the cession (of land). Privately, I freely say to you that I should be delighted if Panama were an independent state or if it made itself so at this moment; but for me to say so publicly would amount to an instigation of a revolt, and therefore I cannot say it." *

It is true also that the United States government mercilessly bullied Colombia in a series of threatening telegrams, to try to

* To Dr. Albert Shaw, Editor of the *Review of Reviews*.

force through the Hay-Herran treaty. And when those tactics failed, Roosevelt himself was prepared in his mind to seize the isthmus whatever Colombia said, and build the canal. A week before the revolution, he drafted a message to Congress, which, as things turned out, he never had to use: "Either we should drop the Panama Canal project and immediately begin work on the Nicaraguan canal, or else we should purchase all the rights of the French company and, without any further parley with Colombia, enter upon the completion of the canal which the French company has begun. I feel that the latter course is the one demanded by the interests of this Nation."

His opponents' enquiries were largely devoted to finding some means by which he could have sent a promise to the revolutionaries. One of the most persistent rumors was that Dr. Amador, not trusting either Cromwell or Bunau-Varilla, had made a secret journey to Washington and been received late one night by the President, who promised to support him. One set of sleuths pursuing this story—they were employed by Joseph Pulitzer, proprietor of the New York *World*—traced it back to Amador's son, who had boasted to his friends, before the revolution, that the old man had seen the President and arranged it all. The investigators extracted from him a letter his father had written him two days before he left New York. They eagerly read it as proof of the government's complicity. But it did not mention Roosevelt; it was all about Bunau-Varilla. And it can now be seen to corroborate exactly the story Bunau-Varilla told long afterwards, and only to prove that poor Dr. Amador thought Bunau-Varilla's promises had Roosevelt's authority.

Many American historians still believe the revolutionaries would not have risked their lives and property without a positive assurance of Roosevelt's support. Yet if he gave it, by some verbal message through Bunau-Varilla, or through Cromwell (although he was in Paris), or through the American consul in Panama, the secret was kept ever after by everyone who was a party to it. Among all the improbabilities, it is hard to believe that when ill-feeling began, as it did soon after, between Panama and the

United States, nobody in Panama would have quoted against the President any promise he had made. All in all, it seems fairest now to accept his own statement. "I did not lift my fingers to incite the revolutionaries," he wrote in his autobiography. "I simply ceased to stamp out the different revolutionary fuses that were already burning."

In the view of many Americans, then and now, this was bad enough, and the use of the *Nashville* was worse. The *Nashville* was able to arrive at exactly the crucial moment because Bunau-Varilla—and observers, no doubt, in Colombia too—had told the State Department exactly when the Colombian troops were due to arrive. Her orders had a superficial air of impartiality: to prevent fighting and keep the isthmus open, according to treaty rights. But the order to stop all landing of troops was loaded on the side of the revolution, because it was only Colombia that was likely to want to land troops. This was certainly a breach of treaty obligations, but it did not have any direct effect, because the troops had been landed before the orders were received. The importance of the *Nashville* was that the revolutionaries believed she had come at their request, so that they assumed, as soon as they sighted her smoke from Colon, that she had come to help them.

It was all perhaps reprehensible: gunboat diplomacy always was. And so was Roosevelt's de facto recognition of the new government within a couple of days of the revolution—for the revolutionaries had not yet performed a single function of government, or shown whether they would ever be competent to do so. The recognition was nothing more than a warning to Colombia to keep her hands off. But through all the fog of doubt and suspicion which still surrounds the affair, one has to remember that morality in international affairs, in those days, was always pragmatical, and that Roosevelt believed that the end—the building of a canal to serve all nations—amply justified him in waving his stick at a minor Latin-American state which tried to obstruct it. And it must be added that he also seems to have been a victim of Bunau-Varilla's deception. In his autobiography he referred to Bunau-Varilla as an eminent French engineer who was living on the isth-

mus at the time. In fact, Bunau-Varilla had never been to the
isthmus since he was relieved as de Lesseps' acting chief engineer
nearly twenty years before. But no doubt, on his visits to Washington, he gave the impression he had come straight from Panama
at the request of the revolutionaries. There is no record that he
ever mentioned Dr. Amador to anybody. It was a shameless double bluff, which he himself thought justified and clever. Neither
side suspected that in fact he was acting entirely for himself, or,
as he conceived it, for the glory of France, and he left a tangle
of misunderstandings behind him which have troubled the American conscience to this day.

   With the revolution, however, Bunau-Varilla had only begun
his legacy of trouble. As soon as his appointment came through,
he started in a feverish hurry to get the canal treaty signed. His
hurry had far-reaching consequences, and one has to look again
at his unusual mental attitude to find the reason for it.
   At that moment, he saw intrigues all round him. Some were
real and some imaginary. To begin with, in Washington itself,
suspicion was already strong that the President had played some
ignoble part in the revolution. A Presidential election was imminent, and Roosevelt was standing for a second term. There was a
genuine risk that his opponents, and the surviving advocates of
Nicaragua, would build up the suspicion to obstruct the ratification of a Panama treaty.
   Secondly, a delegation was known to be on its way from Colombia. Faced with the revolution, the Colombian government
had abruptly changed its mind. It was now offering to ratify the
Hay-Herran treaty at once by decree, without bothering to re-
assemble its senate, if the United States would help it to suppress
the revolution. This was not a genuine risk at all. The delegation
might have confused the issue, but it was really unthinkable that
the United States, after giving de facto recognition, either rightly
or wrongly, to the revolutionary government, would turn round
and hand its members over to Colombian firing squads.
   Thirdly, Bunau-Varilla read in the papers that a delegation

had left Panama for Washington to negotiate the treaty. It included Dr. Amador and a member of the provisional government called Frederico Boyd. This, of course, put Bunau-Varilla in a fury. He had paid or lent $100,000 for the job of minister, and he thought he had made it clear to Amador that this included the privilege of making and signing the treaty. The news reawoke his belief that Amador had what he called a "childish desire" to sign the treaty himself and win the fame of having his name on it. Nothing that Amador did suggests that he had this vain ambition. But Bunau-Varilla had it. After twenty years of frustration over Panama, his mind was not quite balanced on the subject, and to sign the treaty himself was a symbol of personal triumph which he valued very highly. His vanity blinded him to the credible reason for sending the delegation: that the government he now was pretending to represent had not had a chance so far to give him a single word of advice about the treaty, and might reasonably be expected to want to express its opinion. He was perfectly confident he knew best, and the last thing he wanted was to have to explain it all to a couple of Panamanians. So he made the resolve to get the treaty signed before his government's delegates could arrive.

On his way out of the White House after he presented his credentials, he told the Secretary of State, John Hay, that he wanted to conclude the treaty at once. Two days later, he received a draft treaty from Hay. It was the Hay-Herran treaty, only changed to apply to the new republic instead of Colombia. But the sum the United States was to pay for the land concession was left blank. Hay told him there was no intention of making it any less than the $10,000,000 offered to Colombia, but some senators had suggested it ought to be divided between Colombia and Panama. Bunau-Varilla protested at that, and went back to his hotel to think.

Clearly, the State Department was still willing to accept the terms of the Hay-Herran treaty, but he knew that before the treaty was signed Hay would discuss it with the Senators who would have to steer its ratification through the Senate. With the

criticism of Roosevelt, the impending election, and the threat of
a quibble over the money, he was afraid the discussion might go
on too long to suit his plans. So he decided, entirely on his own,
to alter the treaty and make it so favorable to the United States
that the Senate would not be able to resist it. He had never written a treaty, knew nothing of international law, and could not
even write very good English, but none of that deterred him. He
sat up nearly all night, and in the morning he sent for a lawyer
he knew, to correct the grammar and give it a legal air. By the
afternoon, it was finished.

The main change he had made was in the rights the United
States was granted in the canal zone. The Hay-Herran treaty had
given administrative control for a term of a hundred years. Bunau-
Varilla gave sovereign rights in perpetuity. He and his lawyer
friend wrote the very words: "The Republic of Panama grants to
the United States all the rights, power and authority within the
zone . . . which the United States would possess if it were the sovereign of the territory . . . to the entire exclusion of the exercise
by the Republic of Panama of any such sovereign rights, power or
authority." With this phrase, ambiguous, self-contradictory and—
through his ignorance—unique in international affairs, he initiated
argument, ill-feeling, bitterness and bloodshed that lasted sixty
years.

For the moment, however, the unsolicited gift of sovereign
powers had just the effect he had hoped. Secretary Hay, who believed, of course, that Bunau-Varilla was carrying out instructions
from Panama, could hardly believe what he read. His only fear
was that the Panamanians might have second thoughts when they
realized what they had done. Soon afterwards, writing to a senator to encourage the ratification, he said: "As soon as the Senate votes we shall have a treaty in the main very satisfactory,
mostly advantageous to the United States, and we must confess,
with what face we can muster, not so much advantageous to Panama . . . You and I know too well how many points there are in
this treaty to which a Panaman patriot could object. If it is again
submitted to their consideration they will attempt to amend it in

many places ... They will feel that the treaty was safe, that their independence was achieved, and that now it was time for them to look out for a better bargain than they were able to make at first." And one senator, who had supported Nicaragua, spoke for most in describing the treaty as "more liberal in its concessions to us and giving us more than anybody in this Chamber ever dreamed of having." He added: "We have never had a concession so extraordinary in its character as this. In fact it sounds very much as if we wrote it ourselves." Yet nobody suspected that the Minister of Panama had written it entirely to suit his own ends and had never discussed a word of it with any member of the Panamanian government.

On the morning of November 16th, Bunau-Varilla delivered his draft to Hay, together with the modified Hay-Herran treaty, and said he was ready at once to sign either. At almost the same moment, Amador and Boyd were landing in New York. Bunau-Varilla, of course, was much too busy to meet them: he sent them a telegram of welcome. They were met instead by one of Cromwell's staff, who told them that Cromwell was due back from France that afternoon and begged them to wait and see him. Since they had no idea what Bunau-Varilla was doing, they agreed to spend the night in New York.

Nothing could have suited Bunau-Varilla better: he wrote suggesting they should prolong their stay. All that day, he waited for a summons from Hay, but nothing came. At ten o'clock in the evening, impatience overcame him, and he sent a note to Hay. Hay told him to come that night, or early in the morning. He hurried round at once, and they discussed the treaty far into the night. In his autobiography, Bunau-Varilla quoted himself as saying: "So long as the delegation has not arrived in Washington, I shall be free to deal with you alone, provided with complete and absolute powers. When they arrive, I shall no longer be alone. In fact, I may perhaps soon no longer be here at all." The threat was clear: if Hay looked the gift horse in the mouth, the gift would be withdrawn.

Hay took most of the next day to think it over: but he knew
of no reason whatever to refuse such a generous offer. At six in
the evening, he sent for Bunau-Varilla and they signed the treaty.
At seven-fifteen, Bunau-Varilla cabled the government in Panama to tell them he had signed. At nine, Amador and Boyd arrived by train, and he greeted them at the railroad station. At the
news he gave them, Amador, he wrote, "nearly swooned on the
platform . . . It gave me some amusement to embarrass them."

It only remained for Bunau-Varilla to force the Panamanian
government to ratify the treaty. One might have supposed they
would have objected to giving away their sovereign rights when
the United States had not even asked for them. If Amador and
Boyd had made a scene and repudiated Bunau-Varilla, the treaty
could still have been redrafted. But they did not, and one has to
remember what kind of people they were, and what kind of place
they came from. Panama, for all its antiquity, was no more than
an unsophisticated tropical backwater. The four or five men who
by then formed its provisional government had only been in the
job just over a fortnight. Apart from the old doctor, they were
local tradesmen and landowners. None of them knew much, if
anything, about diplomacy or international law, and they had not
had time to engage any experts who might have told them the
difference between the administrative control the United States
had asked for, and the sovereign rights they were giving away
unasked. The only thing that must have been perfectly clear to
them was they were already deep in debt. They simply had to
have the $10,000,000, and quickly, if the revolution was to sur-
vive.

Consequently Bunau-Varilla was able to bully them all. First
he telegraphed a summary of the treaty, and demanded that
Amador and Boyd should be given authority to ratify it. But
Amador and Boyd refused responsibility, and to his intense annoyance he was obliged to send the treaty itself to Panama by
ship, so that the government could see it. While it was on its way,
he bombarded them with threats—that the United States govern-

ment was already displeased at the delay and might withdraw, and that the Colombian delegation was arriving at any minute—and he demanded that they should promise at once in advance to ratify the treaty, without waiting for it to arrive.

The only person who might have called his bluff was Cromwell, and he tried. He had been horrified to find, when he returned from France, that the "unprincipled adventurer" was prancing round Washington in diplomatic dress and making heaven knew what commitments for the new republic. It is unlikely that he had had time to see the treaty. But he informed the President that he and the French company had nothing to do with Bunau-Varilla, or the revolution. And a long telegram was sent through the railroad's employee Captain Beers to tell the Panamanians that Bunau-Varilla had grossly exaggerated his own influence, that his threats were unfounded, and that a Panamanian ought to be appointed in his place.

But it came too late. Bunau-Varilla again had been too quick for everybody. Thoroughly alarmed by what he had told them, the government had already sent him the promise he had demanded—to ratify the treaty they had not yet seen. On the day it arrived, they did so. The United States ratified it afterwards, and on February 6th, 1904, Bunau-Varilla and Secretary Hay signed and formally exchanged the ratifications: the Hay–Bunau-Varilla treaty was in force. On the same day, this remarkable little person resigned from his post and vanished from the scene of history, still thinking in patriotic clichés and happy to believe, whoever was to suffer in the process, that he had proved at last that France was right. "Two strokes of a pen," he wrote nearly ten years later, "were sealing forever the Destiny of the Great Thought which had haunted Humanity during four centuries ... In an instant I beheld, focused before my eyes ... all those heroes, my comrades in the deadly battle, who fell in the struggle against Nature, a smile on their lips, happy to sacrifice their lives to this work which was to render still more dazzling the glory of French genius ... I thought of the shameful league of all the passions, of all the hatreds, of all the jealousies, of all the cowardices, of all the ignorances, to crucify this great Idea, and with it all those who had hoped, through its realization, to give France one more glorious page in the history of Humanity ... I had fulfilled my mission, the mission I had taken on myself; I had safeguarded the work of French genius; I had avenged its honor; I had served France."

For years afterwards, the rumors of scandals continued, and furious accusations were made within the United States against most people who had any connection with the affair. When the rumors at last were beginning to die away, Roosevelt himself revived them by his famous and rash remark: "I took the Canal Zone and let Congress debate." He said this in a speech in 1911. People seized on it as an admission at last of force or complicity in the revolution. His supporters had to explain that he used the word "took" in the sense that he took an opportunity when it was offered. And he remained proud of his quickness in doing that: he often said the beginning of the resurrection of the Panama Canal was the most important achievement of his terms of office.

As time went on, the rumors had begun to concentrate on the purchase of the French company's assets. "Who got the $40,000,-000?" became a headline and a catchword; and it was on this question that Roosevelt, towards the end of his second term, initiated a federal libel action against Joseph Pulitzer, the owner of the New York *World*. The *World* had alleged in outspoken terms that speculation had been going on in the French company's shares, and that some at least of the taxpayer's $40,000,000 had gone to enrich American capitalists. Among the men it implicated were the President's brother-in-law Douglas Robinson, and the brother of the succeeding President, Henry W. Taft. The suggestion was that the President had not only fomented the revolution, but had done it so that his friends could make an enormous profit.

It was in the defense of this case that Pulitzer set his staff to unearth what evidence they could, but the case was quashed on the ground that libel was not a matter for the federal courts, and many of the scraps of evidence they found were never used. Long afterwards, in 1959, a curious book was published by one of his reporters. * It included a facsimile of what seemed to be a signed agreement dated May 1900 between sixteen American banks and individuals to buy shares of the new French company at not more than $20 and sell them at not less than $55. Among the names were Robinson's and Taft's, together with those of J. P. Morgan and Co. and several financiers very well known at the time. All the signatures except two were witnessed by the initials of William Nelson Cromwell. That document did not show whether the people who seemed to have signed it ever carried out their intention, but others listed purchases of shares, or commitments to purchase, which added up to about $10,000,000.

Cromwell denied that he or anyone associated with him had made a penny out of this speculation. The documents, on the other hand, either proved that his friends had intended to try, or else were forgeries; and if they were forgeries, one is left with the interesting question of who could have had the knowledge and skill to forge them, together with the incentive to take such a tremendous risk.

On the whole it seems likely that American speculators had made a handsome profit. It is odd that other Americans should have been so surprised and incensed at the idea. There was nothing illegal about it. It would have been much more surprising if nobody had taken such a tempting gamble, and if no tips had ever leaked out of Cromwell's office. If the treaty and the consequent sale did not go through, the shares were almost valueless. If it did, they were worth an aggregate of $40,000,000. Most of them were originally held in France, but they could be bought there legitimately and cheaply, and Americans were much better placed than Frenchmen to judge what the prospects were. If none of the $40,000,000 found its way back to America, the American financial world had been much less shrewd than it is supposed to be.

Perhaps Bunau-Varilla had served France, although France had not asked for his help. Perhaps he unwittingly served the

* *The Untold Story of Panama,* by Earl Harding, Athene Press Inc., N.Y.

American speculators. He served nobody else. Without his intervention, the United States and Panama would doubtless have worked out a fair and happy treaty. It was his secret motive that gave most of the air of sinister mystery to the affair—the fact that while the United States thought he was acting for Panama, and Panama thought he was a spokesman of the United States, he was in reality acting for a concept of his own, the honor of France, which was meaningless to everybody else.

The treaty which controlled the relations of the two states for the next sixty years was conceived in trickery. But it was not entirely the United States' trickery, as Panamanians have naturally believed. Most of it was Bunau-Varilla's. What he had tried to do, and why he had tried, remained unknown until he published his story in 1913, and by then the Panama Canal was almost finished and was a legitimate source of pride to all Americans. Probably few Americans, even in the fifty years since then, have known how they came to possess their rights in the Canal Zone. If they had, they might have been less adamant in holding on to them so long, against the wishes and protests of Panama. For the treaty was manifestly one-sided, as Secretary Hay admitted after he had signed it, and it is uncharacteristic of Americans nowadays to cling to a national advantage unfair in its function and deceitful in its origin.

(X)

The American Canal

The Land Divided—the World United.

Motto of the Panama Canal Company

To anyone except an engineer, a successful engineering enterprise is duller than one that fails. In failure, there are conflict, drama and emotion: in success, there are only statistics, and a sense of satisfaction which is largely personal. So it must be admitted that the eight years the Americans worked on the Panama canal, after they really got started, are duller in retrospect than than the eight de Lesseps worked. That is not to belittle the Americans' achievement: it was admirable. But most of the pioneering had been done. The engineers acknowledged, more freely than the mass of the American people, how much they were indebted to the French, who had not only dug a respectable amount of earth and left a definitive plan, but had also made most of the possible mistakes. Plenty of books, of every grade of technicality, were written about the engineering achievement just before and after it was finished in 1914, and they still exist in libraries. Half a century later, there is not much need to add to them.

But before the success began, even the Americans' effort fell into chaos and came to the edge of failure: even their narrow strip of the Darien jungle was not made tame and civilized without a final fight. The core of drama in the enterprise was not the earth and concrete, it was still the mosquitoes; and the foundation of the success, or at least an essential stone of it, was laid not in Darien but in India by the British, in the Campagna of Rome by Italians, and in Cuba by the Americans themselves.

By 1904, when the Americans began, the all-important fact had been discovered that the Darien fevers, the yellow fever and malaria, were spread by mosquitoes. Once the fact was accepted, it semed hardly credible that in all those centuries people had died of the two diseases and never guessed—not even the railroad engineers who noticed that veils and window screens of gauze, which they used to keep out the mosquitoes, kept out the diseases too. Yet the acceptance took a long time, for the bizarre life cycles of parasites were also hardly credible—and indeed they still are. Years after the fact was finally proved, there were people who simply refused to believe it, and among them, unluckily, were some of the senior officers on the canal construction.

Among specialists in tropical diseases, the idea had been discussed, though not accepted, for nearly thirty years. When de Lesseps started work, a few doctors in America and Europe were already convinced of it, and if anyone had acted on their conviction then, de Lesseps would quite possibly have finished a lock canal. But it was not until the turn of the century that all the trails of research, both true and false, had been followed to their endings in experimental proof.

The work on malaria came first. The parasites of malaria were seen in the blood of patients, each inhabiting a red corpuscle, by a French doctor in 1880. Italians in the next few years connected the periodic fevers of malaria patients with the periodic reproductions of the parasites already in their blood, and so demonstrated how it was possible for attacks to come on in places where there were no mosquitoes. British doctors tried to infect volunteers by mosquito bites, but it would not work, and many years went by before they discovered that the parasite needed an incubation period in the mosquito. Major Ronald Ross, dissecting mosquitoes in India in 1895, observed the development of the parasites inside them and found the improbable truth: the parasites reproduced asexually in their human hosts, but in the walls of the stomachs of mosquitoes they developed a form of sexual reproduction, and their multitudes of offspring, with a rather horrifying semblance of intelligence, migrated to the insect's salivary glands and waited there until, if it happened to bite an uninfected human, the cycle was complete. It was Ross also who found that only one kind of mosquito, anopheles—and only the female anopheles—performed this baleful task. In 1900, two doctors from the London School of Tropical Medicine lived for four months in the Roman Campagna, which was full of malaria then, and avoided infection by staying inside a mosquito-proof hut from sunset to sunrise every night. They also captured mosquitoes there, sent them to London and infected volunteers at the London school. By then, Ross had published three books on the prevention of malaria, and they had sold in tens of thousands. His methods were simple—essentially, mosquito nets, quinine and the draining of stagnant water—and with care they were very effective.

An American doctor, Carlos Finlay, had connected yellow fever also with mosquitoes as early as 1881, but even after the malaria demonstrations very few people would listen to him. Malaria had an obvious connection with tropical swamps, but yellow fever had not. On the contrary, short devastating epidemics had often occurred in temperate places, many in the United States. It was a more dramatic and more often a fatal disease—although in places like Panama far more people died of malaria because it was commoner. Consequently, most doctors insisted that yellow fever was contagious. The clothes and bedding of people who had died of it were thought to be very dangerous, especially if they were stained with the black vomit which is one of its revolting symptoms. So was the soil of cemeteries where the victims were buried, and one doctor who worked in Panama in the '80s and '90s spent most of his life protesting against the burial customs of the Panamanians.

Yellow fever showed this misleading difference in incidence because, as it turned out, it had not only a different parasite but a different mosquito: not anopheles but stegomyia. Anopheles is a nocturnal mosquito, which bites at night and hides in daylight, and it breeds in swamps and puddles on the ground—anything big enough not to dry up, and small enough not to contain minnows, which eat the larvae. But stegomyia is a house mosquito which operates by day and breeds in waterbutts, discarded pots and cans, blocked gutters and similar domestic situations. Malaria is therefore a swamp disease which is caught at night, but yellow fever is generally urban, and may be caught by day.

As for the parasites, a malaria patient who survives the first attack may have them active in his blood for many years. Most native children in malarial areas have them, without seeming to be ill. Consequently, a stranger in these areas is reasonably safe by day, but almost certain to catch it if he sleeps where the anopheles can get him in the night. With yellow fever, on the other hand, the patient either dies or recovers completely, and if he recovers he is immune, and does not harbor parasites. Most natives of endemic districts are immune, and a solitary stranger is unlucky if he is found by a stegomyia which has bitten an infectious patient. An epidemic requires a certain proportion of nonimmune people among the stegomyia's victims. This may be provided by a sudden influx of nonimmunes into an endemic district—like the railroad men or the French in Darien—or a journey by a man who is incubating the parasite, into a stegomyia area where the people are not immune—which caused the nineteenth century epidemics in North America.

The work on yellow fever was another by-product of the Spanish American War. It was all done in Cuba, and became a celebrated heroic episode in American medicine. Most Cubans were immune, but when an American garrison occupied Havana in 1898 it provided just the right conditions for an epidemic. The army medical officer was a major called William C. Gorgas. Believing the fever was contagious, he set to work to clean up the city. It needed it, but the work had no effect on the yellow fever. The army became so concerned at the number of deaths that it sent a medical commission to study the problem; and one member was Carlos Finlay. The commission set itself to prove or disprove Finlay's theory, with Gorgas as a sceptical spectator.

These doctors captured stegomyiae and let them bite fever patients in the hospital, and offered $250 to any newcomer in the island who would volunteer to be bitten by them. The first to claim the reward were emigrants who had recently arrived from

Spain: they needed the money, and expected to catch yellow fever whether they volunteered or not. The story was that American servicemen, realizing rather late that they were missing something good, collected a quantity of bones and stored them near the hospital, and then spread a rumor among the Spaniards that this was all that was left of earlier volunteers. So the Spaniards were scared away, and the soldiers took their place. But there were at least two who refused the money, and went through the experiments for a higher motive.

Sometimes the disease was transmitted by the bites, but sometimes not. One of the doctors allowed himself to be bitten, and he died. By trial and error, they found that the mosquito had to bite a patient within the first three days of the disease, and then had to incubate it for ten days before it could give it to anybody else. In an especially macabre trial, volunteers slept for three weeks in the bedding, and wearing the filthy pyjamas, of patients who had died: but none of them caught the disease, and so they disproved the old theory of contagion.

Major Gorgas, watching these experiments, was slowly converted from his scepticism to the belief that stegomyia was the agent, and the only agent, that spread the disease. Once convinced, he resolved to get rid of the stegomyiae in the city. He sent round squads to clear out gutters, drains and rubbish dumps, cover water butts and cisterns, and lecture the inhabitants against leaving jars of water in their houses. It was a very tedious job, but it was extraordinarily successful. It started in January 1901. In the previous year, 310 people had died of yellow fever. But by March, the last fatal case had been recorded, and by September the disease had vanished from Havana.

When the Americans, under Bunau-Varilla's treaty, took possession of their strip across the isthmus, enough empirical knowledge existed to make the place healthy at last: the methods of Ross against malaria, those of Gorgas against the yellow fever, and normal methods of sanitation against typhoid and dysentery. And one of the first to arrive was Gorgas himself, whom Roosevelt had brought back from Havana to make the isthmus safe.

It was a daunting place the Americans came to, haunted by the ghost of de Lesseps' failure. Colon was no more than a stinking shanty town surrounding one main street, the waterfront and the railroad station. Panama was much the same, except that its center was the crumbling splendid masonry of the Spanish empire. The two towns were joined by nothing but the single railroad track: all the rest was jungle as dense and wild and wet as when Balboa saw it, except where the muddy scars the French had left were still lying partly open. It had already been called a graveyard of reputations: it was also simply a graveyard. Along the little railroad, beside the banks of the desolate excavations, 25,000 men—a few thousand more or less—lay buried. The French cemeteries, consecrated ground, could still be seen. The vast mass of dead laborers of the past had simply been put underground by their friends and countrymen along the edges of the jungle, and the jungle long since had spread over and hidden their graves. But the newcomers could not forget they were there. And in the jungle also were the other marks of defeat: lost railroad tracks, abandoned trains, locomotives with trees growing out of their fireboxes, great excavators wreathed in greenery as if they were decorated for a summer fête, houses and barracks falling into ruin and empty except for the termites that were eating them away.

And there was another kind of ghost de Lesseps had left behind, the ghost of stories of graft, extravagance and swindling. That haunted the first of the Americans' senior staff to such a degree that they hardly dared to authorize any expense or issue any stores, without wrapping themselves in protective red tape that strangled initiative and progress.

The huge enterprise was put in the hands of a commission of seven men. The president was a retired admiral, and the governor of the newly-acquired territory a retired general. All the rest were civil engineers. They were worthy men in their spheres, but evidently far too small for the job. The general, George W. Davies, antagonized the Panamanians from the very beginning by not calling soon enough on Dr. Amador, who had been made the first President of the new Republic. As for the admiral, John G. Walker, he wore long muttonchop whiskers which were several decades out of date as a fashion, and his outlook of querulous caution was as elderly as his appearance. Under his leadership the new commissioners, meeting in Washington, so involved themselves in discussions of trivial details that they quite lost sight of their objective. They began to create an organization in which nothing could be done on the isthmus without specific authority from themselves—authority which they often withheld or delayed on the ground of economy, or because they could not agree about it, or simply because the papers were lost or forgotten in passing from hand to hand.

Gorgas, promoted a colonel by then, began his new work with eager anticipation. When he reached the isthmus, there was no reported yellow fever there, but he was sure an epidemic would start as soon as the armies of nonimmune workers arrived, unless he could eliminate the stegomyia in time. It did not look a very difficult job. All the inhabited parts of the isthmus put together were smaller than the city of Havana, and he knew from experience exactly what to do. He sent a list of essential supplies to the commission in Washington—drugs, disinfectants, window gauze and so on. And to his astonishment, nothing happened: ship after ship came in, and brought him nothing. Growing anxious, he cabled Washington, and only received in reply an order, sent by post, not to use cables in future because they cost money. Then the commission visited Panama, and he learned that he was expected to do his work directly under the orders of the admiral and the general—and that both of them thought the mosquito theory was a lot of newfangled nonsense. He wasted a lot of time explaining to the admiral what had happened in Havana: the admiral listened, and then laughed at him and told him to get on with clearing up the city streets. Putting Gorgas' latest list away in a drawer of his desk, he is said to have made a comment which summed up his attitude. "Gorgas," he said, "there is one thing certain. Whether we build the canal or not, we will leave

things so fixed that those fellows up on the [Capitol] Hill can't
find anything in the shape of graft after us."

One has to remember, in the old admiral's defense, that in
those days people did not accept medical theories with quite the
unquestioning trust they give them now. Men who were stubborn
by nature, like the opponents of Florence Nightingale a generation earlier, still preferred what they thought was their own common sense. But Gorgas was the last man to merit such a stupid
rebuke. Of all the American builders of the canal, it is he who
most deserves to be recollected: he was the only man in authority
who stayed on the isthmus from the beginning to the end, and
one of the few who made a reputation there instead of losing it.
He was a gentle, quiet Southerner of unshakable integrity, patient, portly, white-haired and middle-aged, loved by his patients
and subordinates and always apt, through his own modesty, to
be trampled on by his more ruthless insensitive seniors. He was
a doctor by nature: what had made him an army doctor was his
boyhood in the Civil War, when his father was the confederate
chief of ordnance and he used to meet his heroes Stonewall Jack-
son and General Lee. He always remained an ardent Confederate
and regretted that the Confederacy had failed, and this may
have been one reason why he was less successful as an officer than
as a doctor. But an officer's habit of obedience was very strong in
him. All through his ten years on the isthmus, he was torn between a longing to do his job as a doctor, and a longing to quit
and escape the frustration his seniors hedged him in with. He
never gave up, but he never rebelled: he never appealed over the
heads of his senior officers to the leaders of the medical profession. He was in a position like Florence Nightingale's and almost
as important, but he lacked her formidable fighting spirit. Even
in his letters home he was diffident. "The work is great work," he
wrote in the early days, "and very attractive to me, though I am
much discouraged at starting. The commission have their own
idea of sanitation, and do not seem much impressed by mine. If
I had myself alone to consider, I would stick it out. The work,
even as it is, is much more important than anything I am

likely to get in the United States." The other person he had to consider was his wife, who was with him in Panama and was thought, wrongly as it turned out, to have an incurable disease and only a year or two to live. With that additional distress, he patiently struggled on, doing his best with the stores and staff the commissioners allowed him—sometimes half of what he asked for, sometimes none.

The first man who was appointed chief engineer had much the same trouble. His name was John F. Wallace. He was a competent railroad engineer from Chicago, but he has the misfortune to be remembered mainly because he arrived on the isthmus bringing two elegant coffins, one for himself and the other for his wife. He suffered like Gorgas from having seven capricious bosses, and also from an outcry in the press at home. The American public, now that Uncle Sam was on the job, expected "the dirt to fly". It was a natural patriotic sequel to the distaste America had felt for the French endeavor. But it was ill-informed, and Wallace took it far too much to heart. He started at once to try to make the dirt fly. He asked for new equipment, but before it arrived he recruited thousands of men and set them digging with the French machinery, the best of which was twenty years out of date.

This was the straightest road to chaos. There was no supporting organization—no adequate accommodation, medical service or food supply, and nothing but the archaic little railroad to connect the site of the work with the world outside. When materials started to arrive, they piled up on the docks at Colon because the railroad's worn-out stock and rickety bridges could not carry them, and because there was nobody in Colon who knew where to send them. And when men began to arrive, they were bundled into trains and then pitched out at wayside halts in the heart of the jungle somewhere near Culebra and told to walk to the engineering offices. They found a slimy track like the ancient Spanish trail, which gave them a first dispiriting taste of jungle. They had been promised furniture and accommodation in the old French houses: what they got, with luck, was a cot and a place to put it in a room with a dozen others, or with a little less luck, a tent in a jungle clearing. Some took lodgings in Panamanian houses at rents which were reminiscent of the gold rush, and all of them had to buy their food, and in the dry season even their water, from local hucksters. Prices went up until the men could not afford to eat: then wages were put up, and prices went up again. There were stories of parties of hungry laborers foraging like buccaneers for bananas in deserted Indian plantations in the jungle. Of course, the men began to doubt if their bosses knew what they were doing. And they were right, for Wallace had started digging before the government had even decided the old familiar question—whether to build a lock canal, or try to dig down to sea level.

The first man died of yellow fever in December 1904. Gorgas doubled his efforts to make people take the right precautions, but the admiral and the general were not the only opinionated sceptics. The epidemic spread in the headquarters building, perhaps because it was close to Panama City, and also because the architect in charge of it refused to look after the screens that Gorgas had managed to install. The architect died: and even in the dry winter season, the disease crept on, in isolated cases here and there, towards the mass of unprotected workers in the middle of the isthmus

To modern eyes, it all seems strangely un-American. It was far less efficient than anything de Lesseps had done. The organization was muddled at the top and discontented at the bottom; and worst of all, it had absolutely none of the patriotic, idealistic fervor which had inspired the French to such pathetic gallantry. Everyone was listless and disenchanted. The only constancy and dedication were shown by Gorgas and his sanitary squads.

But there were people—Wallace and General Davis were among them—who could see what was basically wrong: that a canal in Panama could not be built by a committee in Washington, even if it were a good committee. After a year of almost useless confusion, their protests and suggestions were piling up in Washington. Press reports of discontent and fever were added to them; so were the stories of disillusioned angry workers who had given it up or been sacked and gone home. At the beginning of 1905, President Roosevelt asked the commission to resign and appointed a new one. It still had seven members, because the Senate refused to reduce the number, but the executive power was limited to three: a business man as chairman in Washington, a lawyer as governor on the isthmus, and Wallace as chief engineer. That gave new hope to everyone on the job, especially to Wallace, who had proposed the arrangement. But only two months later, for no clear reason whatever, he suddenly left the isthmus, went back to New York and insisted on resigning. Everyone from the President downwards was furious with him. It is said he thought he was indispensable and wanted more money, or that he had quarrelled with the new chairman; but recollecting his coffins most people believed—and it still seems the likeliest explanation—that he was morbidly afraid of yellow fever.

His disappearance set the spark to panic on the isthmus. The rainy season had started, the first that the new generation of workers had seen: the steaming jungle was sombre and depressing. Rumors of disease were magnified hysterically. The trains crawling by the construction camps seemed always to be carrying sick and dead. Local undertakers, hoping for the best, stacked up a supply of coffins at each of the stations. Any death, and any sudden sickness, was put down to yellow fever. Men looked for the symptoms every morning in themselves, and at the most trivial illness gave themselves up for dead. Remembering the graves among the jungle, they thought the doom of the French was coming to them, and since they lacked the French idea of glory, most of them made up their minds to escape from the isthmus if they could.

In the spring of that year, 500 deserted their posts and took ship for New York. The horrific stories they told were published everywhere, and the families of men who had stayed began to write and beg them to come home. Work was disorganized and almost ceased. Only one thing prevented the total disappearance of the labor force: many of them could not afford to go. On leave, they were allowed a special fare of $20 for the passage home, but the ordinary fare was $75, and that meant months of saving. They were demoralized, scared, and almost useless, but they had to stay.

The strangest thing about this communal nervous breakdown was that it was almost entirely due to imagination, to the haunted malignant aspect of Panama. In fact, among all the tens of thousands of people on the isthmus, residents and employees, there were only about 130 cases of yellow fever in the panic period, and only forty people died of it. The epidemic—as opposed to the panic—lasted for eighteen months, with a total of 246 cases and eighty-four deaths. Of these dead, thirty-four were canal workers: the rest were Panamanians. It was sad, but it was nothing to make a fuss about.

The panic came abruptly to an end with the appointment of Wallace's successor. His name was John F. Stevens: another railroad engineer, but a man much more tough, decisive and intelligent than Wallace—a man, moreover, who knew his job and knew that he knew it, and did not really give a damn for anyone, even the President. Before he went to Panama, Roosevelt summoned him to his home at Oyster Bay and told him, according to Stevens' recollection, that Panama was in a devil of a mess. Stevens demanded a free hand, and the President gave it to him by telling the story of a newly rich man who engaged a butler and said "I don't know what butlers do, but you get busy and buttle like hell." On his arrival in the isthmus, Stevens found the workers, in his own words, scared out of their boots. To them he said, "There are three diseases here, malaria, yellow fever and cold feet. And the worst of the three is cold feet." That Americanism and others like it brought them to their senses. Within a few days, Stevens put a halt to all the excavation and prepared to start afresh where the enterprise ought to have started: rebuilding the railroad and laying a double track, repairing the old French houses, increasing the port installations and organizing a commissariat which, in spite of the protests of Panamanian merchants, began to sell food at cost price to every worker.

Gorgas, like everyone else, had welcomed the new commission, believing that nobody could be quite so difficult as the admiral. But at first, he was no better off. Both the new chairman and the new governor scorned the mosquito theory, and as the change of command coincided with the outbreak of yellow fever, Gorgas found himself blamed for the epidemic. His seniors still laughed at him and his ideas, and even the rank and file, popular though he was, had begun to talk of him as a crank who might have prevented the yellow fever if he had not wasted time and money messing around with mosquitoes. The new chairman tried to get rid of him, and to give the job to a young friend of his who was an osteopath. But the recommendation had to go to Roosevelt, and Roosevelt, fortunately, was better advised than the men he had appointed. He consulted a couple of eminent doctors—one of them had been on safari with him—and both of them said there was no man alive better fitted than Gorgas for tropical sanitation. The chairman was ordered to give Gorgas all the help he needed, and to his credit he became his firm supporter.

But it was Stevens who really gave Gorgas a chance. He had a much more alert and receptive mind than the rest of these men. Perhaps he already knew about mosquitoes. At any rate, he knew a genuine expert when he saw one, and he simply handed over his engineering staff to Gorgas' command. At last Gorgas was able to get to work on the stegomyiae. He did exactly what he had done in Havana: he systematically got rid of the breeding places, to the extent, it was said, of pouring a film of oil on the holy water in Panama Cathedral. And he was perfectly successful. Stevens gave him the men at the end of July 1905: by December, the last case of yellow fever in Panama was over. But for the stubborn ignorance of the first commissioners, there would never have been an epidemic.

While Stevens was sorting out the chaos on the isthmus, the government started at last to consider what kind of canal it was trying to build. In spite of the French experience of landslides and the Chagres floods, Wallace had favored another attempt at a sea-level canal. Stevens came down strongly in favor of locks.

In June 1905, Roosevelt appointed yet another international board to report on this ancient problem, and six months later, to the astonishment of most of the people on the isthmus, it voted eight to five in favor of sea level—the very plan that had been de Lesseps' downfall.

Roosevelt, however, did not accept its advice. Influenced by Stevens, he told Congress that unless he was otherwise directed he proposed to build a lock canal. And early in 1906, two years after the American project had started, a Senate investigation into this basic question was begun. Stevens had to go to Washington as a witness, impatient at answering technical questions put by politicians. The investigating committee voted for sea level by six to five. Against all his own inclinations, he found himself forced to become a lobbyist for the only kind of canal he believed was feasible. The need to do it irritated him almost beyond endurance, but he did it very well. "I talked to Teddy like a Dutch uncle," he wrote in his usual irreverent way. And in June the Senate reversed the two decisions: by 36 votes to 31, it chose a lock canal. It was a narrow escape. In spite of twenty years of technical progress, the sea level plan might well have sunk the Americans as it had sunk the French.

Stevens was exactly the man the enterprise needed to put it on its feet: forthright, self-confident, impatient, often rude, and something of a genius in leadership and organization. Within a year, he transformed the isthmus, creating a system that kept the work at full pitch and the workers tolerably happy. But with the same qualities, he was not the man to stay and see it through, to go on operating the system year after year when once he had set it going. His first brush with the Senate had only been a foretaste. "If I have got to mix and mingle with every politician in the United States," he wrote to the governor, "the sooner I will be able to drop it the better I will be satisfied." And inevitably, in a government project, that was one of the things he had to do.

So he only lasted eighteen months, growing angrier all the time with what he thought was the plain stupidity of people in

Washington. He disagreed with the chairman over a question of putting the work out to contract, and the chairman resigned. Soon after, he wrote an extremely rude letter to Roosevelt. He complained he was always being opposed by people he would not wipe his boots on in the United States, and claimed he could earn a hundred thousand a year more in jobs that were waiting for him—some of which "I would prefer to hold, if you will pardon my candor, than the Presidency of the United States." It was an offer of resignation, and Roosevelt, refusing to pardon his candor, accepted it forthwith. And not even a petition begging Stevens to stay, which was signed by 10,000 men on the isthmus, made either of them change their minds. Roosevelt was sick of resignations, and wrote to his Secretary of War: "I propose now to put it in charge of men who will stay on the job till I get tired of having them there, or till I say they may abandon it. I shall turn it over to the army."

This he did; and from that moment onwards, in 1907, the building of the canal was almost perfectly successful, and in retrospect perfectly dull. The man he appointed was a major of engineers named George Washington Goethals: a man efficient, capable and—perhaps another asset—notably lacking in warmth of personality. Goethals was respected and sometimes feared by the huge international army of workers—over 30,000 men—which grew under his command, but he was never loved as Gorgas was and Stevens had been. He would certainly have said he did not care: he was there to finish a canal, and whether his subordinates liked him or not had nothing to do with that.

Goethals always had the grace to admit that Stevens had created the organization and made the plans: all he had to do was keep it going. That was not a small job: it took another seven years of hard unspectacular labor, and he was becomingly modest about it. But he was extraordinarily mean to Gorgas. For all the years they worked together, the two men cordially disliked each other. Perhaps it was a memory of the Civil War, perhaps simply the difference in temperament of a doctor and an engineer, of a man who put human welfare first and a man who insisted on putting efficiency first. Their antagonism was always under control, but it was common knowledge on the isthmus. The appointment of Goethals came too late to influence the yellow fever campaign: that had already been won. But while the canal was being built, malaria was never entirely beaten. In 1906, eight out of ten of the workers had been in hospital with malaria. By 1911, it was only two out of ten. Gorgas was disappointed. He had got rid of the disease completely in Havana, and he believed he could have done the same in Panama if he had not been hindered by Goethal's opposition.

It was certainly true that Goethals gave Gorgas as little support as he could. And he went out of his way to avoid giving credit to him for the victory over disease. The prevention of both diseases, he pointed out, had been discovered before the work in Panama began. To prevent them in Panama was simply a matter of good organization—and for that he tacitly took the credit himself. But the medical world gave the credit where it was due. On the isthmus, Gorgas suffered ten years of frustration and neglect; he was blamed when things went wrong and seldom complimented when they went right. One might say it was his own fault: he was too gentle, too generous, too humble. But elsewhere, in the United States and all over the civilized world, he was rewarded late in his life by academic honor. When he died in 1920, he happened to be in London. A few days before his death, King George V went to see him in hospital and awarded him a British order. He was accorded a state funeral in St. Paul's. The British government, in a message of condolence to his widow, truthfully said the completion of the canal was largely due to his zeal and energy. President Wilson wrote that his unselfish services to mankind could never be forgotten. But "never," of course, is often too long a word.

The canal that Stevens planned, and Goethals built and Gorgas protected, was exactly the same canal that tens of thousands of travellers still see every year, except that it is always being widened. Stevens reverted to plans that had been proposed and rejected at de Lesseps' International Congress in 1879. When de Lesseps' engineers, including Bunau-Varilla, at last persuaded him to accept a lock canal, they put the locks as close as they could on each side of the Culebra cut; for they had already dug the sea-level canal for most of the length of the Chagres valley, and could not have hoped to persuade him to abandon so much work. But Stevens could afford to be logical and ruthless. In his plan, the Chagres valley was blocked by a large earth dam near the sea. The locks were in the dam, and more than half the work the French had done was drowned and useless under the lake behind it.

For this reason, only one completed part of de Lesseps' canal can still be seen. The present canal crosses it a little way from the entrance on the Atlantic side, and passengers on ships have a glimpse of it if they know where to look. On one side, it leads to the neat suburbs of the modern town of Cristobal: on the other, it disappears into the jungle and becomes a pretty, ghostly little backwater. Men sweated and suffered and died to put it there, and nobody ever used it: nobody uses it now except little boys fishing with bent pins from homemade boats, or an occasional party of American soldiers exploring in a canoe. The jungle leans out over both its banks. Trees have fallen into it, and nobody has any reason to dredge them out. Flocks of huge blue butterflies drift along it. It is as quiet and still and empty as any slow stretch of a Darien river a hundred miles from anywhere. But suddenly, now and again, a ship's siren bellows and frightens the birds, and one may catch sight of a monstrous disembodied funnel or a mast incongruously passing beyond the tops of the trees. The canal that succeeded is close to the one that failed.

This sad deserted waterway ends abruptly. It is blocked, like the whole of the Chagres valley, by Stevens' dam, which stands at the place called Gatun where the first stretch of the railroad reached the Chagres river and the late-comers in the gold rush changed over from trains to canoes. From ships in the locks, going up from the sea level to the level of the lake above the dam, the dam itself is difficult now to distinguish: it is so wide and massive, and the slopes of it so gentle, that it looks like part of the hilly countryside. But over to the west, the spillway can be seen, where the surplus water from the lake runs over, into the bed of the Chagres and out to the sea ten miles farther down, below the ruins of the Fort of San Lorenzo. Those ten miles are all that is left of the ancient river route which the Spaniards, the buccaneers and the forty-niners followed. All the rest of it is under the lake where the ships sail now: and so are the original railroad, many more miles of the French canal, and thousands of the nineteenth-century graves.

As the ships steam south, the lake grows narrower to the point where the canal leaves the flooded valley—the point also where Morgan's men saw the smoke from Las Cruces and hungrily licked their lips. The railroad crosses the valley there by a bridge which is close to the shipping channel: Las Cruces was about two miles above the bridge. It is under the water now, but the paving stones of the Spanish trail still lead up from the water's edge through the jungle that has matted over them. Here the Chagres flows into the lake, and its floods, which baffled so many engineers, spread out over the surface—164 square miles— and are harmlessly absorbed.

Beyond the lake, the ships go through the Culebra Cut, where the French made their greatest effort and met their defeat. It has been renamed the Gaillard Cut, after an American army engineer who finished it under Goethals but died before it was opened. Its banks are green now, but here still are the steep sides where the rock was hard, and the gently sloping sides where the mud poured down again and again and buried the machinery in the bottom. It still looks like a big excavation, but the water in it now is eighty-five feet above sea level, and one can measure with one's eye how vast it would have had to be before de Lesseps' sea-level dream could have been realized.

Beyond the cut, the canal descends by locks to what was the valley of the little Rio Grande. From the canal, it is hardly recognizable now as a Darien valley. The jungle and the old savannah lands have disappeared: there are suburbs, apartment developments, an airfield, barracks, mown lawns and ornamental gardens, all with the confident masculine neatness of a military installation.

The canal was opened in August 1914. The culmination of four centuries of thought and twenty years of labor passed without any celebration, because the First World War had just begun. A steamer called the *Ancon,* which belonged to the Panama Railroad and had been used for years to bring men and supplies from North America, was locked through from the Atlantic to the Pacific. The President of the Republic of Panama, and a handful of local diplomats, were on board. Goethals watched in some anxiety from the land. In the Culebra Cut, the *Ancon* was a rather tight fit, because mud was still sliding into it: it was blocked again entirely in the following year. The *Ancon's* transit was the official inauguration, but several tugs and dredgers had been through before her. Gorgas is said to have stolen a march on everyone by paddling a canoe from coast to coast.

And Goethals had held a rehearsal of the inaugural voyage, using a smaller ship. This was on August 3rd. On the deck of that ship, as a guest, was none other than Bunau-Varilla, who had come back to the isthmus at last, after thirty years of absence, to witness the occasion. As the ship approached the first locks at Gatun, somebody gave him the Panama morning paper which announced the German declaration of war. Theatrical and madly patriotic to the last, he crushed the paper dramatically in his hand and struck a pose, pointing towards the entrance of the canal. "Gentlemen," he declaimed, "the two great and consuming ambitions of my life are realized on the same day: the first to sail through the Panama Canal on the first ocean liner; the second to see France at war with Germany."

(xi)

The Republic

For half a century, the Americans have operated the canal impeccably. But all that time, the mischievous treaty Bunau-Varilla made bedevilled relations between the United States and Panama. His amateurish draftsmanship was not only an affront to common sense: it left infinite scope for rival interpretations, for complications he never foresaw, and for bitter feelings. Clause three of his treaty was difficult enough. Panama, through his bullying and its government's lack of experience, gave the United States all the rights, power and authority in the Canal Zone "which it would possess if it were sovereign of the territory," to the exclusion of any such rights for Panama. And it gave them in perpetuity. But what did this mean? On the face of it, Panama still possessed the sovereignty of the Canal Zone. But what was sovereignty without any sovereign power? How could the Canal Zone be said to belong to Panama, if neither the government nor the people of Panama had any rights there, or any prospect of ever receiving their rights again till the end of time?

That clause, clause three, was written by Bunau-Varilla himself in his hotel bedroom. The preceding clause was one he had borrowed from the earlier Hay-Herran treaty with Colombia, and it made the ambiguity and contradiction worse. His own clause gave the United States supreme power without any limits or conditions. But the borrowed clause gave them merely the use, occupation and control of the Zone "for the construction, maintenance, operation, sanitation and protection" of the canal. This was all the United States had asked of Colombia, and undoubtedly it was all they would have asked of Panama, if Bunau-Varilla had not been in such a hurry.

Conflict began at the moment when General Davis, the first

American governor, arrived on the isthmus, and it grew for the next sixty years. Panama insisted, on the basis of clause two, that the United States had no right to do anything there that was not necessary for the running of the canal. The United States, on clause three, insisted broadly speaking that it could do anything it liked, and that anything it agreed not to do was a concession to Panama. And neither seemed to remember, if they ever knew, that they had both been tricked into this absurd and dangerous situation by a Frenchman's weird conceit.

The practical difficulties were endless. What kind of people, for example, and what kind of jobs, should Panama admit were essential to run the canal? How could customs be organized? Who would supply the postage stamps? Who would give recognition to foreign consuls? Would Spanish, or only English, be the official language? Was Panama to be turned out of its only two ports, at Panama City and Colon? And had the United States a right, as it claimed, to requisition any land outside the Zone which it felt it needed for the canal's defense? Initially, every problem was decided in favor of the United States' interpretation, on the basis that might was right. Many, sooner or later, were conceded in favor of Panama, but many were never solved. Among the most important of these was the administration of justice. Under clause two, Congress could and did legislate for the Canal Zone. Its inhabitants were subject to the laws of the United States, to arrest by United States policemen and to trial by United States judges. Yet it seemed wrong to Panamanians that in territory which admittedly still belonged to them, they should be tried or punished by foreigners under foreign laws. And it seemed absurd that Panama should have no jurisdiction over Panamanian ships in parts of her own territorial waters.

In the course of time, Panamanians learned to live with the practical difficulties, although they never stopped their efforts to have them changed. But emotional difficulties steadily increased. The fact was that Bunau-Varilla's whim had given the United States something foreign to its traditions: a colony. In the early days, Roosevelt had said there was no intention of making

a colony. But inevitably, that was what the Zone became. Perhaps it was technically not a colony, but from the Panamanian
side of its borders it looked exactly like one, and inside them,
among some of the resident Americans, it bred a colonial frame
of mind. Moreover, it was in a more irritating position than most
colonies, cutting an otherwise independent state into two separate pieces.

The isthmus evolved through just the same emotional phases
as the colonies of European powers. At the beginning, Panama,
in spite of its long history, was poor, ignorant and politically
primitive. It made its treaty almost as blindly as African chiefs
made treaties with Queen Victoria. It contributed nothing to the
building of the canal, except a small proportion of the unskilled
labor. The canal, and the presence of the Americans in the Zone,
were always the backbone of its economy. American defense of
the canal made the whole country seem safe for American capital,
and outside the Zone vast tracts of land were bought by American companies for timber, coffee and fruit. American generosity
gave all kinds of extra benefits, and under American protection
the country grew up until it thought itself mature. But as soon
as the infant republic could stand on its own feet, it regretted the
sovereign rights it had given away in its cradle, and as it grew up
it resented more and more the presence of the alien power, and
the thought that a Panamanian was a second-class citizen in a
part of his own territory.

If national jealousy can ever be justified, there was some
justification for this. In theory, a Panamanian could go in and
out of the Zone as he wished, and compete on equal terms for
work there. But in practice, the top jobs were held by Americans
and the lower ones by Panamanians. In the running of the canal,
5,000 Americans earned more than 14,000 Panamanians; and although they may have been worth more, the Panamanians felt
they were not being given a chance because of their race. All the
Americans, therefore, (they sometimes called themselves Zonians) were far richer than almost all Panamanians. Indeed they

were richer than the equivalent Americans at home, because they were given extra pay for foreign service and bought most of their goods at preferential rates.

The distinction of wealth between the two races showed most in Panama City. The boundary of the Zone ran close round the center of the old city, leaving it on a kind of peninsula between the boundary and the sea: so the city could only grow in one direction, and its newer suburbs stretched out like a comet's tail while land in the Zone and close to the city center lay unused. In 1960, after some hostile demonstrations, the Americans put an unclimbable wire fence along the boundary there, leaving only the main roads open. On one side, looking down on the city from a hill, were the prosperous homes and elegant landscape gardens of the colony: on the other, the poverty-ridden crowded tenements of old Panama. The difference was plain and striking, and the fence seemed like a symbol, keeping the Panamanians not only out of the Zone, but out of the richer more privileged life they could see inside it.

The feeling of getting a raw financial deal was national, as well as individual. The annual royalty of $250,000 that the U.S. had promised in the treaty was increased to a final figure of nearly $2,000,000, but Panama governments always thought it was much too small a share of the revenue of the canal. They had an excellent case for changing some parts of the treaty, but they rather weakened them by excessive claims for cash. The canal was self-supporting. It paid interest to the U.S. Treasury on the capital investment, and reimbursed the Treasury for the net cost of the government of the Zone: its net profit was small compared with its revenue, which was huge. And it was really impossible to say how much reward was justly due to the United States for building the canal and operating it, and how much to Panama for being in possession of the isthmus.

The isthmus would have been a happier place if Roosevelt or Secretary Hay in 1904 had had the supernatural wisdom to re-

ject the sovereign powers that Bunau-Varilla dangled in front of
them as a bait. Then the Americans would have had to use constant tact to live with the Panamanians. It would have been
hard: but absolute power, here as elsewhere, made everything
seem too easy. By the time the canal was finished, it was impossible for the Americans to think of sharing control of it. They
had built it and paid for it, and they were proud of it. It was
supremely important in their commerce and naval strategy. And
the Panamanians did not inspire much confidence. They always
managed to remain a democratic republic: but their elections
were unscrupulous, and their presidents and governments were
short-lived and often accused of corruption. Panamanian wealth
and power remained in the hands of the people of Spanish de-
scent—it was said that fifty families ran and owned the country
—and the rest of the population, mixtures in every degree of
Spanish, Indian and Negro, remained abysmally poor. The administration was inefficient, in contrast with the clockwork efficiency of the canal. So the Zonians, especially the increasing
number who had been born and bred there, came to look on the
native people with a typically colonial disdain.

Smoldering enmity came to a head in January 1964, exactly
sixty years after Bunau-Varilla's imposture in Washington. What
brought it to its crisis was a literally childish problem which
arose directly from his drafting of the treaty: the problem of
which national flag should be flown outside a school. The flag on
the isthmus had an importance forgotten long ago in older nations. Since the Panamanians had lost all their sovereign rights
in the Zone, they passionately wanted to fly their flag there as a
last symbol of the nominal sovereignty the treaty had left them.
But the Americans had always flown their own flag. In 1959,
after a riot about this elementary question, President Eisenhower
conceded that both flags should be flown side by side at one
place in the Zone—the very spot in the city where the two cul-
tures confronted each other across the boundary. That satisfied
nobody, and in 1961 President Kennedy agreed that both flags

should be flown wherever the American flag had been flown by civil authorities. That pleased the Panamanians rather more, but annoyed the right-wing Zonians very much. One American even brought suit against the governor on the ground that the order was unconstitutional. The action was dismissed, for the treaty showed that the Zone was not United States territory, as some Zonians had persuaded themselves. But it successfully delayed things for nearly a year. Then duplicate flagpoles were reluctantly erected at several places, outside offices and hospitals, and on the canal locks. By American custom, flags had always been flown outside the schools. But there the governor, rather than fly both flags, decided to fly none at all.

It was an explosive emotional situation, and in the middle of it the American children of one high school, more or less encouraged by their parents, decided to play at politics. Early one morning they hoisted their flag on the empty flagpole. When the school opened, the teachers took it down, but the students put up another. That night, some of them camped round the flagpole in case the authorities tried to take it away. Next morning, they hoisted the flag again, and although it was a clear defiance of the President himself, nobody intervened: for the adults in general thought it a worthy patriotic gesture.

News of it soon spread over the border, and that evening about two hundred Panamanian students marched into the Zone with a Panamanian flag, which they wanted to hoist beside the other. Precisely what their rights were was a question that might have occupied lawyers for months. But the American police stopped them, and allowed only six to carry their flag to the foot of the flagpole. The American students and a crowd of adults made a hostile demonstration and sang their national anthem. A struggle began, the six students were hustled off by the police and a mob of Americans, and in the melée the Panamanian flag was torn.

That was the spark: it set the place on fire. In half an hour, the teen-age foolishness was an adult battle, and people were out to kill. Thousands of Panamanians stormed the border fence, overturned cars on the boundary roads, smashed the street lamps and attacked a railroad station. The Zone police drove them back across the border with tear gas and then with revolvers and shotguns. The crowd started looting shops in the city—first those they thought were owned by American companies, then any that had goods they wanted—and one which sold guns. They set fire to the Pan-American Airways office, which was just on the city side of the border: the building was gutted, and six dead Panamanians, presumed to be looters, were found in the ruins in the morning. The Zone police called in the U.S. Army: soldiers arrived in armored personnel carriers, and the rumor spread that tanks were being used. The crowd had begun to shoot with rifles and revolvers across the border fence. Just inside it, there was a large and elegant American hotel, a wooden building that dated back to Stevens' time. The mob surged up to it and tried to burn it with bottles of gasoline, while others shot at its windows from tenements opposite. By telephone, American senior officials tried to get the Panamanian government to call out its national guard, an armed police force, but nothing was done on the Panamanian side. American soldiers were being wounded, and in the middle of the night the commander brought up a squad of sharpshooters and posted them in the hotel with orders to shoot to kill any snipers they saw across the fence.

The radio, of course, was broadcasting accounts of what seemed to be happening, and within a couple of hours the same thing started in Colon: crowds invaded the Zone, the U.S. Army with fixed bayonets pushed them out, buildings were burned to the ground and wild shots were exchanged in the darkened streets.

In both cities, the fighting ranged up and down the border fence all night, and flared up again and again in the next two nights and days. The Panamanians never penetrated far inside the Zone, and never came near the canal: the American troops and police, for their part, never tried to cross the border. Most American civilians retreated to their own homes and waited there, some defiant, some in trepidation. And then at last the Panamanian national guard appeared on the streets again, and the rioting suddenly stopped, as if everyone knew it had gone far enough and the party was over. In the clearing up of Panama City, it was found that ten American soldiers had been wounded, while eighteen Panamanians were killed and nearly eighty more admitted to hospital. But precisely who had killed whom was never established. Three or four were probaby shot by the American army marksmen, including a little girl on the balcony of her parents' tenement apartment. Others may have been wounded or killed by stray shots, or by shopkeepers defending their property, or even by private enemies who took the chance for vengeance. For it had started in dislike and resentment of the United States, but it had turned into a night out for the lawlessness which is never far under the surface anywhere, a chance for everyone who had an urge to overturn a car or loot a shop or throw a stone at a street lamp.

The episode left both sides rather shamefaced. Some Americans in the Zone were deeply distressed by it: a common comment was "I'd no idea they disliked us so much." Many were afraid months afterwards to go out of the Zone and into the city again. The wilder right wing, of course, said it only showed the Panamanians were not to be trusted, and they put the whole thing down to a Communist plot. One or two of the few recognized Communists in the republic had indeed been seen among the rioters, but there was no evidence that they started it: they merely seemed to have made the best of it after it started, like so many other people.

Most of the Zonians had a feeling that Panama had been ungrateful, after all the United States had done for the country. A few extremists even revived the old stories of Roosevelt, not as scandals but as something else deserving gratitude: "Why, the republic would never have even existed if it hadn't been for Roosevelt." They had still to learn, as the British had painfully learned, that a colonizing power has no right to gratitude for the benefits it brings to a colony, any more than parents have a right to it for feeding and housing their children. Perhaps the most

sensible summing-up was made by one American who lived in
the city, not in the Zone. "Of course," he said, "we've given them
most of what they have. But gifts are no good without the old-
fashioned thing called love, and that's a thing we've never given
them. God knows, they didn't make it easy. But we didn't try
enough."

Lawyers in Panama accused the United States Army and
police of violations of the Universal Declaration of Human Rights,
and asked the International Commission of Jurists to investigate.
The Commission found the accusations unproved, but neither
side came out of the investigation very well. The Commission was
critical both of American and Panamanian authorities: the Americans for not making their schoolchildren behave themselves, and
the Panamanians for not trying soon enough to control their mobs.
It advised the Panamanians to use tolerance, moderation and
understanding in their relations with the United States. But for
the tension and resentment it put the primary blame on the state
of mind of the Americans in the Zone, especially those who had
been born there. "We cannot help feeling," it wrote in its judicial
avuncular style, "that the United States, having regard to the
special situation it occupies in the world, and with its resources
and ideals, should reflect upon these sad facts and take effective
steps to make possible a reorientation and change in the outlook
and thinking of the people who live in the Canal Zone. Undoubtedly this is a difficult and uphill task, but it would yield rich
dividends in healthier relations with the people of Panama."

The explosion did some good. It blew off steam, and it revealed a state of mind in the Zone that was far from typical of
the United States—the very same state of mind that Americans
had often criticized in the older colonial powers. Both sides
seemed to take the Commission's advice to heart. Within a few
months, the United States government agreed to do what it had
often refused to do before: to discuss an entirely new treaty.
Perhaps there was no connection between the two events—but
perhaps the riots reminded Washington of the final lesson the
British had to learn: that no colony can justly last forever, and

that when its native people grow resentful, the only possible thing to do is to give it back to them.

When the discussions began, President Johnson said the United States sought fair play and justice, with a decent respect for the rights of all. The fact that the United States were large and Panama was small would have no bearing on the discussion. And ten months later, in September 1965, he repeated that sentiment—"We are determined to do what is fair and what is right" —and he was able to announce that "areas of agreement" had been reached. The old treaty was to be abrogated: a new and modern one would effectively recognize Panama's sovereignty over the Zone, and integrate the Zone with the rest of the Republic. Panama would share in the management of the canal, and in its benefits. This statement, at last, was an honorable though tacit admission that the United States had not always been fair or right in the past sixty years: and with this change of heart, it seemed that the unhappy chapter in the history of the isthmus would soon be ended, and Bunau-Varilla's mischievous work would soon be buried.

(*xii*)

The Nuclear Plan

THE HUMAN DISHARMONIES of these sixty years have only existed along the canal. The natural harmony of the jungle is never far away. Even in the Zone, there are tracts of virgin jungle: passengers on ships have glimpses of it. Its virginity there has an air of being carefully preserved: some parts of it are used by United States forces for training in jungle warfare, and on the roads in other parts there are signs forbidding litter. But outside the Zone to the eastward, a short walk can still take you into fastnesses that stretch unbroken and undisturbed all the way to the Atrato River and the empty site of Santa Maria de la Antigua del Darien. At sea off Colon, there are always ships in sight. But a little way along the coast in either direction, east into Darien or west into Veragua, takes you abruptly out of the modern world, past the decaying hamlets of Portobello and Nombre de Dios or the abandoned mouth of the Rio Chagres, and right back to the world of Quibian, Comagre and Careta. The descendants of those old *caciques* crept down to the coast again when the Spanish danger was past, and they live there now, pure-blooded, alone, aloof and independent.

In Darien, safety has changed the Indians' mode of life in one way. After Pedrarias, they retreated into the heart of the jungle to avoid the Spaniards: now, they have retreated to the coral islands to avoid the insects and the vampire bats. Most of their villages are built on tiny islands which are covered all over by bamboo huts with narrow paths between them. Some of the villages overflow their islands, and their outermost huts are built on poles in the water. When the villagers want to go anywhere or do anything they have to use their dugout canoes, usually with paddles or poles or sails, but here and there, very fast, with American outboard motors. The villages are remarkably clean and tidy: these Indians do not keep domestic animals, but live on fish and bananas, and trade in coconuts. Noisy, decrepit motor boats come chugging along the coast from time to time to collect this product and to carry what passengers there are. But much of the trade is with sailing schooners which slip across the Gulf of Darien from Colombia. This has been contraband ever since 1904, but the Indians were doing it long before that, and they refuse to see why the revolution—in which, of course, no one consulted them—should stop them selling coconuts where they want to sell them.

These Indians, the Cuna, are indeed the subjects of the Republic of Panama, and so are the Chocos who live in the jungle on the Pacific side of the mountains. But that does not mean much more than when Don Juan Pimienta told the Reverend Shiels that they were subjects of the king of Spain. They have never regarded themselves as anyone's subjects. In 1925, they rebelled: some Negro Panamanian police had been annoying them. United States intervention, backed up by a cruiser, persuaded them to make a pact of peace with the Panamanian government, and also persuaded the government to leave them alone. Since then, the Darien coast and the jungle behind it has been recognized as their hereditary land, and nobody has been allowed to disturb them.

Although most of them have become canoe people rather than jungle people, their society has hardly changed at all. *Caciques* still rule their little territories, including one major village and possibly two or three other smaller settlements. The committees of elders still meet in solemn conclave. There is no authority above the *caciques,* except the distant government in Panama—so far away and so foreign that nobody takes much notice of it. Life is still as simple as human life can be. Nobody is rich, but nobody is oppressed by being poor. There are plenty of bananas, fish teem in the milk-warm shallow sea, and every newborn baby is given a few coconut palms which grow with it

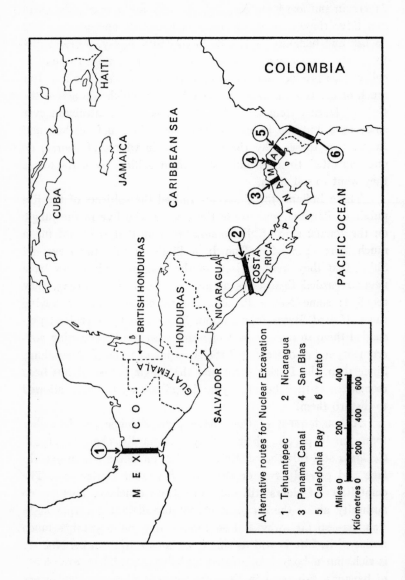

and give it the means of buying all the merchandise it is ever likely to need. When a Cuna needs a house, to get married or because his own is burnt or fallen down, the *cacique* decrees, the village helps, and the house is built in a day. The men have given up noseplates and nakedness and go about in tattered shorts and shirts, but the women dress up in elaborate embroidery and beads. They still wear gold rings in their noses, and some of them still possess magnificent breastplates and necklaces of gold, which no doubt are worth hundreds of dollars—but they like these ornaments, and do not want hundreds of dollars. It is only when a young man covets something like an outboard motor that he goes to the city and works till he can buy it and take it home.

The Indians' dreadful experience at the Spaniards' hands made a permanent mark on their character—or at least a change in their policy. They are still friendly, polite and cheerful with strangers by day. But they are still extremely unwilling to let anyone stay on their coast overnight. They have let a few missionaries live with them, and a very few other outsiders who have proved their sympathy. There is one small hotel on an island in the Bay of San Blas, where tourists are taken by air from Panama and the local Cuna have been taught to embroider and dance for the tourist trade. There are two foreigners at a banana company's airstrip in Caledonia Bay. But these are special concessions, each carefully considered by the local *cacique* and his meeting of elders. In general, the Cuna remain suspicious of anyone who tends to outstay his welcome. It may be a racial memory of the old Spanish custom of accepting hospitality and then slaughtering the hosts when they were sleeping. It may just be a vague and understandable sense of uneasiness. Or it may be a logical suspicion that foreigners do not really change, and may still want to settle and seize the Cuna lands and disrupt their tribal life. Whatever the reason, their policy has been perfectly effective, so far. They have taken back the lands they possessed before Balboa came. Since the rapes of the Spanish soldiers, they have not interbred with other races. They are still themselves, and among the blessed people in the world who are quite content.

After fifty years, the Panama Canal is too small. Its locks are 1,000 feet long and 110 feet wide. When they were built, they were not simply big enough to fit what ships existed then, but big enough for any ship that ever seemed likely to exist. It was an act of remarkable foresight to build them so big as they are, but nobody could see as far as fifty years ahead. Now, there are over a hundred merchant ships at sea which are too wide for them, and about 600 too deep to go through fully laden. And perhaps more important still, the large aircraft carriers of the U.S. Navy cannot use them.

Consequently, the President of the United States has appointed yet another commission to study the isthmian problem. All the old routes have been surveyed again: Tehuantepec in Mexico, which Saavedra considered in 1528; the Nicaraguan route—but skirting the lake, not using it; the routes on the Atrato River which Frederick Kelley's men explored in the 1840's; the shortest route of all, from the Bay of San Blas where Drake met the maroons—a route which nobody ever seriously thought of, although Wyse took a cursory look at it before his successful exploration by railroad train; and finally, the route straight across from Caledonia Bay, where Balboa went, and Paterson dreamed of going, and Dr. Cullen and Gisborne pretended they had gone, and Strain met his awful disaster. Bunau-Varilla's pet scheme has been looked at again, for dredging the lock canal down to sea level. The routes are the same, the isthmus is the same: but the problem nowadays is entirely different, because it is possible to excavate by nuclear explosives.

If the mysteries of nuclear explosives are taken for granted, their application to making a canal is a simple conception. Within a certain depth, any underground explosion, nuclear or chemical, breaks the surface of the ground and throws up debris. Much of the debris falls back into the hole, but some of it is thrown outside, and a crater is left. For an explosive charge of any given power, there is an optimum depth at which the largest crater is produced. Underground charges fired simultaneously in rows can produce overlapping craters—or in effect a ditch—and the debris falls out at the sides of the ditch, rather than at the ends.

Nuclear explosives, even in megatons, are small enough in bulk to be lowered down boreholes made by the kind of drilling rigs which are used for oil wells. The craters that could be produced by the largest devices are far bigger than a mere ship canal would need. A new canal could therefore be excavated by putting through a temporary access road, sinking boreholes at calculated intervals, burying nuclear devices in them and firing them in rows, perhaps twelve or fifteen at a time. By calculating the depth and power of each device according to the height of the land above it, a sea-level canal of roughly uniform width could be excavated without any further labor, except perhaps a little tidying up.

This technique not only brings a sea-level canal into the range at last of practical and economic possibility: it also turns every earlier conception upside down. The cost of a nuclear device is not much different whatever its explosive power is. Consequently, it would be cheaper to make a few large craters, with a few powerful devices buried deep, than to make a lot of small ones. It would therefore be cheaper to make a big canal, say a third of a mile in width, than to make one half the size. And, improbable though it may seem, it would be cheaper to make a canal of a given size through a mountain range than to make it through a low-lying plain. Cheapest of all, no doubt, would be to sink a very few of the most powerful known devices very deep, and blow a large part of the isthmus out of existence. Nothing would be easier, if it were not for the danger from blast, seismic shock and radiation. It is only these side-effects that put a limit to nuclear excavation.

A great deal of work has already been done in analyzing the ancient routes from this new point of view. In nuclear excavation, you do not need to think, like de Lesseps and Stevens, in terms of cubic yards: all that really matters is the length of the route, the size of the charges that can safely be used, the rivers that will have to be controlled, and the number of inhabitants

who, whether they like it or not, will have to be moved out of
the way.

So far, the calculations are not exact, for two reasons: the
routes have not yet been surveyed in sufficient detail, and too few
experimental excavations have been made. The largest underground explosion up to date was one hundred kilotons at a depth
of 635 feet in the alluvium of the desert of Nevada: it left a
crater 320 feet deep and 1,200 feet across. But that was small
as nuclear explosions go, and there is still some doubt in the
mathematics of scaling up the size of the crater for larger explosions and different kinds of rock.

On what basis there is, however, it is clear that nuclear excavation would be far cheaper than mechanical excavation on
any of the routes, and far cheaper also than dredging the present
canal to sea level. The cost of the excavation itself would be less
than one-tenth, and even if the overhead expenses were the same,
the total cost would be less than half: so there cannot be much
doubt that a determined effort will be made to build a brand-new
canal, rather than bring the old one up to date, and to build it in
this brand-new way. There is a natural enthusiasm among American nuclear engineers at the thought of a chance to do something useful, instead of merely threatening destruction, with the
devices they have spent such skill and money on.

The estimates of cost already give a guide to the probable
choice of route. The cost of nuclear excavation alone, for a canal
1,000 feet wide, was reckoned as follows in 1964:

Tehuantepec	$1,084 million
Nicaragua	$1,093 million
San Blas	$269 million
Caledonia Bay	$299 to $329 million
Atrato	$692 to $910 million

The differences in these costs are mainly due to the lengths
of the routes, and hence the number of explosive devices needed,
and the number of boreholes needed to sink them in—957 of them
on the Nicaragua route, which is 139 miles long, and only 271 at

San Blas, where it is only forty miles from sea to sea. The estimates assume that "over-excavation" would not be allowed: in other words, that the charges used would be the smallest that would do the job, although they would be most expensive. For a larger canal, 1,500 feet wide, only 724 devices would be needed in Nicaragua, and 218 at San Blas, and the cost would be correspondingly less: but of course the total explosive power, and the dangerous side-effects, would be larger.

On these figures alone, San Blas would seem the obvious choice. But San Blas, as it happens, would need the largest single shot: fifty megatons to blast a hole 1,500 feet deep and nearly three-quarters of a mile across, through the ridge which at that point is 1,100 feet high. And the place where this fearsome charge would have to be fired is only thirty-five miles from Panama City and Colon. The hazards to these cities, to quote an engineering report, "cannot be fully determined until certain blast safety work has been undertaken." It seems very doubtful whether they could ever be determined to the satisfaction of the people who live there. And if they object, the next best choice would be Caledonia Bay, which is over a hundred miles from anywhere— except the villages of the Indians.

There may be political considerations in the final choice which will override the mere matter of expense. When the quarrels between the United States and Panama were at their worst, many Americans would have favored building a new canal outside the Republic, even though it would have cost far more. But with the new air of agreement between the two countries, there seems to be no common-sense reason for looking beyond San Blas and Caledonia Bay, which are both in Panama. There will be some hard bargaining for the right of way, wherever it is. But luckily, the problem is smaller now than it was in Bunau-Varilla's heyday. One of the attractions of a new canal, in American eyes, is that a huge force of men would not be needed to run it or defend it. Defense of the present canal has always been magnified by the fear that quite a simple act of sabotage could put locks out action, or even drain the lake. But a big sea-level canal w be almost indestructible, and even if an enemy blocked it with a nuclear bomb, it would not be very difficult to blast the blockage out again with another. Such a canal might be run by five hundred men, instead of the present thousands: they would live in a small town built for them at the Caribbean end. The jungle itself would provide the best possible defense, as it always has, against marauding armies. Air and sea defense would not have to be based on the spot. Nothing like the Canal Zone, with its colonial complications, would ever be needed again.

There is something peculiarly shocking about an underground nuclear explosion, even though one can only watch it at close quarters through slow-motion moving pictures made by automatic cameras. To the most sophisticated city dweller, there is still something important in the solidness of the ground he walks on: it is still an instinctive symbol of stability. To see a wide stretch of placid countryside bulge upwards in a monstrous blister, and then split open with tongues of flame and smoke, disturbs something fundamental in an ordinary person's emotions. Nobody is likely to think unmoved of the mountains of Darien, wild and useless though they are, being burst apart, and the trees and animals, rocks and streams and valleys, all the primeval panorama of the jungle, suddenly flung into nonexistence. But of course, one knows this is sentimentality. If one man with a button can do in a microsecond what would take an army of men a lifetime with picks and shovels—well, so much the better: that ˙ progress.

ᵗʰe first difficulty to be overcome—after persuading the ⁿf the Nuclear Test Ban Treaty to agree—will be to in general, and the people who live on the isthmus ᵗt nuclear engineers know what they are talking say it will be safe. The experts have proved to ion that most of the radioactivity in explosions ped in the glass formed from melted rock at ᵉr, and that only a very small amount escapes will certainly have to answer some searching questions, and some silly ones. What happens to a jungle swept by an atomic blast and bombarded by radioactive rocks—which may fall up to five miles away? What happens to the animals which escape being incinerated but are dosed with radioactivity and run away? Or to Indians who catch them and eat them? What about radioactive fish and birds? Who will find the Indians in the heart of the jungle—not much easier now than it was when the Spaniards tried—and make them go far enough away at the crucial moment? Where will the radioactive dust come down? And is it safe to upset the geological stability of a place where earthquakes are already not unknown? The more innocently foolish the questions, the harder they will be to answer.

But if they can be answered, it seems most likely that the chosen route will be Caledonia Bay. If it is the choice, the only people for whom the thought of all the destruction will be more than sentimental are the Indians. An engineering report about it says: "The evacuation problem and potential damage to buildings is relatively slight on this alignment." That is an understatement. There are no buildings except the bamboo houses of the Cuna on the Caribbean coast—the houses they build in a day —and the shacks of some halfcastes on the Gulf of San Miguel. Nobody knows precisely how many people there may be in the jungle, but it would be surprising if more than 5,000 have homes in the thousand square miles which would have to be emptied. To move these 5,000 the same report allows no less than $35,-000,000. For their share of this gold mine, the Pacific halfcastes, who have no very deep roots, will certainly move anywhere. The Chocos Indians, whose jungle shelters have always been expendable and seasonal, may simply retreat farther east and disappear into places that will still remain unravaged. But the Cuna, who have guarded their coast so long against intruders, will be deeply disturbed.

Exactly opposite the mouth of the planned canal in Caledonia Bay is the village, on a little coral island, of the *cacique* who is called Winston Churchill. Its name is Mulatupo. It is not marked on the published maps of the engineers, so insignificant does it

seem to be. But there it is, a home, the center of a little kingdom,
placid and quiet now in the beautiful bay which had so many
lifetimes of violence. On the shores of the mainland, and on the
other islands, are the banana groves and the coconut palms—
each tree belongs to somebody—and on the reefs are the fishing
grounds, where the sea comes sparkling in incredibly blue and
breaks incredibly white, and the young men balance their dug-out
canoes in the lee of the coral rocks. The life the Cuna lead there
still seems as idyllic as it seemed to the buccaneers in the moments when they grew tired of gold and slaughter. Of course, a
sophisticated person could never join it and enjoy it: but a
glimpse of it can give him an uneasy feeling that this may be
how mankind was meant to live.

If this is the choice, Mulatupo, to say the least, will never be
the same again. The scorched and scarred shores, when it is all
finished, will surround an international anchorage full of ships. No
doubt the *cacique* and his people will be treated very generously:
the world has changed since Pedrarias, even though the Cuna still
suspect it never changes. Perhaps other *caciques* along the coast
will find room for them. But whoever has the distressing job of
going to Mulatupo, and telling its people what the world has
decided, will know—as they will know themselves—that dollars
cannot buy back everything they will lose.

It will be an odd coincidence if the history of Darien starts
again in Caledonia Bay, the scene of 200 years of bloody history
and then of 265 years of undisturbed oblivion and peace. This
was Comagre's country: it was here that Comagre's admirable
son told Balboa about the other sea. The mouth of the new canal
will be in sight of the Scotsmen's lookout on the point above Fort
St. Andrew. Ships steaming in towards it will make their landfall
off Golden Island, where the buccaneers met so often and Don
Juan Pimienta's fleet blockaded the harbor. The construction
camp will be exactly in the place where Balboa's lost city of Acla
is thought to have been, and the new permanent town will not
be far away: perhaps somebody will think of reviving the old

name in his honor. When the first men go ashore to clear the route, they will climb the ridge precisely where Balboa's men staggered up with the planks and ropes and anchors to build the first brigantines on the South Sea. Inland, beyond the mountains, in the steamy valley of Rio Chucunaque, they will cross the confusing country where so many of their predecessors lost their way —Oxenham's crew with their stolen pearls, Wafer and his buccaneering companions, and in later generations Dr. Cullen, Lionel Gisborne and Isaac Strain. Beyond that again, it is quite possible they will blast away the unidentified peak where Balboa knelt and prayed on the morning of September 26th, 1513.

These new pioneers will find the jungle of Darien just the same formidable obstacle that it has always been. Of course, they will bring new weapons to force a way. Men will be lowered from helicopters, if they can find a big enough space between the trees. Others will land on the beaches with armies of machines. But first of all, before even the bulldozers can go in, somebody will have to find a way for them: and he will have to go on his own two feet, with his machete in his hand, like all the other adventurers who have ever been there.

Sources

This is very far from a complete bibliography of the isthmus, but I think it includes most of the original stories on which all history books are ultimately based. In some episodes, such as the crossing of the forty-niners, there is a superfluity of these stories, and I have made a rather arbitrary choice.

A very good general history is *The Land Divided*, by Gerstle Mack (1944).

CHAPTER I: THE EXPLORERS. There are four firsthand accounts of this episode: by Columbus, in a letter to Their Highnesses of Spain, written in Jamaica in July 1503; by Ferdinand Columbus in his *History of the Life and Actions of Admiral Christopher Colon* (1582); by Diego Mendez in his will; and by one of the brothers Porras. I have not relied on the last of these, because in Jamaica later in the same voyage these brothers led a mutiny against Columbus, so they must be expected to be prejudiced. I used translations of Columbus and Mendez published by the Hakluyt Society in 1933, and a translation of Ferdinand Columbus from Churchill's *Collection of Voyages and Travels* (1704).

CHAPTER II: THE WAY ACROSS. There is very little strictly firsthand information about Balboa. Peter Martyr, in Seville, made a practice of interviewing anyone who came back from the Indies, and wrote a wise and often amusing narrative in the form of letters to the Pope, which were published with the title *De Orbe Novo* in 1516–1530, and translated in part by Richard Eden as *The Decades of the Newe World* in 1555. Other details are found in the histories of Oviedo y Valdes, who was in Darien for a while under Pedrarias, and Bartolome de las Casas, who lived a long time in the Indies and became a bishop in Mexico. Oviedo was inclined to defend the Spanish colonists' treatment of the Indians; Las Casas attacked it fiercely. Both their accounts were written soon after the events, but not published in full until the nineteenth century. Antonio de Herrera's *Historia General de las Indias* was written later but published in 1601.

CHAPTER III: THE ELIZABETHANS.   Saavedra's plans for a canal are in Antonio Galvao's *True Discoveries of the World unto 1555*, translated and published in 1555. The story of Drake's voyage of 1572 was published in 1628 with the title *Sir Francis Drake Reviv'd: Calling upon this Dull or Effeminate Age to follow his Noble Steps for Gold and Silver. Written from reports by members of his crews by Philip Nichols, Preacher, Reviewed by Sir Francis Drake himselfe before his death, and much holpen and enlarged by divers Notes with his owne hand here and there Inserted. Set forth by Sir Francis Drake, Baronet (his nephew) now living.* Oxenham's voyage, since there were no English survivors, is only known from the Spanish reports written in Panama at the time; they are published in the Hakluyt Society's Vol. LXXI, Series II. The firsthand account of Drake's last voyage is *Drake His Voyage,* by Thomas Maynarde, also first published by the Hakluyt Society (1849).

CHAPTER IV: THE BUCCANEERS.   John Esquemeling's account of Morgan's raid is in *The Bucaniers of America* (1704), which also includes stories of Darien by other notable buccaneers. Lionel Wafer's *New Voyage and Description of the Isthmus of America* was published in 1699.

CHAPTER V: THE SCOTTISH COLONY.   The main source is the Company's papers, which are preserved in the National Library of Scotland. A selection of them, *The Darien Papers,* was published in Edinburgh in 1849. *Memoirs of Darien,* by the Rev. Francis Borland, was published in 1716, but according to its subtitles it was written mainly in 1700, while its author was in the American regions. It starts as a graphic story of the second expedition, from the ministers' point of view, and then it turns into a sermon. A pamphlet called *The History of Caledonia, by a Gentleman lately Arriv'd,* was published in 1699. It is said to have been made up at second hand from other documents, including Wafer's book, but it adds some details of the first expedition which seem authentic. There is a very sarcastic tract called *A Defence of the Scots Abdicating Darien,* by Walter Herries, who was a surgeon on the first expedition: I do not think his story can be trusted. *The Writings of William Paterson* were collected and edited by J. Bannister in 1859.

CHAPTER VI: THE LOST CANAL OF RASPADURA. The letters Humboldt wrote during his journey are in the *Life of Alexander von Humboldt*, edited by Karl Bruhns and published in English in 1873. His account of the journey is in his *Personal Narrative* (1814). His argument with Frederick Kelley about the Raspadura Canal may be found in the Journal of the Royal Geographical Society around the year 1856. Captain Cochrane's book is *Journal of a Residence and Travels in Columbia* (1825). Dr. Cullen's is *The Isthmus of Darien Ship Canal* (1853), and Lionel Gisborne's is the *Journal of the Expedition of Inquiry for the Junction of the Atlantic and Pacific Oceans* (1853). Lieutenant Strain's disaster is described by one of his companions in *Harper's New Monthly Magazine* of March 1855.

CHAPTER VII: THE RAILROAD. The main source is the *History of the Panama Railroad* by F. N. Otis (1861). *Panama in 1855*, by Robert Tomes (1855) describes this period, and *Panama, a Personal Record of 46 Years*, by Tracy Robinson (1907) starts only a little later, and also has much to say about de Lesseps. The Bishop's crossing is from *The Early Days of my Episcopate*, by Rt. Rev. Wm. Ingraham Kip (1892). The army's crossing I have only seen in a typed copy of the medical officer's report in the library of the Panama Canal Company, in the Canal Zone. There is a mass of material in the United States about the forty-niners' adventures on the isthmus, and I have probably only seen a small portion of it: a good summary is *Sea Routes to the Gold Fields*, by Oscar Lewis (1949). From this period onwards, the files of the *Panama Star and Herald* are full of information.

CHAPTER VIII: THE FRENCH CANAL. De Lesseps' autobiography, *Souvenirs de Quarante Ans* (1887) reveals much of his character, but of course it stops before the disaster. A thorough and fair account of the scandal and trials is in *The Life and Enterprises of Ferdinand de Lesseps* by C. Barnett Smith (1893); it has the merit of having been written when the events were fresh in living memory. Much of the criticism of French behavior on the isthmus seems to have had its origin in *Five Years in Panama*, by Wolfred Nelson, an opinionated doctor who must have had a grudge against the Frenchmen. An elaborate forecast of failure was *The Panama Canal*, by J. C. Rodrigues, which was published as early as 1885. Philippe Bunau-

Varilla's own egocentric view is in his *Panama, the Creation, Destruction and Resurrection* (1913), and *The Great Adventure of Panama* (1920). A continuous exposition of De Lesseps' opinions was given in his company's bulletin. Among modern biographies, George Edgar-Bonnet's is authoritative, while those of André Siegfried (*Suez and Panama*, 1940), Hugh J. Schonfield (1937) and Charles Beatty (1956) are more readable.

CHAPTER IX: THE REVOLUTION. There is a jungle of comment in books and newspapers (as there is about de Lesseps), but anyone who explores too deeply in it risks losing his way and finishing farther from the truth than when he started. I have discarded what is emotional, partisan, hypothetical and secondhand, and restricted myself to the few—but I think sufficient—original sources.

By far the most detailed personal narrative is Bunau-Varilla's *Panama, the Creation, Destruction and Resurrection*. It is almost crazily prejudiced, but no book ever revealed its author's weaknesses more clearly, and with care and practice one can disentangle the truth, and confirm much of it from other sources. President Roosevelt's actions and opinions can be found in his *Autobiography* (1914), in biographies such as J. B. Bishop's (1920) and in his speeches and writings. Cromwell published nothing about his part in the affair, but his biography, *William Nelson Cromwell*, has been written by his legal colleague Arthur H. Dean (1957). Among official publications, the most comprehensive is *The Story of Panama: Hearings on the Rainey Resolution before the Committee on Foreign Affairs of the House of Representatives* (1913). United States documents, such as the State Department's communications with the consul in Panama, and the reports of the Isthmian Canal Commissions, are easily found, but I have not heard of any on the Panamanian side which clarify the story: revolutionary governments, of course, are not inclined to keep files of documents until the success of their revolution is assured.

CHAPTER X: THE AMERICAN CANAL. This field has been well ploughed by others, and I hope I may be forgiven for not reading all the technical reports and treatises. *And the Mountains Will Move*, by Miles P. DuVal, Jr. (1947), provides a well-documented narrative. Among the many books published about the time the canal was finished, *The Panama Gateway*, by J. B. Bishop (1913) carries authority, since he was secretary of the second Canal Commission. A biography of Gorgas is called *Physician to the World*, by John M. Gibson (1950). Mosquitoes have a bibliography of their own: among it, Ross's books are still most interesting.

CHAPTER XI: THE REPUBLIC. Coming nearer to the present, I have been guided partly by conversations with Zonians and Panamanians. *The United States and the Republic of Panama*, by William D. McCain (1937), is an excellent account of relations between the two countries from 1904 until the eve of the Second World War; its author, as a United States citizen, is more critical of his country's policies than I would presume to be. The riot of 1964 is described in the Canal Company's journal *Spillway* (January and February 1964); so are the benefits brought to the Republic by the American presence. The riot is further analyzed in the *Report of the International Commission of Jurists* (1964). The governments of the Canal Zone and the Republic have both issued many statements on the points at issue between them.

CHAPTER XII: THE NUCLEAR PLAN. My sketch of nuclear technique is based on documents of the U.S. Atomic Energy Commission, and its future application to the isthmus on engineering reports and the preliminary report of the Commission appointed in 1965. I have seen Cuna Indians myself, and a sympathetic account of them is *San Blas—The Forbidden Land*, by Fred McKim (1947).

Index

About the Author

David Howarth was born in London in 1912. He attended Cambridge University, where in 1933 he received a B.A. in physics and mathematics. As his first job, he worked for John Logie Baird, a pioneer in television, in the days when it was worked by a large revolving disk. He then joined the British Broadcasting Corporation, working first as a technician and then on news and editorial jobs.

Mr. Howarth served for the first eight months of World War II as a war correspondent for the BBC with the British and French armies in France. During the evacuation from Dunkirk he joined the navy, and spent the next nine months in command of an old motor yacht patrolling the southeast coast of England hoping to repel German invasion. From 1941 to the end of the war in Europe, he was stationed in the Shetland Islands as second in command of a private navy, first of Norwegian fishing boats, later of American-built subchasers, which landed arms and agents in occupied Norway. This experience provided the material for his first book, *Across to Norway*.

After the war Mr. Howarth stayed on in the Shetland Islands and worked there for five years designing and building fishing boats and yachts. But as a result of the success of his first book, he decided to devote his full time to free-lance writing. In the years since, he has written nine more books, including *We Die Alone*, *The Sledge Patrol*, and *D Day*. While he was doing the research for this book he visited Panama and, among other things, had a U.S. Army helicopter set him down in the middle of the jungle so he could walk out, to get the feel of jungle living. In the book, he makes brilliant use of the experience in vivid recreations of the sights, sounds, and feel of the steaming, ominous, mosquito-ridden terrain through which all of Panama's adventurers have explored, traded and built.

Mr. Howarth now lives in the country outside of London with his wife, Nanette, and their four children.